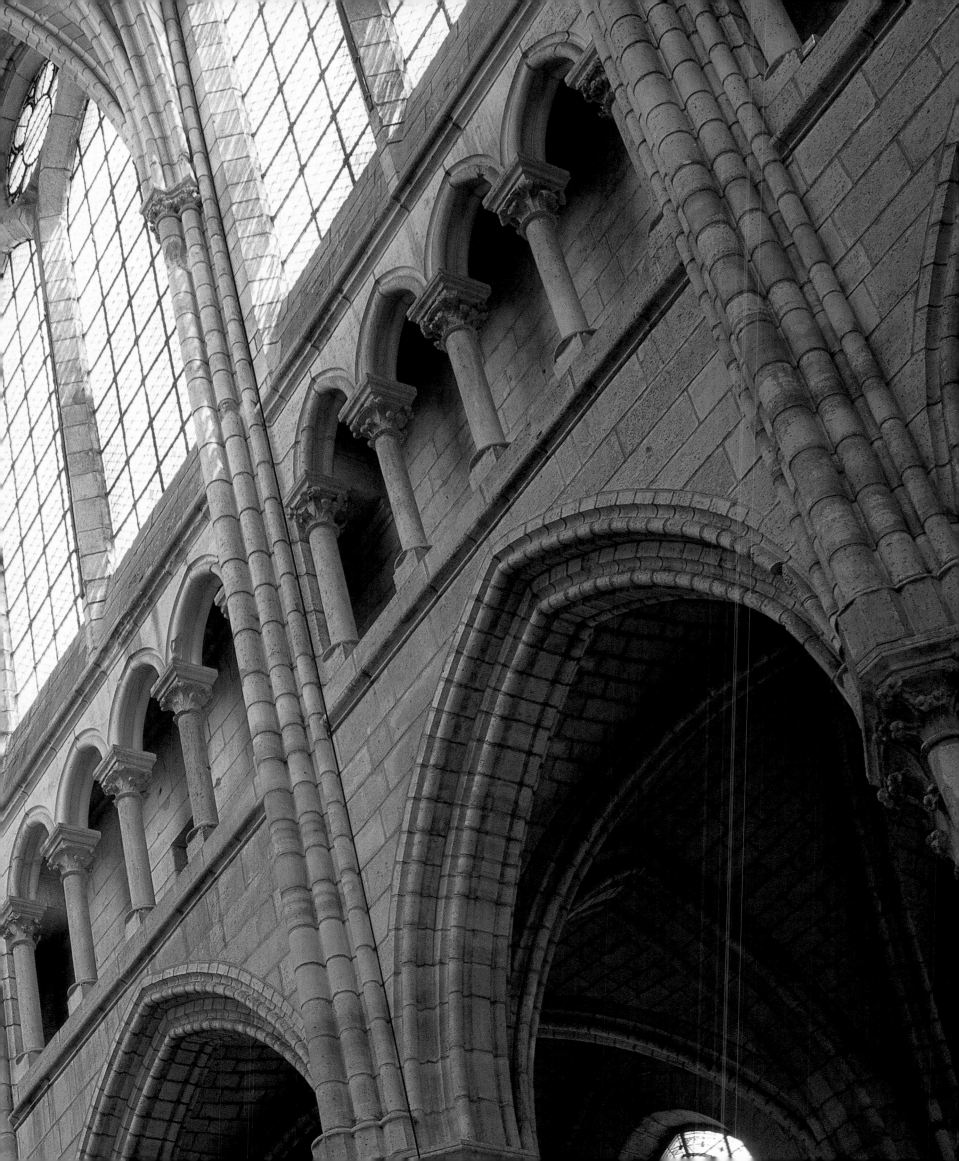

THE ROSE WINDOW
SPLENDOUR AND SYMBOL

PAINTON COWEN

With 381 illustrations, 301 in colour

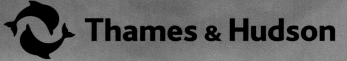
Thames & Hudson

TO MY MOTHER

The author would like to thank the following for their kind support: Tony & Tere Axon, Francis Atwater, Geoffrey Bateman, Ian & Rose Battye, Jeremy & Elisabeth Best, Derek Blades, Pamela Bowles, Alessandra & Martin Brackenbury, France Buono, Duncan & Meg Campbell, Steven Cantle, Peter & Lucy Chadlington, CriCri & André Chanas, John & Sandy Cleland, Nic & Margot Cooper, Richard Cooper, Rick Cordell, Mrs R.E.Court, Bob & Lucy Cranmore, Andre Crepin, Douglas Day, Fiona Duby, Geraldine Dunbar, Lavinia Ferguson, David & Joanna Fitzgerald, Anne Cooke Yarborough & Brendan Flanagan, Mark Fletcher, Annick Gaillard, Jean Pierre Gaillard, George & Brigitte Gaillard, Geoffrey Gallimore, Pamela Gordon, Caroline Gordon & Mike Salmon, Matthew Greenberg, Rosalind Grimshaw & Patrick Costeloe, Mike Hall, Richard Hallows, Bob Harris, Diana Harris, R. A. Hohler, Francis Jenkinson, Roger Jones, Lauri & Sally Khurt, David Li, Sue Leonard, Charlotte & David Lloyd Williams, Celia Lowenstein, Joanna Lumley & Stephen Barlow, Gillian Lynn, Piers & Janie Marson, Michael & Auriol Marson, Guy & Sam Marson, John Matchett, Colin & Sissie McCall, Brian McCarron, Ivan McCracken, Iain Morrison, Linda & David Nancekievill, Peter & Katrina Norbury, Julia Nott, Nicole & Jo Offredi, Jo Ouston, Hugh Purcell, Charles Radford, Jane Reeves, Anya Sainsbury, Andrew & Anabelle Sanders, Alastair & Em Sawday, Nicola & Karine Schwartz, George & Mollie Sinclair, Tony & Indira Sleight, Graham & Diana Snell, Peter Sowerby, Rosemary Van Allen, Jonathan Warr, Julian Watson, Simon Watson, Michael Williamson, Tim Wilson.

p. 1 Exterior of north rose, Notre-Dame, Paris
pp. 2–3 The Last Judgment in the south rose at Sens Cathedral
pp. 4–5 The north transept of Soissons Cathedral
pp. 6–7 Flamboyant rose, west façade, S. Giovanni, Syracuse
THIS SPREAD Ruined rose at Lieu-Restauré

First published in the United Kingdom in 2005 by Thames & Hudson Ltd, 181A High Holborn, London WC1V 7QX

www.thamesandhudson.com

British Library Cataloguing-in-Publication Data
A catalogue record for this book is available from the British Library

ISBN-13: 978-0-500-51174-9
ISBN-10: 0-500-51174-8

Printed and bound in Singapore by C. S. Graphics

CONTENTS

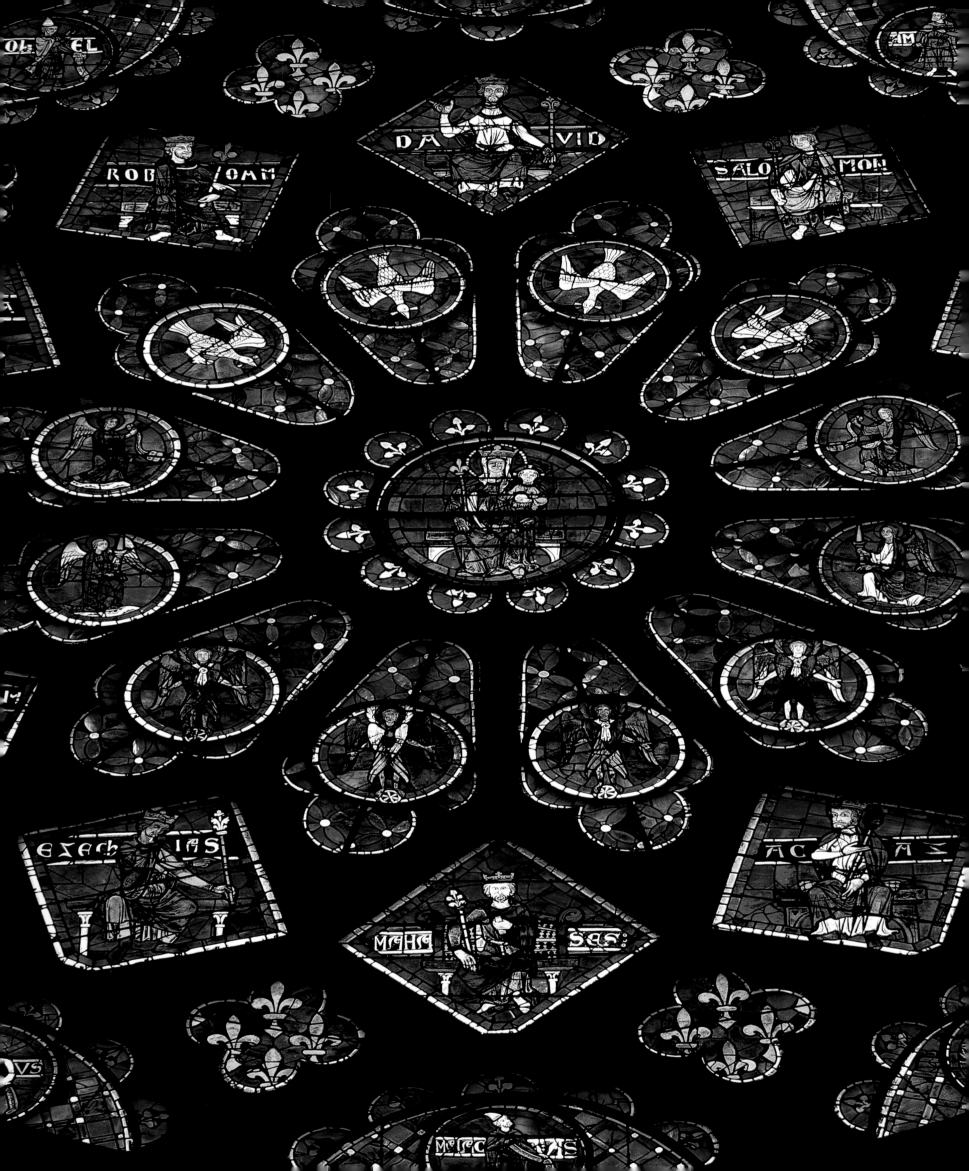

PREFACE

It is a wonderful opportunity to be able to put together a second book on rose windows some twenty-six years after the original *Rose Windows*. The intervening period has seen the publication of a great deal of excellent and useful material on Gothic architecture – much of which can be found in the Bibliography – and hopefully the approach taken in this book reflects these developments. Although the original *Rose Windows* had much to say about the meaning of these remarkable structures, my attitude toward their interpretation has evolved somewhat over the years, and I am much happier now to let each window speak for itself. Accordingly, this book places far greater emphasis on chronological development, allowing a full exploration of the origins and evolution of the form. Nevertheless, there is an extensive chapter on the iconography of rose windows and their glazing, and another on their geometry and construction. And in each of the four chronological chapters there is a special spread, called 'The Spirit of the Rose', that looks at what the rose might have meant to each age.

Although I have travelled far and wide to see and photograph hundreds of rose windows in their settings I have often had to rely on the work of numerous scholars in order to locate, learn about and date many of them. In particular I would like to thank Tim Ayers, Paul Crossley, Jean-Luc François, Rosalind Grimshaw and Patrick Costeloe, Martin Harrison, Stuart Harrison, Meredith Lillich, Nicholas Rank, Buffy Tucker and Joan Vila-Grau, for their help and suggestions. This book also owes an enormous debt to the many friends and acquaintances who have sponsored photographs and particularly to my mother in this respect; to my partner Annick Gaillard who has helped carry cameras and tripods all over Europe as well as providing a second pair of eyes and helping with translation; to Geraldine Dunbar, Anne Cooke-Yarborough and Michael Hall for their help with translation; to the many priests, church wardens, Deans and Chapters of cathedrals, the Monuments Historiques and city Communes in France, Italy and Spain for allowing me to photograph the buildings in their charge; and to the many libraries and librarians in Britain and France, including the Bibliothèque Nationale, the Médiathèque du Ministère de la Culture et de la Communication, Westminster Abbey Library, the National Art Library, the British Library, the Warburg Institute Library, the Courtauld Institute Library, and Cambridge University Library. I would also like to say a special thank-you to John Matchett and Rick Cordell for their photographic advice, to Tad Mann for his help with the drawings, and to Jean-Pierre Lagrange for his photography. I should like to thank everybody at Thames & Hudson, in particular Anna Perotti for her sensitive design, and Susanna Friedman, who ensured that every picture is shown to its best advantage. Nor could I ever thank sufficiently my editor, Christopher Dell, who has shown an exceptional interest in and enthusiasm for rose windows, made numerous suggestions, and carried out research, while his editorial functions have often exceeded what might normally be expected.

The gazetteer at the end of the book lists the more notable, interesting and important rose windows around the world, but with unlimited space one might easily include many more. For this reason, photographs of many other rose windows can be found on a dedicated website, www.therosewindow.com. This also includes forums and additional information, and readers are invited to consult it, and to add comments, amendments and additions (for which they will be credited) that can be of help to students and fans of the genre alike.

OPPOSITE Detail of the north rose, Chartres Cathedral

INTRODUCTION
THE ROSE WINDOW AND THE GOTHIC EXPERIENCE

The rose window is one of the most spectacular of all the creations of the Gothic era. Its power to impress in today's world – a world saturated with visual spectacle and a seemingly infinite variety of multimedia diversions – is something of a miracle in itself. Although generally of a different genre to those of the Middle Ages, today's 'pilgrims' to the great Gothic cathedrals and churches, mostly tourists, still often stand mesmerized by the startling displays of colour and geometry afforded by the rose windows in cathedrals such as Paris, Chartres, Reims, Palma or Strasbourg. Like all great works of art such rose windows seem to 'speak' directly to the individual, catching us unawares and slipping past the enquiring intellect by the impact solely of their form, light and colour.

One person whose life was certainly changed by the powerful image of a rose window was the young Eugène Viollet-le-Duc (1814–79) who, when taken to Notre-Dame 'by an aged domestic' in the early 19th century, was seized by *une belle terreur* – a beautiful terror – in the presence of the cathedral's south rose:

> The cathedral was shrouded in darkness. My gaze was
> focused on the stained glass in the south rose window
> through which the rays of the sun passed, sparkling with
> great subtlety.... Suddenly the great organ came to life;
> for me it was the rose before my eyes that was singing....
> As I looked I came to believe in my imagination that some
> of the panes of glass produced the low sounds and others
> the high ones: I was seized by so beautiful a terror that
> I had to be taken out.[1]

Viollet-le-Duc later wrote that in that moment he knew his destiny was to be bound up with the then crumbling cathedral (and many others in France). One beneficiary of his restoration work there is the current organist at Notre-Dame, Olivier Latry, who writes:

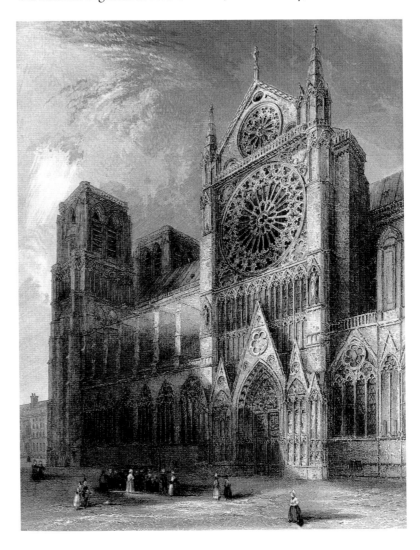

OPPOSITE Detail of the west rose, Strasbourg Cathedral, c. 1300

ABOVE RIGHT The south façade of Notre-Dame in 1837, very much as Viollet-le-Duc would have seen it as a child – and before he rotated the rose by fifteen degrees as part of his 'restoration' of the cathedral. It is clear from this engraving that even in the 19th century rose windows were tourist attractions.

Situated midway between heaven and earth on the west wall, the organ of Notre-Dame, Paris, projects its sonorities under the cathedral's vaults like a musical extension of the medieval rose window playing with the colours just above it.[2]

However, mysticism is not enough for the modern mind and once we have regained our composure we want to know more about these strangely beautiful webs of glass and stone, woven into intriguing flowers of light: how and when were they built; what imagery they contain; who invented them. Perhaps above all, we want to know what they *mean*.

This book hopefully goes some way to answering these questions. It is an exploration of the rose window as an architectural device, a phenomenon even, central to the High Gothic style of the early 13th century in western Europe, especially France, but considered an essential element in great church building for a long time afterwards – arguably right in to the 21st century. It is also an investigation into the meaning or meanings of these creations, both generally and specifically. In this context it is useful to see the rose window as being formed of two mutually dependent parts: the stone tracery within a monumental masonry circle, and the glass. The tracery gives architectural form both inside and out; the glass (which only very rarely has survived intact) gives a specific meaning to the form. Often this meaning is part of a larger architectural programme; on occasions it is at the very heart of the programme. These two themes – the formal development of the rose window, and the development of its iconography or meaning – are reflected in the division of this book into a chronological survey of the rose window from tentative origins in Spain or even Syria to the present day (Chapters 1–4), and a chapter on the meaning both of the form and of the stained glass (Chapter 5). The geometry that governs the form of rose windows (and which is sometimes crucial to its meaning) is discussed in the final chapter.

WHAT IS A ROSE WINDOW?

For such a familiar feature the rose window is surprisingly difficult to define. The French names *la rose* or *rosace* can be used to cover a number of architectural details in churches and cathedrals incorporating round windows and related unglazed forms. In English the term is commonly used to denote round windows containing stone tracery that radiates in a symmetrical pattern from and around the centre, like the spokes of a wheel: the classic examples would be the mid-13th-century transept roses at Notre-Dame (see pp. 102–103). However, this definition is clearly not sufficient, since a number of so-called rose windows do not exhibit radiating spokes. Indeed, by these criteria such famous examples as the early rose in the north transept of Laon Cathedral (see p. 70), or the so-called 'Bishop's Eye' in the south transept of Lincoln Cathedral (see p. 25), would not qualify. Neither would the huge round panels of glass that are found particularly in Italy and Spain from the 15th and 16th centuries containing a single scene, even though they are often referred to as such. Nor, even, would the giant 13th-century window in Siena Cathedral that seems to patch together lancet windows to fill a circular space (see p. 17).

This book includes all of these examples, alongside many other variations, with the assumption that all monumental, circular, typically axial openings, glazed and unglazed, with or without tracery, may reasonably be called 'rose windows'. Another argument for inclusion would be that a rose window is almost always designed to be appreciated from outside as well as inside – indeed many Italian roses, covered in rich sculpture, are often far more impressive from the outside. This book also discusses, from time to time, carved stone rosettes of similar form to a rose window but which are purely decorative and have never carried glass, nor were intended to do so. Finally, the book includes some roses that have been wholly or partially destroyed, including ruins that once housed giant roses, such as at Longpont, St-Jean-des-Vignes at Soissons and Crépy-en-Valois.

Every rose window is a balance of stone, glass, iron and lead, each element requiring very specialized skills. Here the beautifully carved spokes hark back to the rose window's origins in the 'wheel' window. In the glass we see angels surrounding a personification of the Church Triumphant (north rose, Lyon Cathedral)

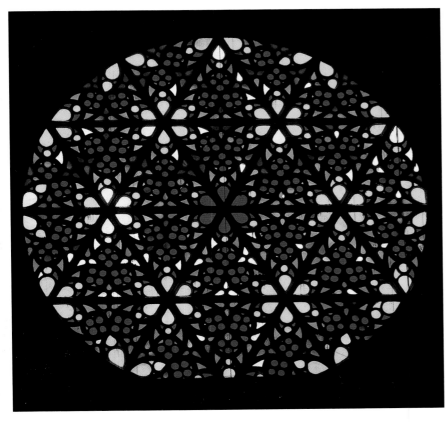

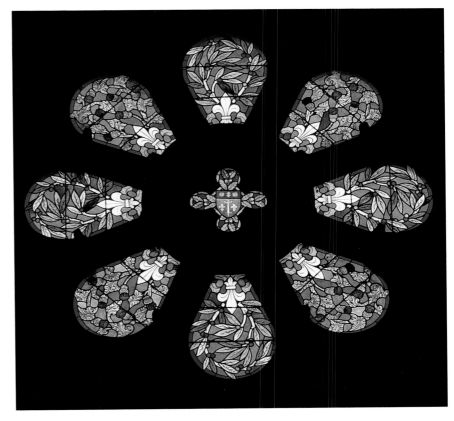

What is a rose window? Most people think of a classic
Rayonnant rose, such as the one opposite at Clermont-
Ferrand Cathedral, dating to the early 14th century.
However, many other forms exist, as can be seen in the
examples above. Clockwise, from top left: east rose,
Siena Cathedral, showing the Death, Assumption and
Coronation of the Virgin Mary, by Duccio, 1287–8;
an Art Deco rose at St Nicholas, Outines, 1936; the south
rose at Domrémy-la-Poucelle, early 20th century; the
huge crossing rose at Palma Cathedral, originally 14th
century, but rebuilt later, glass largely modern

That many rose windows have not survived is due to their inherent fragility, some of them being a kind of architectural challenge to utilize as little stone as possible in order to support as big an area of glass as possible.

While we can say what is or is not a rose in structural terms, there remains the fundamental question of where the name comes from. The English, French, Italian and Spanish words – rose, *la rose*, *rosone* and *rosetón* respectively – seem all to share a derivation in *rosa*, the Latin name for the flower, and this particular use probably originated in the 17th century.[3] However, Camille Enlart has suggested that the word may in fact derive from *roue* or *roe* in old French, meaning wheel.[4] Certainly the word 'wheel', or its Latin equivalent *rota*, was in use by the mid-13th century, as we see at Cremona Cathedral in Italy (see p. 155). The west rose window at Reims Cathedral, meanwhile, was referred to as the 'O' by the Master Mason Bernard of Soissons on a plaque previously in the cathedral, and it is as the 'the fourth vowel' that Jean de Landun refers to the transept roses at Notre-Dame in Paris when writing in 1323:

> I would be happy to learn where [else] one might find two circles like this directly facing each other, resembling the fourth vowel. [Within] are lesser circles and others even smaller, artistically positioned, some round, others lozenge-shaped, containing sparkling stained glass of precious colours and figures painted with great delicacy.[5]

Villard de Honnecourt referred to the Chartres rose that he sketched in the early 13th-century (see p. 241) as *fenestra* (Latin for window) and the rose at Lausanne as *une reonde veriere* ('a round stained-glass window', in old French). All these examples point to a common origin in the oculus, and this essential and ancient form is central both to the formal characteristics and the meaning of every rose window.

OPPOSITE Clockwise, from top left: main façade, S. Pietro, Tuscania, mid-13th century; gable, Notre-Dame de Roscudon, Pont-Croix, mid-15th century; ruined rose, Longpont Abbey, before 1217; Ancien Collégiale St Thomas, Crépy-en-Valois, late 13th/early 14th century

TOP RIGHT Villard de Honnecourt's drawing of the Lausanne rose window, showing the description *une reonde veriere* written in the rim, *c.* 1235. The drawing contains many inaccuracies (see p. 251)

ABOVE RIGHT The ruin of an early 14th-century rose at Winchester Palace, Southwark, London, which was destroyed in a fire in 1814

ROSE WINDOWS IN GOTHIC ARCHITECTURE

While its origins predate the 12th century, the true rose window is a specifically French Gothic creation. In contrast to the preceding Romanesque style, which was characterized by thick, solid walls, round arches, barrel vaults and small windows, the Gothic style used an array of new structural techniques to give a sense of airiness, weightlessness and pronounced verticality. This is a rather simplistic distinction: Romanesque elements can be found well into the 13th century, while some early Gothic churches, such as Laon Cathedral, do not feel particularly airy. But all in all it amounted to an architectural revolution, heralding a golden age for architecture not just in France, but right across Europe.

The main innovations of the new style first appeared together in the Abbey of St Denis, just outside Paris, in around 1140–50. The rebuilding of this important church was masterminded by Abbot Suger, whose views on his creation survive in two works, *De Consecratione* and *De Administratione*. While later changes make it difficult today to get a sense of Suger's scheme, several important features remain. First, the ambulatory at the east end, with its breathtaking stained glass. Second, the imposing west end, with the distinctive arrangement of a triple portal flanked by two towers (which would appear again a little later at Chartres). The key innovations at St Denis were an accentuated verticality, the triple portal, and, of course, the rose window – perhaps the very first, though since lost. The one innovation not exhibited at St Denis, but which was vital to the further development of the High Gothic, was the flying buttress. This allowed architects to channel most of the forces created by the weight of the vaults to *outside* the building. This meant that for the first time substantial areas of wall could be turned over to glass: one direct result was the development of the giant rose window. By 1260 some of these roses have annexed entire façades, and the style was no longer confined to in and around Paris but could be found in Spain, Britain, Germany, Italy, and beyond.

ABOVE The west end of Reims Cathedral with its two mid-13th-century roses. The First World War took its toll on the building, and the glass in the upper rose is about one-fifth original, while the lower window contains a design of the Litany of the Virgin by Jacques Simon, 1937

OPPOSITE In this aerial view of Chartres Cathedral we can clearly see the key innovations of Gothic architecture: the flying buttresses flanking the nave; the twin towers at the west end; the recessed triple portal of the south transept; and, of course, the rose windows. Here we can see the west and south roses, of which the west is the earlier

This new monumentality in architecture was driven by many factors beyond the technical, however. First, it was the result of the growing secular authority of the Church throughout Europe, coupled with a period of great economic growth. Second, from the early 12th century, changes in religious practice led a growing demand for complex iconographic programmes such as the Tree of Jesse or the Life of the Virgin (see Chapter 5). These programmes grew to encompass stained glass, sculpture and architecture, creating artistically unified structures. The best example is Chartres Cathedral, in which every piece of glass and stone echoes with a common message: the power of beauty, even more than the spiritual and temporal power of the Church. Power is a word that easily comes to mind when discussing rose windows, even discounting the message of the iconography. Their forceful presence on three – and sometimes even on all four – of the axes of important churches and cathedrals seems to indicate something beyond the forces of mere fashion and competition. It is often the form alone of those windows that impresses us with its 'power' to force light into kaleidoscopic displays governed by precise and brilliant geometry.

After the High Gothic and Rayonnant trends of the 13th century the Gothic style developed many regional variations, but the rose window remained a central feature almost everywhere (except, curiously, in Britain, where the rose had enjoyed great popularity early on). Roses of the late 14th to 16th centuries are characterized by their use of 'Flamboyant' tracery – so called because of its particularly flame-like forms – and while the roses of the period up to the mid-16th century may lack the grandeur of their 13th-century predecessors, they more than compensate in terms of innovation and imagination, and are often virtuoso in their detail. After around 1540 the Gothic style fell out of fashion almost everywhere, and although a few non-Gothic roses were dreamt up in this period, it would not be until the Gothic revival of the 19th century that the rose window would regain its former glory or importance.

These six engravings show the basic developments of
the rose form in the medieval period: first, at top left,
one of the three simple, yet inventive, west roses from
Peterborough Cathedral. The shapes of the petals are
similar to those at Beauvais, which dates to around 1150
(see p. 56); below that is the Chartres west rose, from
c. 1215, which still retains colonnettes. Top centre is
the Laon west rose, one of the first giant roses that
dominated the façade, dating to around 1200, while
below in the centre is the north rose at Notre-Dame,
Paris, a masterpiece of Rayonnant design, with clearly
radiating tracery, dating to c. 1245. On the right, above,
a transitional rose at St Mary's, Cheltenham, from the
early 14th century, shows the Curvilinear style, the
gradual introduction of curving tracery, which
eventually led to Flamboyant windows such as
that at the Sainte-Chapelle, c. 1485, bottom right

THE MEDIEVAL EXPERIENCE OF THE ROSE WINDOW

The symbolism and iconography that rose windows transmit can speak to us at many levels. Hugh of St Victor, who almost certainly advised Suger as he planned the rebuilding of St Denis, commented generally on Suger's creations that:

> The foolish man wonders at only the beauty in those things; but the wise man sees through that which is external, laying open the profound thought of divine wisdom.[6]

There are few accounts of the reactions of medieval contemporaries to the architecture that was evolving in their midst: Hugh of St Victor's writings offer one viewpoint, but his follower Richard of St Victor upheld that there were four different levels of seeing Biblical truths.[7] The few medieval accounts that do exist seem to be somewhat prosaic, and one cannot help but wonder whether our 21st-century reactions to rose windows may, on occasion, contain much latent romanticism and perhaps even a longing for something miraculous to be revealed.

There is one particularly apposite contemporary account, however. It comes from the *Metrical Life of St Hugh* and concerns the two rose windows at Lincoln Cathedral as they were in the 1220s:

> The double majesty of the windows displays shining riddles before men's eyes; it is emblazoned with the citizens of the Heavenly City, and the arms with which they overcame the tyrant of Hell. And the two larger windows are like two blazing lights, whose circular radiance is looking at the north and south end, and surpasses all the windows with its twin light. The others may be compared with the common stars; but of these two, one is like the Sun, the other, the Moon. Thus two candelabra make sunlit the head of the church, imitating the rainbow in semblance and variegated colours; Nay, not imitating, but rather outdoing it; for when the sun is broken up in the clouds it makes a rainbow; but these two shine without a sun, and glitter without a cloud...

And later:

> Illuminating the world with heavenly light is the distinguished band of the clergy, and this is expressed by the clergy....
> The twin windows that offer a circular light are the two Eyes of the cathedral and rightly the greater of these is seen to be the bishop and the lesser the dean. For the north represents the devil, and the south the Holy Spirit and it is in these directions that the two Eyes look. The bishop faces the south in order to invite in, and the dean the north in order to avoid; the one takes care to be saved, the other takes care not to perish. With these Eyes the cathedral's face is on the watch for the candelabra of heaven and the darkness of Lethe.[8]

ABOVE Rose windows have always had mystical associations. Here a rose is the conduit for the conception and Heavenly blessing received by Mary (central panel of the *Aix Annunciation*, Barthélémy d'Eyck, 1445)

OPPOSITE This rather spectacular and unorthodox rose at Lincoln Cathedral was known even in medieval times as the 'Bishop's Eye' (the one opposite is known as the 'Dean's Eye') as seen in the account in the *Metrical Life of St Hugh*. It is filled with glass recovered from the aftermath of the Civil War, reset in a glorious jumble that plays with the light. The original scene was probably the Last Judgement, as in the rose in the north transept (south rose, Lincoln Cathedral, *c.* 1330)

In this extract rose windows are clearly ascribed specific properties and meanings. However, it is still difficult for us in the 21st century to 'get into' the mind of an age over eight hundred years ago, since its whole world image must have been fundamentally different from ours. Medieval man clearly experienced beauty as a moral and psychological reality – as E. R. Curtis stated, 'When the scholastics spoke about beauty they meant by this an attribute of God.'[9] For Suger at St Denis, the jewels and coloured glass in his new church possessed the ability to:

> transform that which is material to that which is immaterial....
> Then it seems to me that I see myself dwelling, as it were,
> in some strange region of the universe which neither exists
> entirely in the slime of the earth nor entirely in the purity
> of Heaven; and that, by the grace of God, I can be transported
> from this inferior to that higher world.[10]

This 'transportation' was what is often referred to as the mystical or 'anagogical' effect. Whether the rose window on the façade of St Denis was designed to have such an effect we cannot say, though filled with 12th-century glass the effect must have been magical.

Suger's commentary also raises another point pertinent to the study of rose windows – indeed, all stained glass – in the medieval period: the importance of the symbolism of light. A famous work by the late 5th-century Syrian mystic known as Pseudo-Dionysius the Areopagite called *The Celestial Hierarchies* expounded a theory of Divine Light by which humans could experience a greater reality, 'fittingly tempered to our natures by the Providence of the Father.'[11] Seeing light as a transforming power goes back to the New Testament, particularly St John's Gospel, where Christ is presented as the Logos, the creative principle in the universe (he is seen as such in three small rose windows at Chartres – see p. 194).[12] The metaphor of light as a transformatory agent was

developed by, among others, St Augustine and Pope Gregory the Great in the 6th century, and by the 12th century had been combined with theories derived from the newly rediscovered Plato. *The Celestial Hierarchies* had an enormous influence on the Byzantine world, and was translated into Latin by an Irish monk, John Scotus Eriugena, in the 9th century, who added a commentary: it was this version that Suger and his fellow monks would have studied. For Robert Grosseteste (who also translated the Pseudo-Dionysius) in the 13th century, light was the mediator between 'bodiless and bodily substances, a spiritual body, an embodied spirit'.[13]

It was not only light that interested the Neo-Platonists. Geometry and music also reflected 'pure form', since both were founded upon numbers and therefore potentially acted as manifestations of God. It was only natural to use numbers and simple proportions in architecture to reflect this. The rose window, as a marriage of light and number, clearly blossomed in this metaphysical climate.

OPPOSITE Light has always had mystical associations, which are often played with in rose windows (S. Maria Maggiore, Tuscania, mid-13th century)

ABOVE RIGHT The circle within the square symbolizes the finite and infinite, the reconciliation of earth with heaven, of time and eternity; Christ appears at the centre of both. Around the square are fifty-two heads, probably symbolizing the weeks of the year (main façade, Orvieto Cathedral, 14th century)

OVERLEAF The personal experience of the rose window can be (and probably always has been) one of constant surprise and elation (Sant Cugat, Sant Cugat del Vallès, 1337–50, glass 20th century)

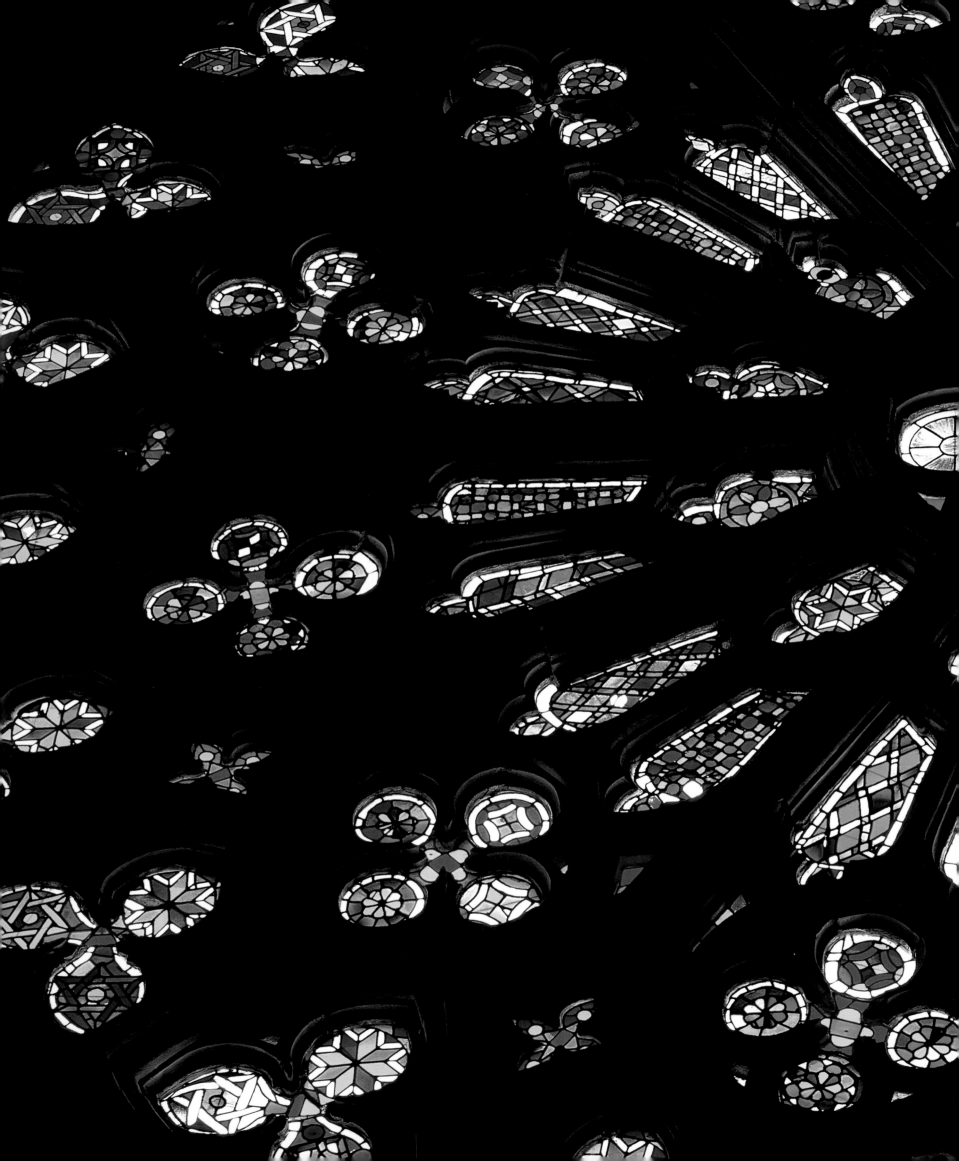

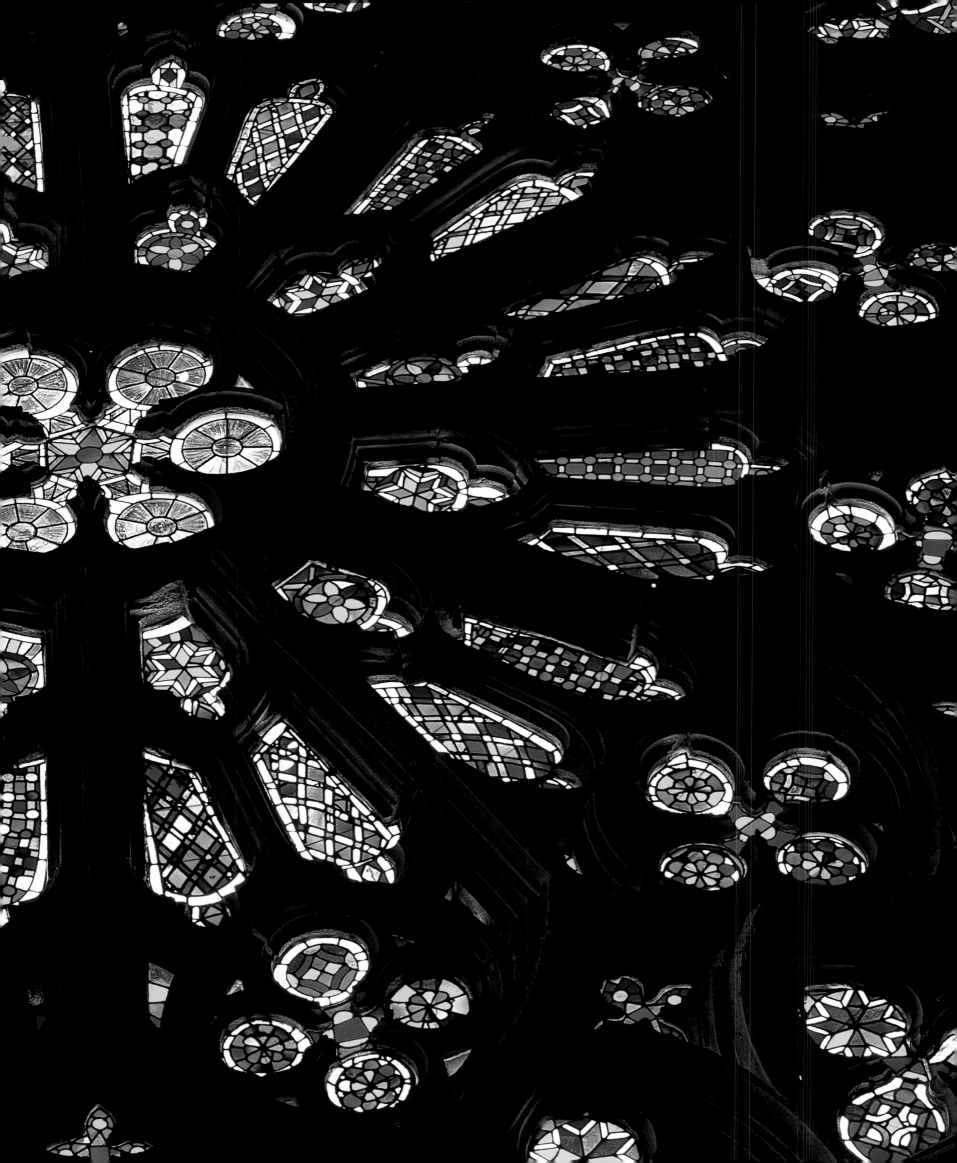

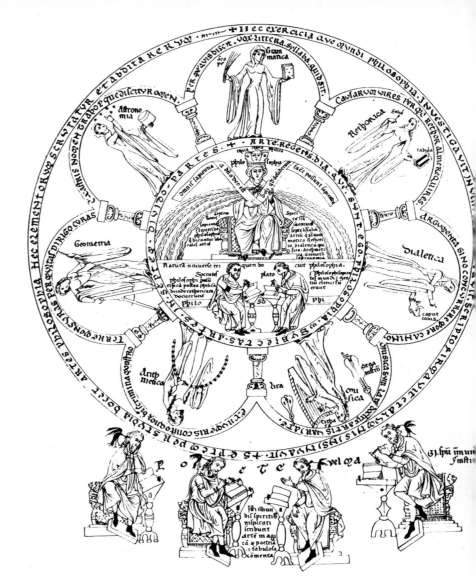

When considering medieval attitudes to the rose, it is also useful to look at the scholastic interest taken in cosmological schemes, specifically the Microcosm–Macrocosm relationship. Stemming from Bede's *De Temporibus* in the 9th century, this scheme showed relationships between the four elements, the four seasons, the four directions, the months, and the signs of the zodiac, as well as with the four humours and the four ages of man.[14] Much of this cosmological cycle appears in the rose at Lausanne Cathedral (see pp. 208–11). As is discussed in Chapter 5, which deals with iconography, order was something of a medieval passion. The rose window was particularly suited to portraying and linking these numeric-based philosophical 'systems of relationships.' So, the rose frequently symbolized divine order, and, in its perfect roundness, could also stand for the universe.

In trying to understand how the medieval viewer saw the rose, it is instructive to look at how, why and where it was depicted. Roses and rose-type patterns appear often in many other media, including sculpture, metalwork, manuscript illumination and pavements. An example of the latter is the marble pavement at S. Miniato al Monte (see p. 53), which dates to 1207 – about the same time that the first really large rose windows were being constructed. This example is useful since it shows the twelvefold form seen most commonly in rose windows, in this case perhaps because it houses figures representing the signs of the zodiac. Its indebtedness to early rose window designs can also be seen in the carrying over of colonnettes. Some hundred years later, at Westminster Abbey, we find tiles based on the rose window of the north transept. This suggests that the rose might function as an emblem or symbol of the foundation, almost like a brand, something instantly recognizable.

Another rose hovers above an effigy on a tomb at Saint-Germain-lès-Corbeil. Here, it seems to function almost as a protective device, or a symbol for the soul of the deceased.[15] The 13th century saw an explosion of interest in microarchitecture – essentially the use of Gothic forms on a miniature scale. Another wonderful example is the reliquary of St Gertrude, at Nivelles, which featured four finely worked Rayonnant roses, one of which was based quite accurately on the west rose at Reims (though this type originally stemmed from the transept roses at Notre-Dame in Paris). Its delicacy seems in keeping with the Virgin appearing below (the connection between the rose window and the Virgin Mary is discussed in Chapter 5). Sadly, like so many real rose windows in northeastern France and Flanders, the reliquary was very badly damaged in the Second World War.[16] A late medieval painting of the Annunciation to the Virgin by Barthélémy d'Eyck (see p. 24), meanwhile, tellingly has the heavenly light of the blessing directed (rather awkwardly) through a miniature rose. The rose here is a vehicle for divine communication or revelation, with clearly mystical overtones.

A similar mystical association can be seen in the *Romance of Alexander the Great* manuscript, made in Rouen in around 1445. Looming at the back of the room, behind the Caladrius birds that brought healing, it seems to stand for the numinous. Intriguingly, there are very few spiral roses, perhaps because of the inherent difficulty of designing and constructing them, though this particular design recalls the rose in the Bourbon Chapel at Lyon Cathedral (see p. 151) or the spiral on the façade of Milan Cathedral (p. 268).

OPPOSITE Depictions of rose windows in the medieval period can tell us much about how they were viewed, and perhaps give us a clue as to their original meanings. Clockwise from top left: tiles from the Chapterhouse of Westminster Abbey, early 14th century; an illumination from the *Hortus Deliciarum* by Herrad of Landsberg, shows Philosophy surrounded by the Liberal Arts, similar to the north rose at Laon Cathedral (see p. 70), 19th-century copy of 12th-century original; the reliquary of St Gertrude, Nivelles, by Nicolas de Douai and Jacques de Nivelles, 1272–92; the tombstone of Magister Johannes, a curate, in Saint-Germain-lès-Corbeil, dated 1340.

ABOVE RIGHT An illustration from the mid-15th-century manuscript *The Romance of Alexander the Great*, shows the emperor seated in the throne room before a fine helicoidal spiral rose window, with the Caladrius birds.

THE GLASS

If the massive changes seen in faith and society since the 13th century make interpreting medieval roses difficult, this disadvantage is compounded by the fact that only very rarely has a rose retained its original glass. Where it does survive, however, the effect is breathtaking, both in the overall impression, and, where we are able to get close, in the detail of the individual panels. Stained glass was an expensive material in the Middle Ages so the production of the huge rose windows that appeared after 1200 represents a tremendous investment in terms of materials and manpower. At Chartres we know that two of the rose windows were paid for by the King of France and the Count of Dreux, both wealthy men.

There is some question over how the earliest roses were glazed. In all likelihood the first known rose window, at St Denis, would have had coloured glass, since it was very much to Suger's taste. However, those eager early proponents of the rose, the Cistercians, forbade the use of figurative, coloured glass, and would have probably used either clear glass or grisaille. Even in non-Cistercian foundations we cannot be entirely certain what originally filled the window – possibly thin sheets of alabaster were used in some cases, as we find today at Orvieto Cathedral in Italy. Good quantities of glass survive in roses only from the late 12th century onwards, but even then survival is sporadic. Generally speaking the earlier glass tends to be darker and richer, with blue and red predominating; later glass is lighter and more painterly, with yellow and green used extensively in the 14th century. By the 16th century the rose is often being treated as a large canvas, in the Renaissance manner.

In more recent times, roses have tended to be glazed (and reglazed) with more abstract designs, and new techniques such as dalle de verre (slab glass, often set in concrete) have been employed. At Washington Cathedral the rose designed by Rowan le Compte incorporates prisms, which throw the light in different directions (see pp. 184–5). Sensation has always been at the heart of the rose.

ABOVE LEFT A detail of Christ teaching in the temple, from the 'Dean's Eye' at Lincoln. It may originally have been elsewhere in the cathedral, but it is not uncommon for glass to be reused or moved around (north rose, Lincoln Cathedral, c. 1230)

OPPOSITE A beautifully painted angel with six wings in the famous reds and blues characteristic of the 13th-century glass at Chartres (north rose, Chartres, c. 1230)

While the form of a rose window may be the first thing to impress us, the glass is vital to the specific meaning of any rose. Since the rose was one of the focal points of any church, the glass is often of very high quality. However, it has also been frequently replaced, and modern schemes have had varying degrees of success

TOP ROW Three panels from the rose window in York Minster with the red and white roses commemorating the union of the Houses of York and Lancaster by Henry VII's marriage; modern glass in the east rose window at Crema Cathedral; a detail from one of the windows in the dome of Florence Cathedral – the sleeping disciples with Christ in the Garden of Gethsemane, by Ghiberti, c. 1443–5; a detail from the Last Judgment in the rose window at Ste Radegonde, Poitiers, c. 1270

BOTTOM ROW St Andrew and a bishop in the south rose of Notre-Dame, c. 1260; musical angels in the Flamboyant north rose window at Sens Cathedral, c. 1518; modern dalle-de-verre glass at St Luc, Romainville, 1931

OVERLEAF The south rose window in Lyon Cathedral features the Redemption: twelve angels surround the dove of the Holy Spirit, while at the summit is Christ and the four Evangelist symbols, and below scenes from Adam and Eve – here we can see the creation of Eve, the Temptation and the Expulsion (south rose, Lyon Cathedral, 1235–40, some 19th-century glass)

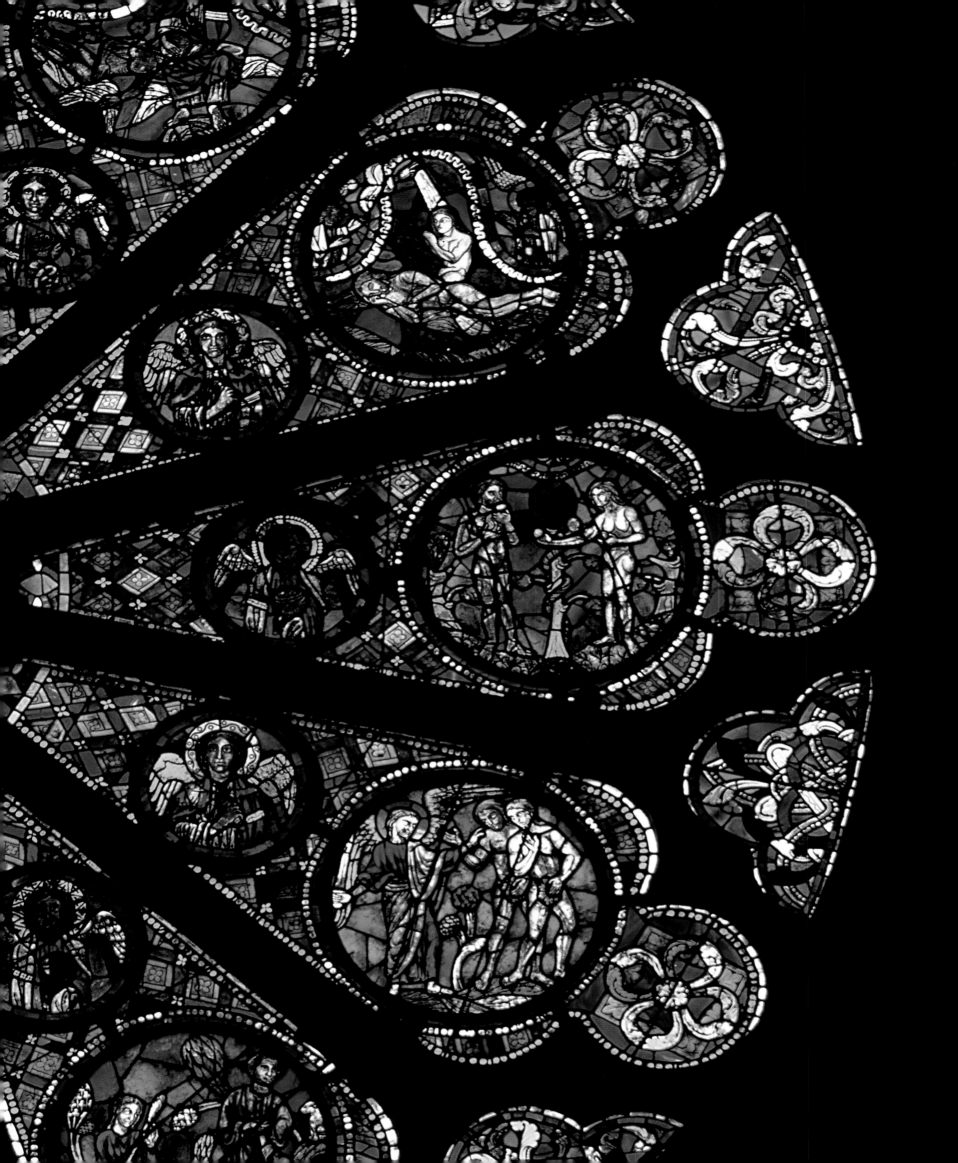

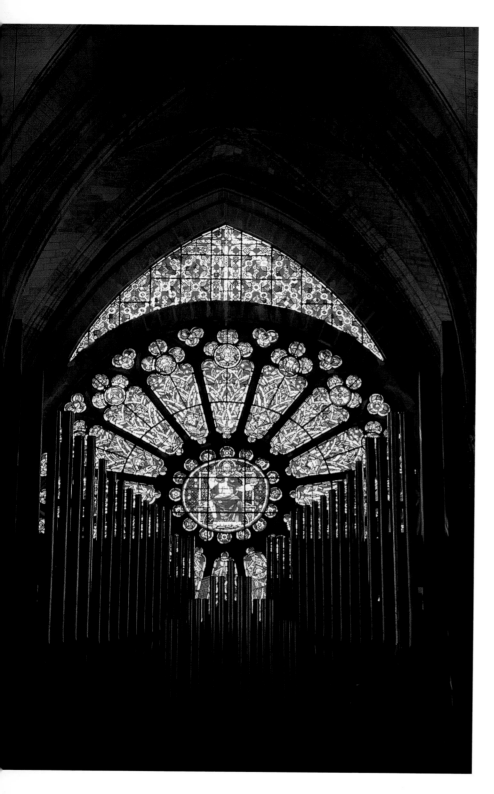

THE ROSE WINDOW TODAY

With the Gothic Revival of the 19th century came a renewed interest, in Britain, France and Germany at least, in the art and architecture of the medieval period, and the first serious attempts to document and conserve this heritage. Champions of the style such as Viollet-le-Duc worked hard to restore such important monuments as Notre-Dame and St Denis (where as recently as the 18th century the important early rose window had been lost to make room for a clock), sometimes perhaps imposing their own ideas a little too heavily. Today, conservation efforts are more scrupulous, as we can see in the recent projects at Lincoln, Lausanne and Chartres, where the glass has been cleaned and protected, and the stonework made secure, or even very carefully renewed (see pp. 262–3). In more drastic cases, where roses have lost their original glass completely, they have been reglazed, often sympathetically. While one may initially worry about the historical accuracy of such reglazing, such renewal is entirely in keeping with the medieval view of things – we will encounter a few instances of earlier roses being replaced with more fashionable designs, as was the case with the Sainte-Chapelle in 1485. In addition, such reglazing can give the rose, as an object of religious meditation, a new lease of life, ensuring that it remains relevant in the modern church.

Ironically, as Europe was waking up to its rich medieval inheritance, and wave after wave of publications was appearing dealing with the nature of Gothic art, society was already beginning to drift ever further from the political and spiritual origins of these creations. Today we have largely lost the ability to read the complex yet illuminating iconographic programmes, to disentangle the references to scholastic thought, to comprehend the precise geometry or the sheer scale of the task of constructing these cathedrals.[17] As this book hopefully demonstrates, however, with a little effort and a sympathetic attitude, roses can give us the most fascinating insights into the medieval way of looking at things.

ABOVE LEFT This rose at Soissons, badly damaged in First World War bombardments, was given a new lease of life with striking Art Deco glass by Gaudin in 1931 (west rose, Soissons Cathedral, tracery c. 1260)

OPPOSITE A rose at Notre-Dame, Le Folgoët, 15th century

CHAPTER 1
FROM DARKNESS TO LIGHT: THE ORIGINS OF THE ROSE WINDOW

Traditionally, the birth of the rose window has been seen to coincide with the birth of the Gothic style at St Denis. There the rose in the western façade – which, as we saw in the Introduction, was sadly destroyed in the 18th century to make way for a clock – dated from between 1140 and 1144, and took the form of a simple wheel shape, probably with twelve spokes. While St Denis deserves its place as a key innovator in Gothic architecture we must question the miraculous appearance of a fully formed (if primitive) rose at that church, especially when we consider the structural risks that the earliest architects must have taken. Needless to say we are hampered in our efforts by the severe lack of documentary and physical evidence, but also by constantly shifting chronologies. The other frequently cited early rose, at St Etienne in Beauvais – which is the earliest surviving Gothic rose window – almost certainly postdates St Denis by about ten years.[1] In trying to piece together the origins of the rose window, then, it is more fruitful to examine its constituent parts. We begin by looking at three key pre-rose window trends: the development of the oculus, the independent development of tracery, and the symbolism of the circle.

THE OCULUS

The most obvious precedent for the rose window is the simple oculus, a circular opening designed to let in light, and often not glazed. This probably strikes us as a fundamentally Romanesque device – circular, static, iconic – and it is interesting that both Jean Bony and Erwin Panofsky have pointed out that despite its enormous popularity, the rose is largely out of keeping with the Gothic

mentality.[2] In fact, the oculus dates back at least to Antique Roman architecture where it is sometimes found at the summits of domes (for example, in the Pantheon), but it is in Early Christian architecture – specifically in the region covered by modern-day Syria – that we find it assuming some sort of apparent symbolic function. An example of a 6th-century Syrian oculus could recently be found at the chapel at Burdj Hêdar, located at the centre of the pediment.[3] Helen Dow, in her thesis on the origins of the rose window, has suggested that the placing of oculi (or other circular motifs) above doors and windows, often at the four points of the compass, 'emphasizes the protection aspect' of these devices.[4]

Assuming – what an assumption! – that one might draw a continuous line from these early oculi to the 12th-century Ile-de-

ABOVE RIGHT Some of the earliest oculi in a religious context can be found in the Near East, particularly in Syria. Typically these openings are axial and placed in pediments or above doors (chapel at Burdj Hêdar, Syria, 6th century AD)

OPPOSITE A moment of transition from oculus to rose (east rose, Silvacane Abbey, c. 1200)

France, a likely point of contact would have been Spain, with its links to the Byzantine Empire and the Near East,[5] and it is interesting to note that in the past Spain has been seen as a possible channel for the introduction of the Gothic pointed arch. However, the oculus did not seem to play a significant role in Carolingian or Ottonian architecture, judging by the very few surviving examples (the oculi at Saint-Généroux in France may date from as early as 950), and it is in the late 11th century that oculi began to make a more widespread appearance, in Romanesque churches. An impressive example from the early 12th century can be found at Cefalù Cathedral, in Sicily. The tradition continued into the 12th and even the 13th centuries, and the advent of the rose window by no means spelt the end for these oculi.

Some of them are wonders to behold: St Gabriel near Tarascon, churches in Berson, Gassicourt, Fleurial and Gouzon in France and Uzzano in Italy are just a few examples of impressive oculi. In Italy the oculus went on and on – right up to the 16th century in parallel with the evolution of rose or wheel windows.[6] It is tempting to imagine that as the oculi grew larger they required glazing, and that as they grew still larger tracery was developed as a support for this glass. Certainly some later 12th-century oculi – good examples would be the Cistercian abbeys at Pontigny and Preuilly, both in France – begin to sprout cusps, presumably to support ever-larger areas of glass. This reminds us that new architectural devices might be taken up at very different speeds in different areas. Such windows also seem to point forward to the lighter 'bar' tracery typical of 13th-century roses, discussed in Chapter 2. The earliest surviving glazed oculus, meanwhile, can be found not in France nor in Italy, but in Britain, at Canterbury Cathedral. The transept oculi there date to around 1180 (see pp. 46–7), the north one containing a scene representing the Old Law, symbolized by Moses and Synagogue, surrounded by the cardinal virtues and Old Testament prophets (the south containing 19th-century glass).

OPPOSITE The Carolingian church at Saint-Généroux is one of the oldest surviving in France, though much restored. The twin oculi at the east end are almost certainly original, though they are not necessarily a common feature of Carolingian churches (Saint-Généroux, Poitou, c. 950)

ABOVE RIGHT This large oculus is roughly contemporary with the building of St Denis. It was heavily restored in 1852–5, and may originally have had tracery. There are traces of two small naked figures on the perimeter, suggesting that this might originally have been a Wheel of Fortune, similar to the surviving wheel at St Etienne, Beauvais[7] (Cluniac Priory, Gassicourt, c. 1150)

ABOVE This fine oculus at the isolated church of St Gabriel in southwestern France is surrounded by the symbols of the four Evangelists. Its decoration with floral and natural motifs, which is original, is highly reminiscent of Roman designs found in the area (St Gabriel, Tarascon, c. 1200)

OPPOSITE This large cusped oculus at the magnificent Cistercian abbey-church of Pontigny appeared after the first fully formed rose windows, but offers an attractive alternative. The design is reminiscent of other Cistercian oculi on façades of similar date, as at Noirlac, Silvacane, Heisterbach, Fontfroide, Orval, Sylvanès and the eastern wall of Fossanova in Italy (cusped oculus, south transept, Pontigny, abbey built 1160–80)

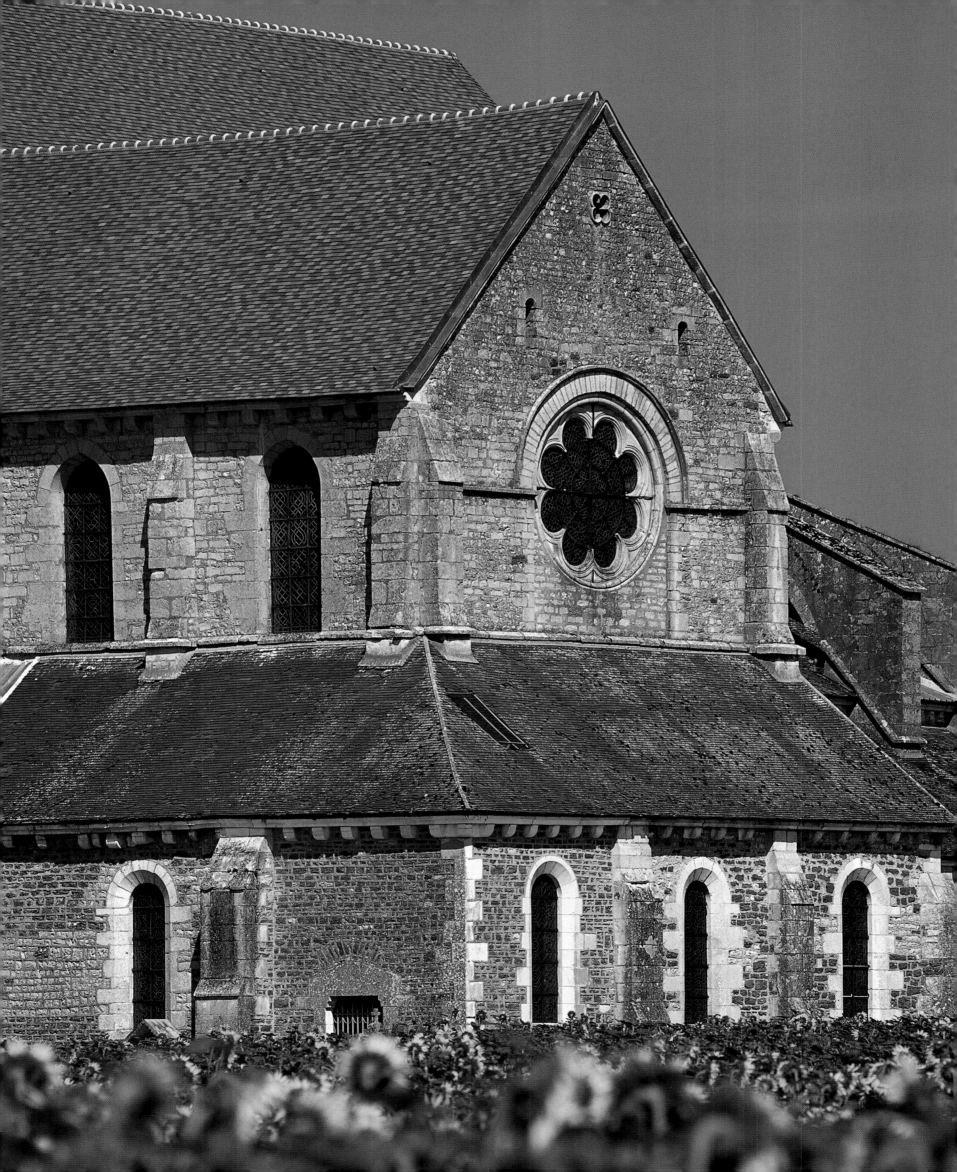

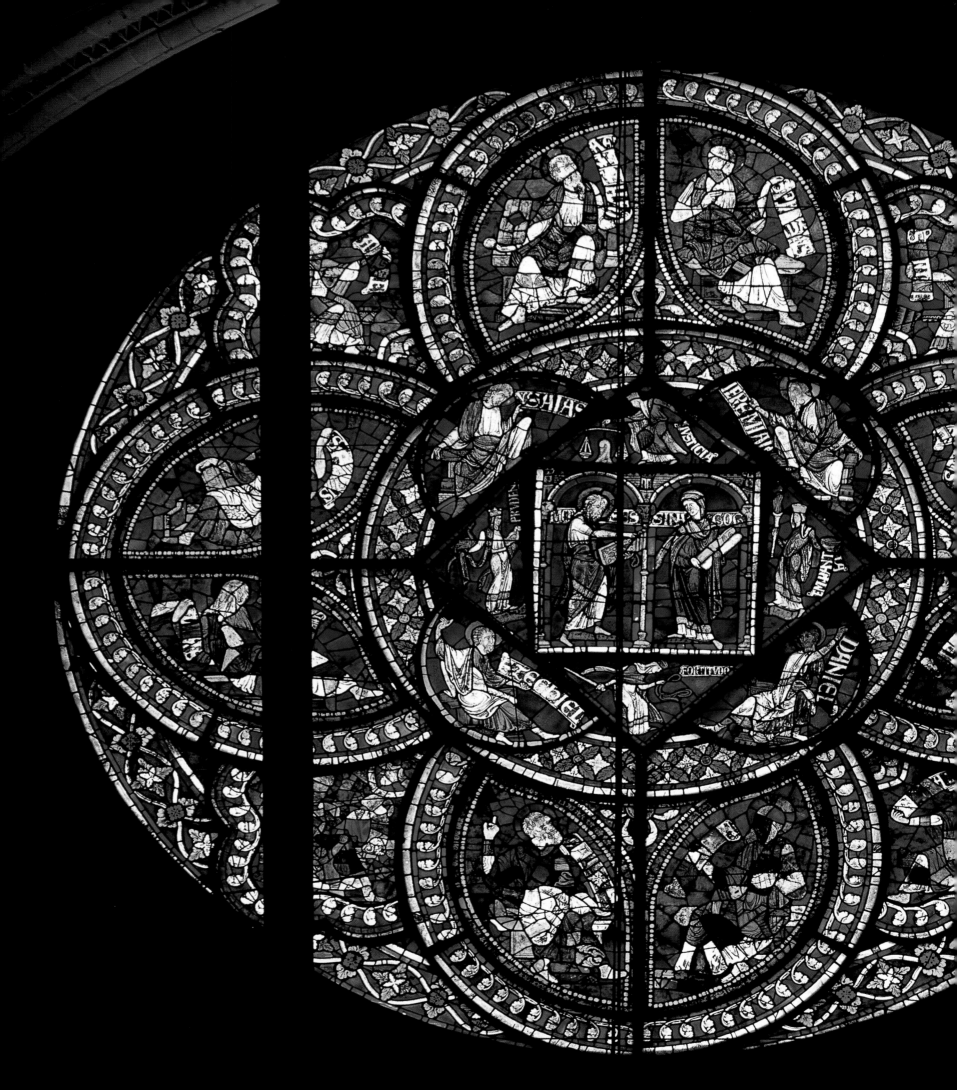

The oculus at Canterbury is the oldest surviving glazed example anywhere. It shows the Old Law, symbolized by Moses and Synagogue, surrounded by the cardinal virtues (Prudence, Justice, Temperance and Strength), with the prophets Isaiah, Jeremiah, Ezekiel and Daniel in the half-roundels. The south transept probably originally contained the New Law (north oculus, Canterbury Cathedral. Stonework and glass c. 1180 and 19th century)

THE EVOLUTION OF WINDOW TRACERY

Examples of pre-12th-century window tracery are widespread and varied. Indeed, attempts to fill windows with some kind of system that admitted light yet kept out adverse weather go back to Roman times. Filling the void with a sheet of alabaster, marble or glass was one solution, but larger windows needed some form of internal support, perhaps made of wood, lead or even iron.[8]

If we return to 5th- or 6th-century Syria, we find a primitive 'plate' tracery, where a single, flat piece of stone has had openings chiselled out of it, before being set into a wall. In some cases circular

or radial patterns in the tracery, usually set within a square, hint at rose windows, as can be seen at Haouran.[9] A very interesting example, again dating from the 6th century, though known to us only through 19th-century drawings, is the circle hollowed out to form a cross in the gable of a basilica at Dêr Termanîn. We cannot be sure of the exact function of this device, but its axial positioning suggests importance.

Such windows are often known as transennas: later examples might be made from lead, stucco, or even a single piece of stone that is carved into a geometric pattern and can be fitted into a window to allow light to enter. Transennas were popular in the Islamic world with its particular interest in geometry. Examples can be found on two sides of the 9th-century Visigothic church at San Miguel de Lillo in Oviedo, Asturias, Spain (where Islamic influence was felt strongly), as well as at the nearby church of San Julian de los Prados. Also in Asturias, at Priesca, is the wonderful transenna at the church of San Salvador. Dating to after 921, this has a clear radiating form, with eight spokes, and semi-circular forms filling in the corners. A tiny oculus also survives at this church, above the door on the west façade. A good example of a claustrum with wheel-like form, meanwhile, is the 6th-century Visigothic screen in the church of San Vicente, Cordoba, with its striking radiating tracery. Interestingly, there was originally an almost identical screen in the Grand Mosque in the same city. Other early small one-piece traceries can be seen at Ravenna (S. Apollinare in Classe), the Baptistery in Albenga, and Petit Niort, western France (see p. 50).

Another possible point of entry into Europe for the oculus with tracery could have been Sicily, where Early Christian, Islamic and, later, Romanesque styles were fused. Certainly it has been suggested that the early 12th-century oculi at Cefalù Cathedral might originally have had some kind of tracery, in wood, lead or stone.[10] This could easily have been like the pierced ornamental medallions found at Pomposa from the 11th century (see p. 51).

An example of a transenna: tracery carved from a single plate of stone that is inserted into an opening in the wall. The technique was particularly popular in Visigothic Spain (transenna, San Salvador, Priesca, after 921)

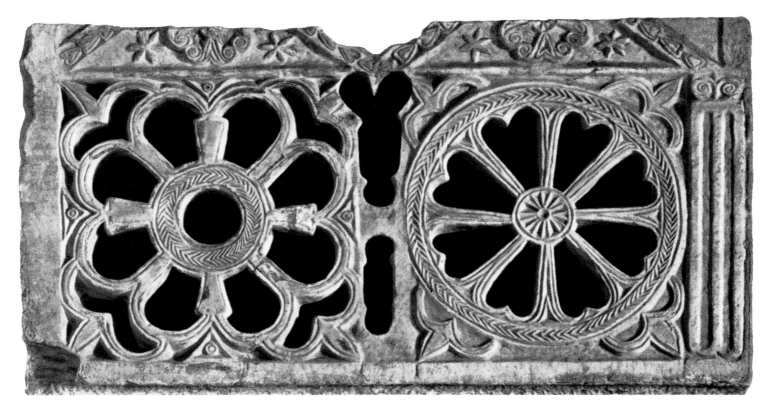

TOP LEFT AND RIGHT Pierced plaques, presumably used as transennas, from Haouran. As with many later rose windows, the number of divisions seems to have particular significance (plaques from Haouran, Syria, before 8th century)

ABOVE Two wheel designs in the Visigothic ambo at the church of San Vicente, Cordoba. The right-hand wheel prefigures a rose window design with alternating spokes and cusps popular in late 12th-century France and Spain (ambo, San Vicente, Cordoba, 6th century)

OVERLEAF LEFT A rare early French transenna created from two slabs of stone perforated with a pattern of holes. Such window fillings were common before the use of glass became more widespread (transenna, Petit Niort, late 11th century)

OVERLEAF RIGHT One of two circular windows on the façade of the narthex at Pomposa. The tracery at the centre of each window is formed from two mythical creatures. Inside the building the floor has a huge wheel mosaic, at the centre of which is the date of the reconstruction (Pomposa Abbey, church reconstructed 1026)

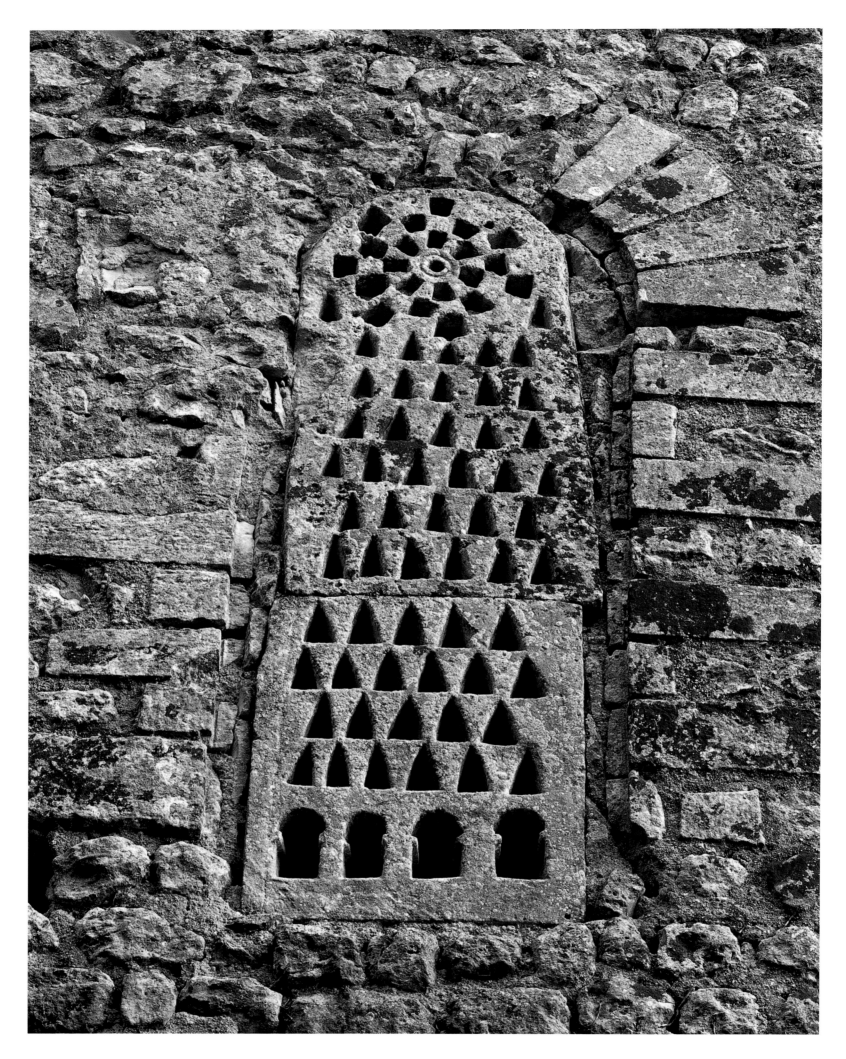

THE SYMBOL OF THE CIRCLE

Although art historians tend to look for precedents and sources for artistic and architectural features it has to be said that there is something rather inevitable, even archetypal, about circular or radiating patterns. The image of the wheel seems to be deeply ingrained in the human sub-conscious: it often appears in Buddhist art and architecture from well over a thousand years ago, as well as in ancient Greek and even Babylonian art. From the very earliest Christian times, when the faithful relied on covert symbols to identify themselves, one of the most popular was the 'Chi-Rho'. The Greek letters X and P combined within a circle can still be seen, for example, as graffiti on some the streets of 1st-century AD Ephesus, in Syria, and for the next two thousand years this symbol can be found in numerous different forms and places, typically embellished into the form of a six-spoked wheel.[11] Rosettes, crosses, spirals, wheels, stars and other forms based on the circle can be found as decoration carved onto door lintels, architraves, tombs, altar fronts, pillars, capitals and friezes for many centuries before Romanesque and Gothic architecture evolved. These devices may well have originated in the sun symbols associated with pre-Christian religions, notably Mithraism, yet they remain popular well into the 12th century and can be seen decorating many Romanesque churches in France – as for example on a lintel at Moissac, St Vivien in the Guyenne, or Levinhac – and in Italy at Bominaco and Albenga. Circular patterns abound in profusion at the eastern ends of Monreale Cathedral and Palermo Cathedral, both in Sicily and both late 12th century.

Circular form was, moreover, a convenient and popular way of presenting ideas and philosophical schemes, a mode that also goes back at least to late Roman times. It is common even today to talk about 'cycles', meaning narrative sequences, even when the form is not circular. So, we find in manuscripts and wall paintings throughout the early medieval period the vices and virtues, signs of

the zodiac, labours of the month and ever-popular Wheels of Fortune, each of which uses the wheel structure to emphasize either their polarities or their transitory and time-dependent nature. Christ at the centre of a dome surrounded by angels, apostles and the elect in Paradise is an awe-inspiring representation of circular form making a theological statement: examples can be seen in paintings and mosaic from Istanbul to Venice and Rome.[12] More down to earth is the splendid depiction of the Creation in the 11th-century tapestry at Girona Cathedral, in northeastern Spain, where the six days surround Christ as Creator.

In Italy, floor mosaics with elaborate geometrical layouts based on squares and circles demonstrate that Antique Roman tastes still prevailed in that region after the year 1000 – as can be seen, for example, in the floor zodiacs in the churches of S. Miniato al Monte and S. Giovanni, both in Florence, as well as at Aosta, where Christ occupies the central circle and is surrounded by the labours of the months. In the case of the zodiac pavement at S. Miniato, which dates to 1207, the tradition has itself been overtaken and is influenced by rose window design.

ABOVE Circular patterns can be very useful for organizing information. In this tapestry, which depicts the Creation, God sits at the the centre surrounded by scenes and characters from Genesis. The four rivers of Paradise enclose the corners, while in the series of squares that enclose the rivers and the circle of creation are the months of the year, the Year, the Sun and the Moon (Creation Tapestry, Girona, c. 1100)

OPPOSITE This marble pavement in S. Miniato, Florence, synthesizes the tradition of radiating pavements with a rose-window type design (complete with capitals). As with many rose windows the division into twelve neatly coincides with the subject matter: the signs of the zodiac (pavement, S. Miniato al Monte, Florence, installed 1207)

THE FIRST ROSE WINDOW?

Bearing in mind these three trends – and particularly the oculus in the religious context and the development of tracery – the earliest remaining example of a rose window is arguably in northwest Spain, at San Miguel de Lillo, near Oviedo. After the Moors had invaded Spain in 711 the first victory of the resistance occurred at Covadonga in eastern Asturias only eleven years later in 722. Thereafter the Kingdom of Asturias was born. Alfonso I (the Chaste) ruled from 791 to 841 and established his capital at Oviedo, but it was his son Ramiro I who, in the 840s, built the Summer Palace (now a church) just outside the city, with the attendant church of San Miguel de Lillo a few hundred yards away.

San Miguel de Lillo has been much altered over the ages: its nave has been shortened and it is possible that some of the windows have been rearranged. The rose window is only a few feet in diameter, but manages to contain two layers of openings with another layer of decoration, all centred around a hub. The innermost layer has six petals while the outer has fourteen, and it seems unlikely that the window was ever glazed. There is also a smaller rose with longer petals to the right of the façade, while rosettes adorn the remarkable relief sculptures that flank the door, and a series of circular and spiral patterns are carved into the arch over a door on the first floor. Even the capitals of the columns bear little rosettes and a border or frieze of rosettes runs at floor level round the whole interior of the building. The rose is very much the theme of this building, even if its significance is not immediately clear to us today.

One other church of the same age and in the same region, San Martín in Argüelles, has a similar rose, although almost certainly it is not in its original location. Two other nearby churches have radiating tracery: San Miguel in Villardeveyo (which has been reset) and San Salvador in Priesca (see p. 48). Although neither of these are true roses, there is considerable evidence that a certain type of radiating tracery flourished for a while in this corner of Spain.

Asturias not only has ports that regularly traded with France at this time, but, more significantly, Oviedo is on one of the pilgrimage routes that ran from France to Santiago de Compostela, the home of the relics of St James in northwestern Spain. These routes have long been seen as possible conduits of trends and ideas (though there has been some disagreement over the direction in which the currents flowed). While there is no existing evidence of rose windows in 9th- and 10th-century France, and it would be foolhardy to propose any direct influence, certain similarities in the design of the western end of St Denis, with its rose window looking into a room above the portal rather than the body of the church itself, and the arrangement at San Miguel de Lillo, leave the chance of influence having been transmitted through now lost windows.

ABOVE AND OPPOSITE The Visigothic church of San Miguel de Lillo. The central rose appears to have been cut from a single piece of stone. The photograph above was taken in the late 19th century, when the photographer was able to climb on the roof. Today the church is a UNESCO protected site (San Miguel de Lillo, near Oviedo, begun 848)

LEFT This piece of a Visigothic screen from near Oviedo bears almost exactly the same pattern as the rose at San Miguel, testifying to its popularity and authenticity (part of a screen (?), now in Oviedo Museum, 9th century)

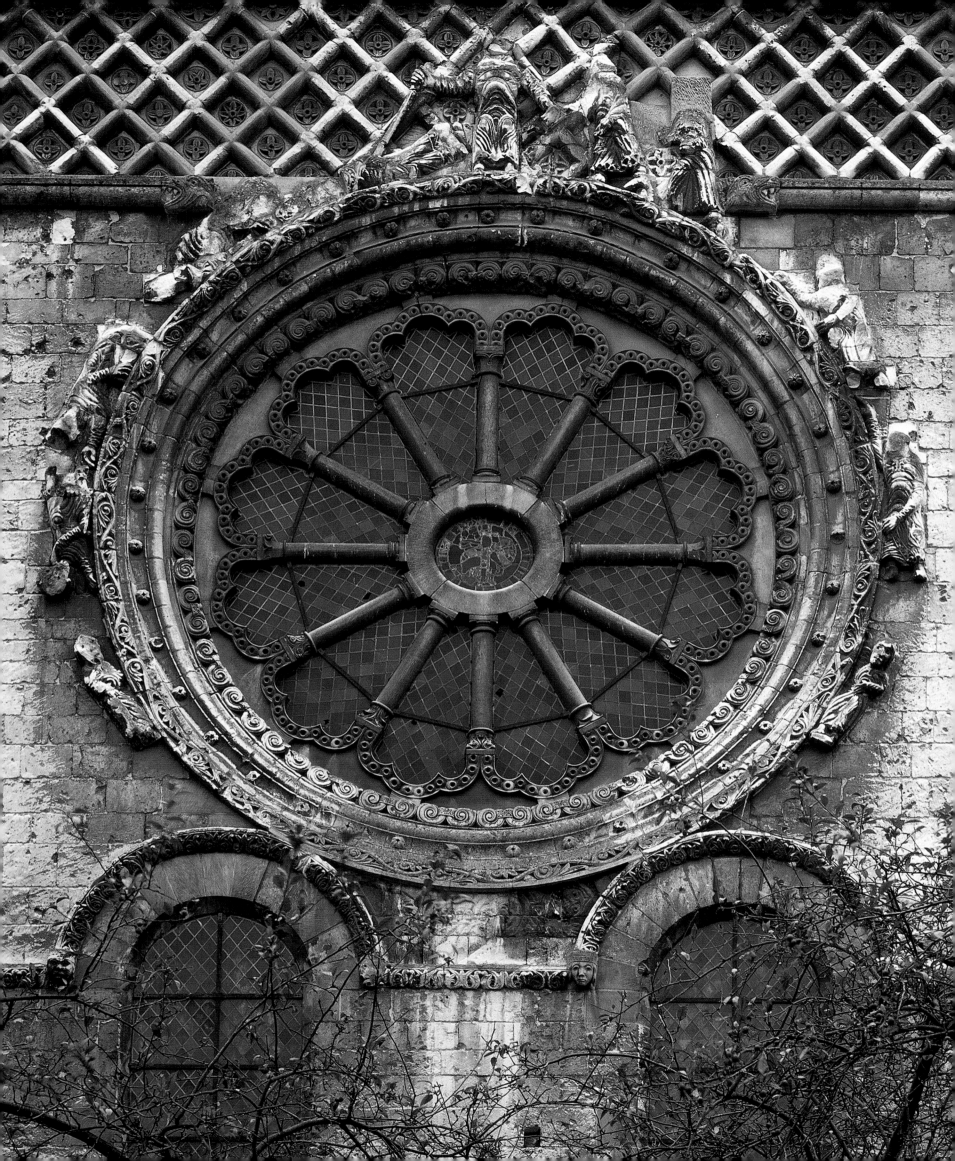

THE EARLIEST ROSE WINDOWS IN FRANCE

We return now to the 1140s, and to St Denis. Regardless of whether the innovations found in Suger's new church actually originated there, it is certain that the design inspired many imitations in France, and the west end arrangement with twin towers and a triple portal obviously exerted an influence on the early Gothic west façade of Chartres Cathedral (see p. 77). It is interesting to note, however, that the Chartres façade, which is like that at St Denis in so many ways, did not adopt the oculus or rose at this point, perhaps because the window at St Denis opened onto a chapel and not onto the nave as it would at Chartres. However, as we shall see later, Chartres's west end did get a rose soon after 1200, presumably by which time it was deemed an essential part of any modern façade.

As to the question of whether the St Denis window had tracery from the beginning – our earliest record, a 17th-century drawing by the Italian architect Vincenzo Scamozzi seems to show very simple tracery, but this could conceivably have been added later – a wheel window high up in the transept of St Etienne in Beauvais may offer some support. Dating from about 1150, this rather splendid creation is decorated around its edge with figures, hapless actors caught in the cycle of virtue and fortune. The Wheel of Fortune is often illustrated as an actual wheel (see Chapter 5), and so it seems reasonable to assume that the 'spokes' dividing the oculus were integral to the overall conception at Beauvais. A further argument for the window at St Denis having had a simple, spoke-like tracery, is that the consecration of Suger's church in 1144 was attended by the bishops of both Sens and Senlis, both of whose churches soon after gained rose or wheel windows high up on their façades. At Sens the now blind wheel or rose was placed at the top of the western façade, set inside a square frame, sometime during the period 1160–70. A similar rose was installed a few years later at Senlis.

These windows are still fairly small (especially when compared with what was to follow just thirty or forty years later), and often only illuminate the space above the vaults, suggesting that initially at least they were designed to be seen from the outside more than the inside (and also making it unlikely that the earliest roses had elaborate glass).[13] This idea seems to be supported by Beauvais's obviously didactic sculpture, which, it has been suggested, played an important role in the local community – in the more recent past the Mayor of the town was sworn in underneath the rose, presumably to remind him of the changing fortunes of worldly office.

OPPOSITE The earliest surviving rose – or perhaps more correctly wheel – window in France is a curiously polished and refined affair. The sculpture around the rim shows the rise and fall of fortune. At this early date the spokes are still treated as colonnettes, with miniature capitals (north transept, St Etienne, Beauvais, c. 1150)

ABOVE RIGHT The proportionately tiny rose at Sens Cathedral is yet to grow to fill the space between the towers, as it would at Laon. The cathedral also has two spectacular transept roses dating to the early 16th century (west rose, Sens Cathedral, c. 1160–70)

THE ROSE ARRIVES IN BRITAIN

While the large-scale Gothic rose window indisputably originated in the Ile-de-France, it was not long confined to that region. The first area to adopt the rose outside France was Britain, most notably in a series of spectacular roses built by the Cistercians from 1150. This monastic order, founded by Robert de Molesme in the early 12th century (though more fully established in Cîteaux under its famous Abbot St Bernard) established a series of large monastic foundations, built in an up-to-the-minute, if pared down, style throughout Europe, though especially in France and Britain.

The roses built by the Cistercian order in Britain form a cohesive yet diverse group. Sadly, almost all were destroyed in the mid-16th century during the anti-monastic fervour of the Reformation, and it is only through painstaking analysis of ruins and fragments that a picture is emerging of a string of impressive roses built right through to the mid-13th century. The classic British Cistercian type (also adopted at York Minster and by some Augustinian foundations) has at least two layers of columns, often arranged around a central cusped void (good examples are Byland, Guisborough, Elgin and Fountains east – see p. 61), though some, such as Kirkstall, are rather more idiosyncratic.[14] The most important thing about these roses was their size: even the earliest examples spanned almost the entire façade, and the later ones ranged from six metres (twenty feet) to over eight metres (twenty-six feet) in diameter. The other features that quite possibly had great impact on later rose windows were the relationship between the rose and the lancets underneath, and the positioning of smaller rosettes at two or four corners of the rose, which recall Italian Cosmatesque pavements.

Not all early roses in Britain were Cistercian, however: two other noteworthy windows of this early period in England are at Barfreston, in Kent, and St James's, Bristol, the former with an impressive sculptural surround, the latter now much mutilated and neglected but still retaining some of its strangeness.

TOP LEFT This small window at Barfreston is richly decorated with beasts, birds and foliage; the wheel's pillars seem to emerge from the mouths of heads acting as capitals. It recalls early primitive wheel windows in Italy, Spain or France (St Nicholas, Barfreston, Kent, c. 1180)

ABOVE LEFT The design of this very early rose is intriguing and unique: essentially a large opening surrounded by eight small ones, the design is animated by the criss-crossing string moulding (St James's, Bristol, c. 1160)

OPPOSITE The famous 'Marigold' window at York Minster represents the later stages of the Cistercian style of rose in Britain (south rose, York Minster, c. 1230–40)

OPPOSITE Byland Abbey was abandoned in the 16th century, but masonry fragments and some miraculously preserved tracings (see p. 258) have allowed the reconstruction of the original design of the rose window (above, top left), which was close in style to the one at York Minster. The remains of the façade show the classic Cistercian arrangement of the rose above three lancets – similar to the east end of Laon Cathedral (Byland Abbey, façade c. 1190, rose c. 1240)

ABOVE, CLOCKWISE FROM TOP LEFT Byland Abbey, c. 1240; Kirkstall Abbey, c. 1155; Elgin Abbey, c. 1220–40; west rose, Fountains Abbey, c. 1150 (Drawings and reconstructions by Stuart Harrison)

Crucial to the early spread of the rose was the Cistercian order of monks. Founded in the 12th century, it flourished throughout Europe, and by the middle of the century had foundations in France, Britain, Germany, Spain and Italy. The Cistercians came to prominence under the famous Abbot St Bernard of Clairvaux (c. 1090-1153), and today are best known for their distinctive pared-down, yet decidedly progressive, style of architecture. As a large centralized order their buildings share many features, leading to a distinct Cistercian vocabulary. An important part of this vocabulary was the oculus, which soon became the rose window. Both invariably appear atop two or three lancets. Early examples include Fountains Abbey, Kirkstall, Pontigny (see p. 45), Léoncel, Flaran, Sénanque, Fontfroide, Moreruela, Noirlac and Fossanova, but many, many more could be listed. Indeed, the frequency with which we find this device at Cistercian foundations surely indicates some special significance.

The Cistercian roses are even more intriguing since, because of St Bernard's famous intolerance of excessive decoration, they would have been glazed with grisaille – white glass painted with monochromatic decorative elements. This suggests that the significance of the rose, for the Cistercians, lay in the form rather than the iconography contained in the glass. That many Cistercian foundations had oculi, usually cusped, rather than proper rose or wheel windows, suggests that it was the circular aspect that the Cistercians found appealing or important. It is reasonable to conclude that the early roses were statements of a sort of divine geometry, but also perhaps symbols of the divine itself. Certainly this is supported by such curious arrangements as that seen at Villers-la-Ville, in Belgium, where nine circles appear in a grid.

The Cistercian love of the rose evolved into the 13th century – some wonderful later roses can be found at Otterberg in Germany, or Byland Abbey in England. Its influence was felt particularly, however, in buildings such as Laon Cathedral, where we find a rose atop three lancets in the east end – a highly unusual setting, but entirely Cistercian.

CLOCKWISE, FROM TOP LEFT Abbey, Otterberg, exterior (rose 1249, glass later); Abbey, Flaran (late 12th century); Vercelli, east window (before 1227); Fossanova (early 13th century); St Léger, Royat (early 13th century); Abbey, Otterberg, interior

OVERLEAF LEFT Abbey, Vaux-de-Cernay (1180–90)

OVERLEAF RIGHT Abbey, Villers-la-Ville (c. 1220)

THE END OF THE TWELFTH CENTURY

The next important development takes place in France, at the Royal Abbey at Braine, not far from Paris, which had three large late 12th-century rose windows. Sadly the glass of all of them was lost during the French Revolution and only a few dispersed panels survive (some of which were reset in Soissons Cathedral[15] – see p. 207). The west end of Braine was demolished altogether, though fortunately reasonable records were made of the form and content of the roses in the 18th century. The two identical transept roses, which survive, have a central hub and twelve spokes radiating to the circumference, where there is additionally a small cusp between each spoke. Madeleine Caviness suggests that these can be dated structurally to around 1185–95,[16] roughly the same date as Saint-Michel-en-Thiérache. The 'source' for the design of the Braine windows was probably the rose today in the sacristy of Noyon Cathedral or a ten-spoke rose at Etampes. They represent a model that was widely adopted around the region into the next century, with examples surviving at Vaux-sous-Laon, Vorges, Bonneval, Mezy-Moulins, Mons-en-Laonnais – and even as far away as Santes Creus in northeastern Spain and Worms in Germany.

The spokes of the wheel at Braine are, as at St Etienne in Beauvais, architecturally inspired columns complete with plinths and capitals that uphold arches. Such rose-wheels can be divided into two families: those that point inwards – centripetal – with plinths on the perimeter and capitals at the centre, and the centrifugal with the plinths at the centre and capitals on the perimeter. At Beauvais the system is centrifugal, as they are with the other early roses at Noyon, Etampes and Chartres west. Meredith Lillich suggests that beginning with the transept roses at Braine a reversal to the centripetal type becomes popular.[17] The two styles coexist during the 13th century with centrifugal systems being adopted at Notre-Dame, Paris, until plinths and capitals gradually disappear completely with the onset of the Rayonnant.

ABOVE LEFT The early 13th-century rose in the west choir at Worms was narrowed with the addition of two stabilizing buttresses (west rose, Worms Cathedral, c. 1220)

OPPOSITE The later 12th century saw the first widely popular rose window pattern, with alternating spokes and cusps. Clockwise from top left: north rose, Braine Abbey, c. 1185–95; sacristy rose, Noyon Cathedral, c. 1170; SS Pierre & Paul, Mons-en-Laonnois, early 13th century; Saint-Michel-en-Thiérache, c. 1190

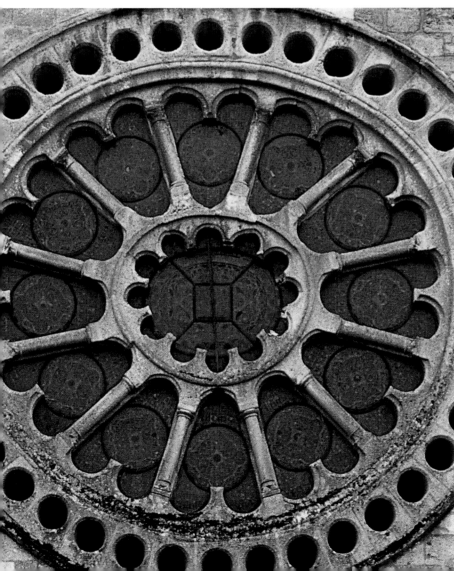
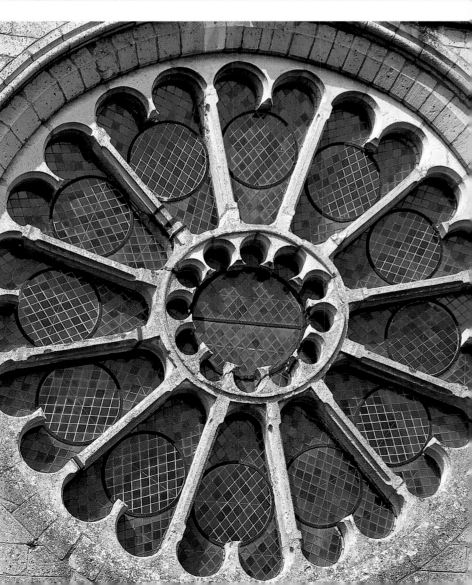

LAON CATHEDRAL

Built on an imposing hill-top site, Laon Cathedral typifies the early Gothic. It relies still on thick-wall construction rather than flying buttresses, and retains a four-storey elevation, yet at the same time it aspires to something grander, more spacious. Nowhere is this more evident than in its three spectacular rose windows.

The first to be built, in around 1180–90, was the north rose (see pp. 70–71). Looking at it from inside it appears to be made up of eight oculi punched through the wall surrounding a slightly larger ninth at the centre, though from outside the bounding circle is quite clear. The design itself is not particularly complex: we see an unlobed version at Guignicourt (which looks positively Romanesque in its simplicity). Hovering above five lancet windows, it is constructed in plate tracery, with a very high masonry/glass ratio: a sign, perhaps, of caution on the part of the architect. Originally it would probably have had a companion in the south transept, although this was later replaced by a strange Rayonnant window (see p. 261). The north rose is the first large rose window anywhere to retain a decent proportion of its original glass, which is of very high quality. The programme is the Liberal Arts, with personifications of Rhetoric, Grammar, Dialectic, Astronomy, Arithmetic, Medicine, Geometry and Music, each with their attribute, surrounding Philosophy in the central rosette.

The building of the west rose a few years later marks a turning point in rose-window design, chiming with the advent of the High Gothic. In all probability it has a similar structure to the now-lost west rose at Braine of around 1200. Distancing itself from the heavy plate tracery of the north rose – perhaps encouraged by the fact that after a few years it still hadn't collapsed – the west rose introduces another row of openings around the perimeter, greatly increasing the amount of glass. It did this by setting the rose under a deep semi-circular arch, ensuring that the loading of the wall bypassed the rose completely. The stone tracery that fills the great circle exists primarily to support the large panels of glass, but also to provide a decorative aspect sufficiently powerful to make the rose the focus of the façade. By taking the number twelve as the geometrical basis of the design it also provides a useful structure for the subject matter of the glass – the Last Judgment – reflecting the emphasis on the number twelve in St John's Book of Revelations. Here, perhaps for the first time, we see the glass and the architecture working in genuine harmony.

The wheel aspect has all but disappeared in this window, and it is hard to tell which way up the colonnettes are, unlike its near contemporaries at Mantes (see pp. 74–5) and Chartres (see pp. 80–81), where the colonnettes still 'support' arches radiating from the centre. In addition, another layer of twelve five-sided openings has been introduced between the hub and the outer layer of semi-circles around the perimeter. Clearly this was in response to the increased radius of the rose. We see the same arrangement at Mantes, also from the second decade of the 13th century, although there the intermediate layer of twelve sharp-pointed pentagonal panels have been elongated and have acquired round bases by the hub. Yet more refined versions of this type appear at Précy-sur-Oise (see p. 73), and at Notre-Dame-en-Vaux at Châlons-sur-Marne: there the central hub has been reduced in size and the intermediate layer has evolved into a series of tapering panels that are more characteristic of the next generation of rose windows, those influenced by the west rose at Notre-Dame, Paris.

The east rose at Laon was the last to be built, between 1205 and 1215 (see p. 72). Its form is a mirror of the west rose, though it is slightly smaller. Eastern roses are comparatively rare, since in the 13th century the rise of the curved ambulatory at the east end prohibited any easy insertion of a rose. The programme is rather complex, incorporating the Elders of the Apocalypse in the outer ring, the twelve apostles in the intermediate ring, and St John and Isaiah surrounding the Virgin at the centre.

RIGHT Laon Cathedral plan showing the earlier and final designs of the east end

OPPOSITE The west façade of Laon was built soon after the north transept front, and was probably complete by 1200. This is the first Gothic façade to incorporate a full-width rose window between the towers and above the portals.[18] The window itself marks a revolution in rose window design, and at nearly 10 metres (33 feet) in diameter is the first giant of the species (west façade, Laon Cathedral, c. 1180–1200)

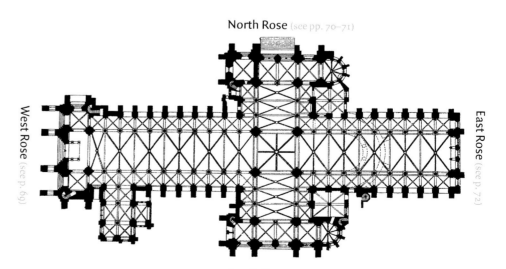

North Rose (see pp. 70–71)

West Rose (see p. 69)

East Rose (see p. 72)

South Rose (see p. 261)

This window, dating from around 1180–90, is actually an arrangement of eight cusped oculi around a larger central oculus, while smaller plain oculi complete the composition. Little attempt has been made to integrate the rose into the façade – in fact it seems to have been added as an afterthought, interrupting an arch which springs from the right. The original parts of the glass date from some twenty years after the window was built, and depict the seven Liberal Arts, together with Medicine, surrounding Philosophy (north rose, Laon Cathedral, window c. 1180–90, glass c. 1205)

ABOVE Laon north and west roses reflect two currents in
rose window design in the late 12th/early 13th centuries.
One approach, related to Laon north, built the rose out of oculi;
the other current, exemplified by Laon west, used a thinner,
more pliable tracery. Clockwise, from top left: SS Pierre & Paul,
Wissembourg, window and glass 1190–1200, reset after 1262;
SS Pierre & Paul, Guignicourt, late 12th century; SS Pierre &
Paul, Précy-sur-Oise, early 13th century; Notre-Dame de la
Nativité, Donnemarie-Dontilly, 1220–40

OPPOSITE Probably drawing influence from the Cistercian model,
the east rose sits atop three lancets. This was clearly a popular
arrangement, and it may be that Laon was also influenced
by the now-lost Benedictine church of St Vincent, Laon, built
between 1174 and 1205 (east rose, Laon Cathedral, c. 1205–15)

The west rose at Mantes, which clearly builds on Laon west, can be dated by the style of the glass to *c.* 1220 or possibly even earlier, making the window almost contemporary with the west roses at Chartres and Notre-Dame. Eight metres (26 feet) in diameter, it features the Last Judgment with Christ in a mandorla at the centre, surrounded by angels and the Virgin and St John. In the outer circle are scenes of the resurrection of the dead, the weighing of souls, souls being led to Paradise and to hell, Paradise being symbolized by the Bosom of Abraham at the summit (west rose, Mantes Cathedral, *c.* 1220)

THE BIRTH OF THE HIGH GOTHIC: CHARTRES

Where Laon so obviously straddles eras, with its up-to-the-minute roses trying to compensate for slightly old-fashioned architecture, other churches had the good fortune to be able to begin almost totally afresh. Thus, when Chartres Cathedral was largely destroyed by a fire in 1194 (which spared only the recently built west end, and, happily, the church's most precious relic, the tunic of the Holy Virgin), the clergy seized the opportunity to create something really modern and spectacular. The tripartite elevation inside was radically new, following Soissons, and the thinner wall construction was supported with flying buttresses – advanced technology at the time. The ambulatory was enlarged, and given radiating chapels, and three spectacular rose windows were installed in the west façade and transepts.

The huge Chartres west rose, which echoes the north Laon rose with its cusped oculi, would have been planned soon after the fire – indeed, probably around the time that Laon's west rose was being built – and was probably completed by 1216. Built above the existing mid-12th-century lancets, this masterpiece still retains a distinctly wheel-like character with the spokes being modelled as pillars complete with plinths, capitals and arches, 'supporting' the twelve cusped oculi. The structure of this rose is something of a wonder, each of the main oculi being built from seven pieces of stone, while hidden geometrical relationships and figures indicate the hand of a master at work.[19] The west roses at Chartres and Laon are perhaps the first roses deliberately designed to impress and amaze, and just as in the Laon and Mantes west roses, the subject of the glass at Chartres is the Last Judgment.

By the 1220s rose window design had picked up considerable momentum, and the transept roses at Chartres mark an important step. The south rose (see p. 85) was begun around 1220, the more sophisticated north one (see p. 84) some ten years later. They derive aspects of their tracery design from the Laon west window – and

possibly from Longpont (see p. 18) – but at Chartres another layer of structure has been added. As well as growing in delicacy and increasing the numbers of concentric layers, these two roses show great efforts to integrate the rose with the lancets below. At Laon the east rose is widely separated from the lancets by a string course, but at Chartres, in the south window, this line has thinned considerably and the rose touches the central lancet when viewed from outside. The effect inside is for the rose to become less isolated, no longer suspended alone in space but associated with the lancets below. In the case of the south rose this proximity is revealing, since it allows us to associate the subject matter of the rose (the Glory of Christ in the New Jerusalem) with that of the lancets (the four major prophets carrying the four Evangelists – see p. 245).[20] The window is thus a declaration of the fundamental doctrine of the Church.

Over in the north transept, meanwhile, the 'Rose de France' (as it has become known) may employ the same array of semi-circles around the perimeter but the intermediate layer is made up not of circles but of squares, which give the extraordinary illusion of rotation. Furthermore, the north rose begins to fill in the gap between the circle and the square frame of the façade with lancets of graded height. This development had first been hinted at in the Cistercian roses of northern England, where small oculi filled the spandrels; Chartres, however, took this idea to its logical conclusion in a way similar to the seminal transept roses of St Denis and Notre-Dame. Externally, the tracery of this rose is more embellished than that of its southern counterpart, while the spandrels above the rose are filled with statues, again reconciling the circle of the rose with the framing square of the façade. This window was donated to the church by Blanche of Castille, the mother of the future King Louis, and depicts the Glorification of the Virgin: Mary with the Christ Child surrounded by angels, doves of the Holy Spirit, prophets and kings symbolizing her ancestry and the prophecies that foretold Christ's coming.[21]

RIGHT A plan of Chartres Cathedral

OPPOSITE The great west rose of Chartres Cathedral was built above the existing Romanesque portals and lancets after the fire of 1194 (west façade, Chartres Cathedral, 12th and 13th centuries, spires 16th and 12th centuries, respectively)

pp. 78–9 An extraordinary photograph of the interior of Chartres in the 1940s, when the glass was removed for safekeeping. The west rose appears on the left, the north on the right. We can also just see the rosettes above the paired lancets in the clearstorey

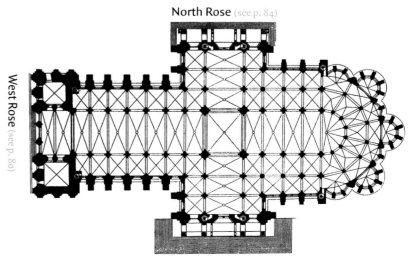

North Rose (see p. 84)

West Rose (see p. 80)

South Rose (see p. 85)

With an external diameter of 13.5 metres (45 feet), the stunning west rose at Chartres feels closer to a wheel window than the more 'modern' design that had just appeared on the west façade at Laon. It is made from a series of templates of Berchère limestone: each of the twelve main lobed openings is made from seven pieces, in addition to the colonnettes and the central boss which is made from twelve pieces. The subject of the glass, as at Mantes, is the Last Judgment: Christ sits at the centre, surrounded by angels and the Evangelist symbols, while the twelve apostles sit in pairs to his left and right. Below, St Michael weighs the souls: a devil leads the sinners to hell on the right (Christ's left) while an angel conducts the elect to the Bosom of Abraham at the top of this circle. In the outermost circle souls can be seen rising from their graves as the trumpets at the top sound; at the summit two angels carry the instruments of the Passion, while at the bottom the damned are tormented in hell (west rose, Chartres Cathedral, window 1205–10, glass 1210–15)

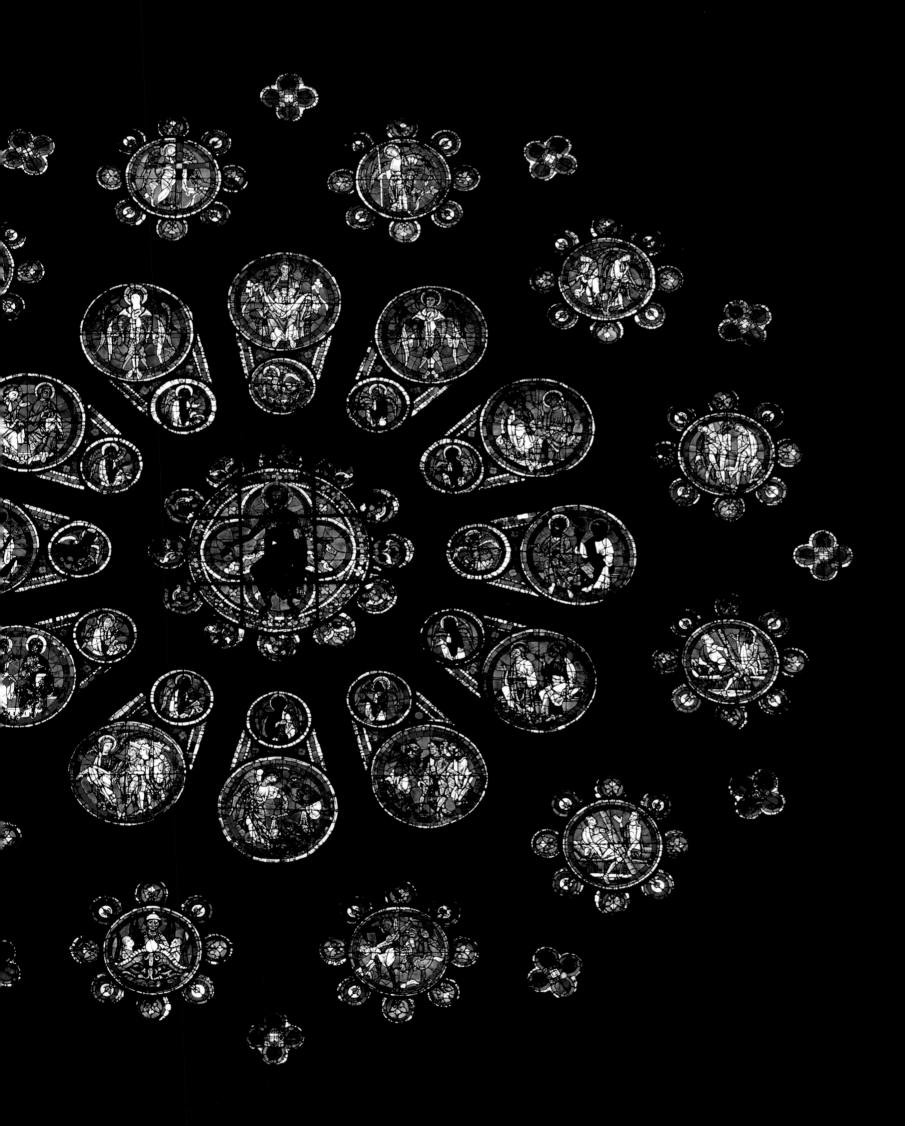

THIS SPREAD The north and south façades at Chartres were constructed a decade or so after the great west window. The south rose is slightly larger with a diameter of 10.5 metres – 35 feet (north transept façade, 1223–34; south transept façade, 1212–26)

OVERLEAF LEFT The north rose portrays the Old Testament, culminating in the Virgin Mary with the Christ Child. Eight angels and four doves immediately surround the Virgin and Child, while the squares are occupied by Old Testament kings (David is at the summit) and the outer layer by prophets. In the lancets below are four Old Testament figures (Melchisedek, David, Solomon, Aaron) with St Anne and the infant Mary in the centre. Beneath them are a series of Old Testament scenes relating to the figures above. The window was given by Queen Blanche of Castille, mother of St Louis and whose portrait is said to have been used for the Solomon lancet. The arms of France and Castille fill the spandrels (north rose, Chartres, glazed by 1234)

OVERLEAF RIGHT The south rose features Christ in Glory, surrounded by the twenty-four Elders of the Apocalypse, each carrying a phial and a musical instrument. In the circle immediately surrounding him are the four symbols of the Evangelists and angels. The blue and yellow checky squares are derived from the coat of arms of Pierre Mauclerc, Count of Dreux, who donated the window. In the lancets below are the four major prophets with the four Evangelists on their shoulders – carried 'so they can see further', with the Virgin Mary carrying the Christ Child in the centre (south rose, Chartres, glazed by 1226)

The north rose at Chartres contains Christ's forerunners: prophets foretelling his coming, kings indicating his lineage, and the dove (shown from four different angles) symbolizing the Holy Spirit. The glass is of the very highest quality, and was made at or near Chartres: these particular examples show off the famous blues and reds for which the cathedral is so well known. Clockwise from left: a dove symbolizing the Holy Spirit; the prophet Jonah; the prophet Abadia; King Asa. The prophets hold banderoles, while the kings hold sceptres.

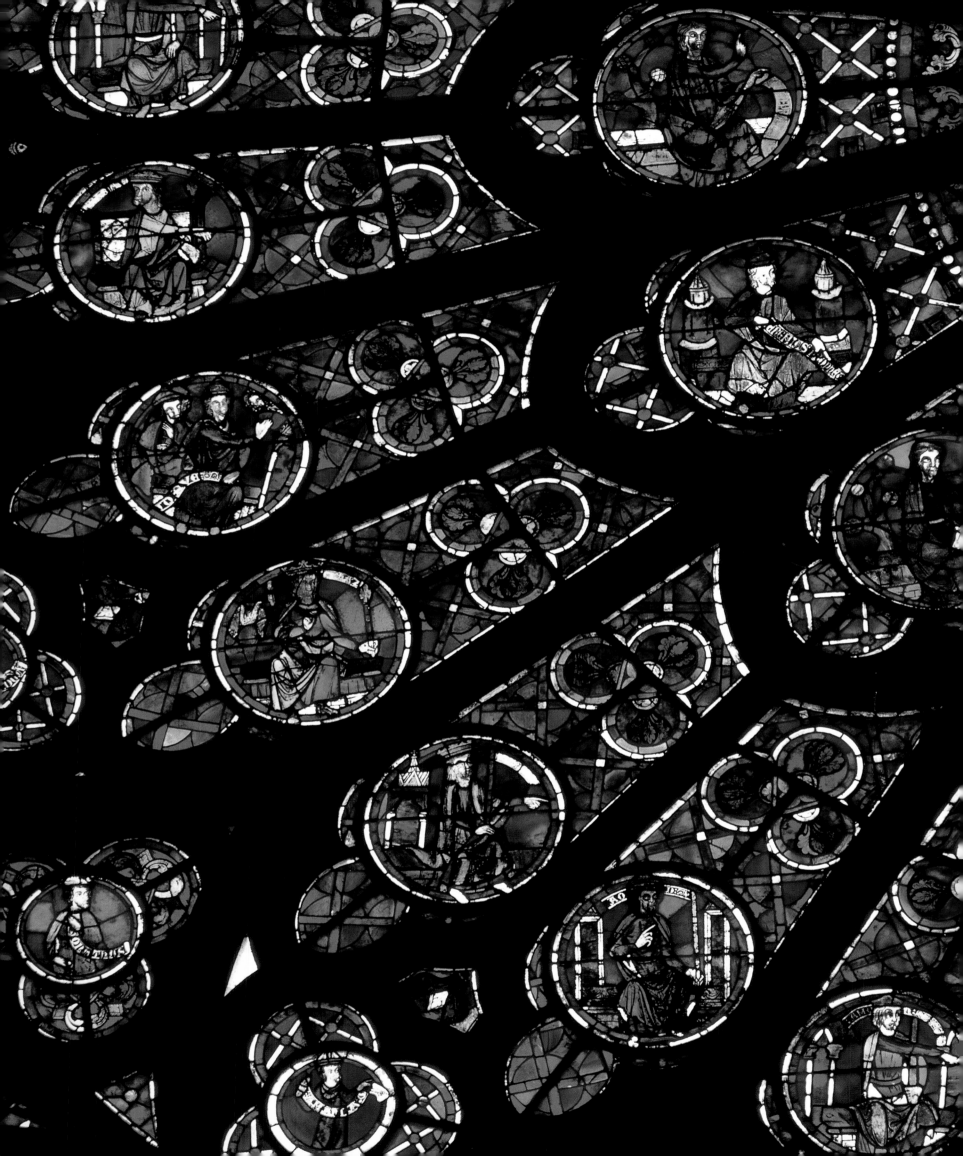

CHAPTER 2
THE AGE OF THE ROSE: INNOVATION IN THE THIRTEENTH CENTURY

The 13th century was a period of marked self-confidence in France. This came in part from the economic boom that resulted in Chartres and a thousand other projects, and in part from the long and energetic reign of Louis IX – later to become St Louis – between 1226 (from 1236 on his own) and 1270. In terms of architecture the king's patronage was prolific, stimulating innovation to the point that many historians still refer to the Louis 'Court Style'.[1] Among his many achievements was the Sainte-Chapelle in Paris, built around 1240, which marked the uptake of a new style, the 'Rayonnant'. This new strain of Gothic architecture emphasized verticality, thinness of tracery, delicacy: the rose window, which at Chartres was already becoming more attenuated, more integrated into the façade, proved an excellent vehicle for virtuoso essays in the new style. To this period belong the sublime creations of Notre-Dame, Amiens, Reims, but also a host of other smaller churches; it also saw the rose window catch on outside France (notwithstanding the earlier roses in Britain), in Germany, Spain and Italy. We begin, however, at the close of the High Gothic style, with Notre-Dame.

NOTRE-DAME, PARIS

The west façade of Notre-Dame is in many respects the tidiest of all the High Gothic façades. This is due in part to Viollet-le-Duc's rather enthusiastic recutting of much of the ornament (and addition of gargoyles) in the 19th century, but he cannot take credit for the fundamental geometry and pleasing proportions. Unlike Laon, where the rose pushes up the string course running across

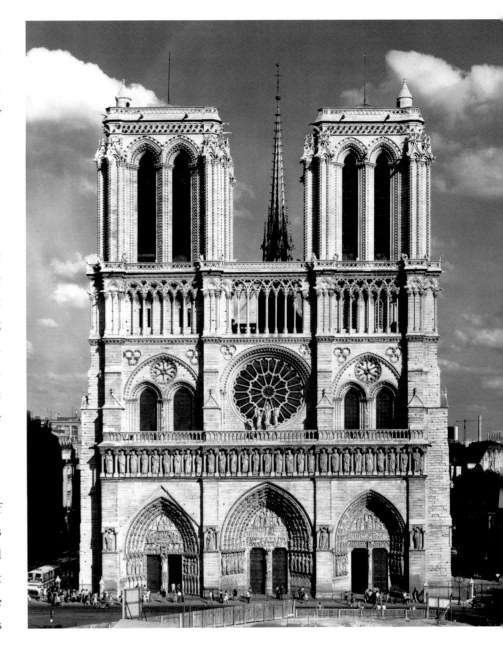

OPPOSITE Detail of the north rose, Notre-Dame, Paris, c. 1255–8

ABOVE RIGHT The west façade of Notre-Dame in Paris is one of the most distinctive of the 13th century. For the first time the rose window feels essential to the composition of the façade, bounded by the towers, the gallery below and the arcade above. While it is still set under a broad and deep semi-circular arch, as at Laon, the rose itself has achieved a new lightness (west façade, Notre-Dame, Paris, c. 1210–25)

the top of the façade (see p. 69), the west rose at Notre-Dame, which dates to 1215–20, fits comfortably, and is no longer so deeply recessed into the façade. Looking at the design of the rose itself, Notre-Dame west is very different either to Laon west, or to the two marginally later Chartres transept roses: the tracery radiates in slim unbroken lines to the edge of the circle, where the division into twelve segments then gracefully subdivides into twenty-four. The wheel character with hub and spokes is still there: so too are the plinths and capitals whereby the colonnettes 'support' the arches. But what is really daring is that every other colonnette of the outer group of twenty-four is set on top of a trilobed arch, displaying the confidence of the master mason in the ability of this structure to transmit the loads of glass, stone and metal – in the upper panels, at least – safely through the system. Combined with a thinner, lighter, more uniform tracery, the overall effect is one of grace and refinement – a proper spider's web – even if it does lack some of the eccentric charm seen at Laon or Chartres west. Its impact was almost immediate, and by the 1220s we see signs of the same attenuated, refined tracery at Brie-Comte-Robert (see p. 202).

The proportion of glass to stone in this window surpasses anything that had gone before, and glaziers were suddenly faced with the challenge of devising larger programmes that could work within this new pattern of subdivisions. In this respect it is interesting to compare the Laon west rose with the scheme at Notre-Dame. Laon contains twenty-five panels; Notre-Dame has thirty-seven, further divided into sixty-one scenes. The solution for the Notre-Dame glazier was to turn to cycles, to combine theology with teaching, so that we get the complete signs of the zodiac, labours of the months, the vices and virtues, all illustrating the struggle of the soul – the 'Psychomachia' – throughout daily life. A corner had been turned in rose window design, and it would be difficult to argue that the winner had been clarity. In the centre we find the Virgin surrounded by twelve prophets.

RIGHT A plan of Notre-Dame (showing some later additions)

ABOVE AND OPPOSITE The west rose at Paris is dedicated to the Virgin, although it is not certain that this was originally so. It has undergone numerous restorations, particularly in the 16th and 19th centuries, when some of the panels were completely renewed. The upper half of the outer circle contains the virtues, and the corresponding vices are in the next inner layer; in the lower half of the outer circle are the months, corresponding to the zodiac signs in the inner layer. The innermost layer contains twelve prophets. At the centre is the Virgin' (west rose, Notre-Dame, 1215–20)

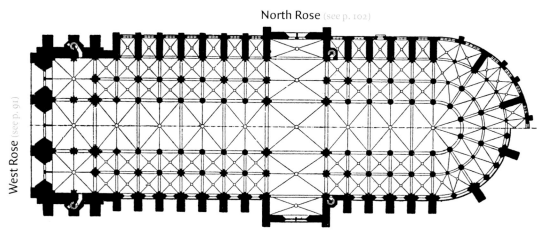

North Rose (see p. 102)

West Rose (see p. 91)

South Rose (see p. 103)

ST DENIS AND THE SAINTE-CHAPELLE

Almost a century after Suger's radical rebuilding of St Denis, the church once again found itself at the cutting edge of architecture in France. In 1231 Pierre de Montreuil (one of the earliest occasions that we have a named architect) designed two new transept roses which are generally acknowledged as heralds of the new Rayonnant style in architecture. The design of the north rose builds on Notre-Dame west, adding a ring of rosettes to the edge of the design (see pp. 94–5), while the south places the rosettes in the central layer. While the spokes have not quite lost every trace of their columnar origins (some capitals are still visible), the roses have already begun to compromise their self-contained roundness as the lower gaps

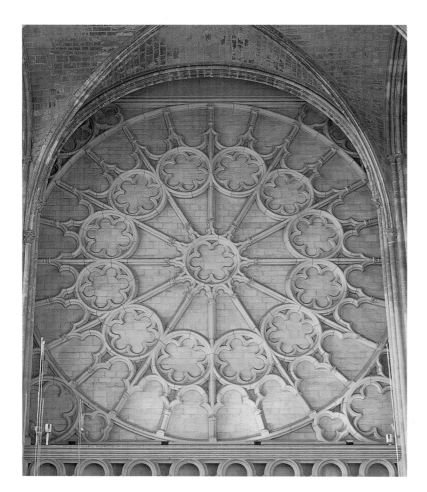

between the circles and the squares that bound them are filled with glazed trefoils, quatrefoils, and mini rosettes or sexfoils – an extension of the process also seen in Chartres north. In fact, these roses also dominate the entire widths of the façades as at Chartres, in the process merging with the lancets below. These lancets in turn adopt a consistency of tracery thickness and 'rhythm' similar to that seen in the rose above, so that they become part of the same composition. The effect on contemporary viewers must have been spectacular, and as with every new invention or novelty at this time it was soon imitated.

The other important early Rayonnant monument is the Sainte-Chapelle, also on the Ile de la Cité, central Paris. Built by Louis as a royal chapel to house the holy relic of the Crown of Thorns, and consecrated in 1246, this astonishing and unprecedented building is far smaller in scale than much of what we have looked at so far. The upper chamber is a clear statement of the new architectural approach – relentlessly vertical, with the tracery reduced almost to nothing in favour of the glass. The original rose window in the west end, which most likely resembled those at St Denis, was replaced in 1485 by the Flamboyant masterpiece that is still there (see pp. 140–41).

To get a sense of the feel of the original Sainte-Chapelle rose we should look at a contemporary window, again by Pierre de Montreuil, the now bricked-up rose in the west wall of the royal chapel at Saint-Germain-en-Laye. This is essentially a smaller version of the south rose at St Denis, with its twelve rosettes in the central layer. One final hint of what the Sainte-Chapelle might have looked like is a rose in a chapel attached to the Benedictine abbey-church at Saint-Germer-de-Fly in Normandy. Said to have been modelled on the Sainte-Chapelle rose and the rose in the Chapel of the Virgin (now demolished) at St-Germain-des-Prés, it is based on the number sixteen, dividing into thirty-two in the outer layer, like the north rose at Notre-Dame.

ABOVE LEFT This rose at Saint-Germain-en-Laye is perhaps the closest to the original rose at the Sainte-Chapelle. Designed by Pierre de Montreuil, it was bricked in later, though has lost nothing of its structural beauty (chapel, Château de Saint-Germain-en-Laye, begun 1238)

OPPOSITE The rose at the Benedictine Abbey of Saint-Germer-de-Fly, built 1259–66, was inspired by the Sainte-Chapelle, though with grisaille glass it gives very different impression (Abbey of Saint-Germer-de-Fly, c. 1260 grisaille replacement, but possibly to original design)

pp. 94–5 North transept, St Denis, c. 1231

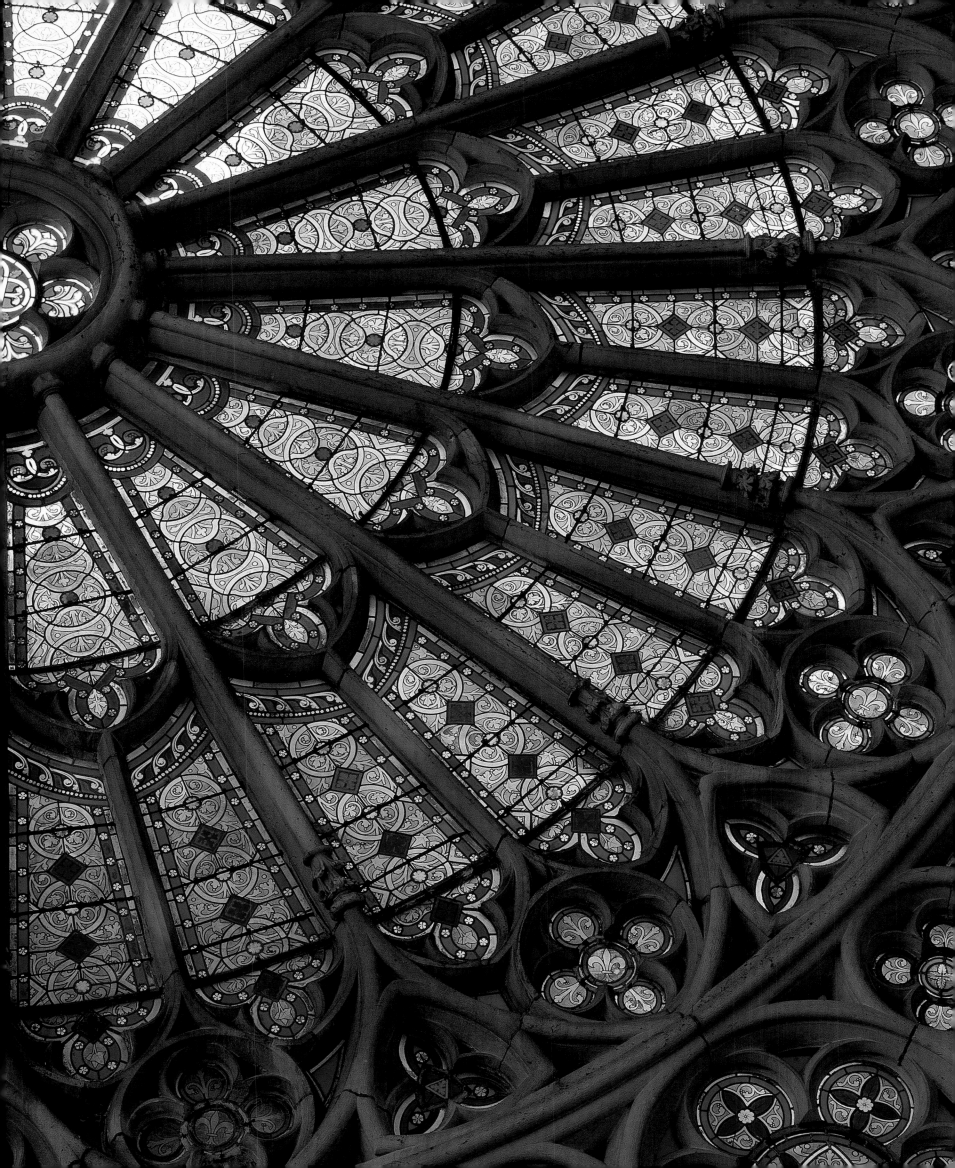

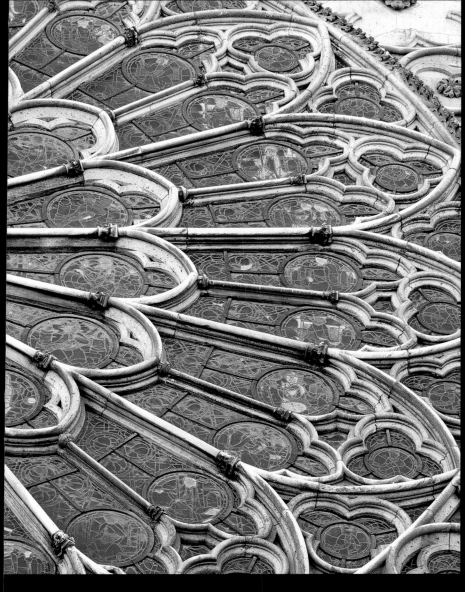

The leap from the early, experimental roses of the late 12th and early 13th centuries to the refined Rayonnant versions of the mid-13th century was great. Beginning with the west rose at Notre-Dame, but finding its fullest expression in the transept roses of the same church, the rose increasingly became attenuated and weightless, but also more regularized. In a sense this was a trend toward decoration; in another sense it marked acceptance of the rose as a key feature of Gothic architecture, to be treated in the same manner as the other elements, with no attempt at differentiation. Of course, the transept roses at Notre-Dame are spectacular to behold, but one feels that they are first and foremost feats of engineering, works of virtuosity – that once begun, there was only a race to thinness. For this reason, Rayonnant roses may seem more ethereal, but lack the mystical – some might say interestingly erratic – qualities found in earlier, more inventive, roses. The perfection came at a cost.

Instead they were hierarchical, ordered, orthodox, relentlessly linear. Everything was logical, ordered, almost standardized: Aristotle had seemingly triumphed over Plato, Reason and Dogma dominated Faith, Orthodoxy over Heresy. We get a sense of the massed ranks of the Church, and this increased emphasis on the glass almost certainly was deliberate: one of the key features of these Rayonnant windows is a great increase in the number of openings, leading to smaller scenes. Prophets, kings, apostles, saints and martyrs are all arranged around Christ and the Virgin Mary in spectacular, hierarchies, but in a sense the glass is coming to the fore and dominating the design just when it was getting less interesting in itself.

CLOCKWISE FROM TOP LEFT   North rose, Notre-Dame (c. 1258); Santa Maria del Pi, Barcelona (first half 14th century); south rose, Notre-Dame (c. 1265); north rose, Rouen Cathedral (1270–80); Abbey, Ebrach (mid-13th century); grisaille, north nave aisle, Poitiers Cathedral (second half 13th century)

OVERLEAF   North rose, Tours Cathedral (late 13th/early 14th century)

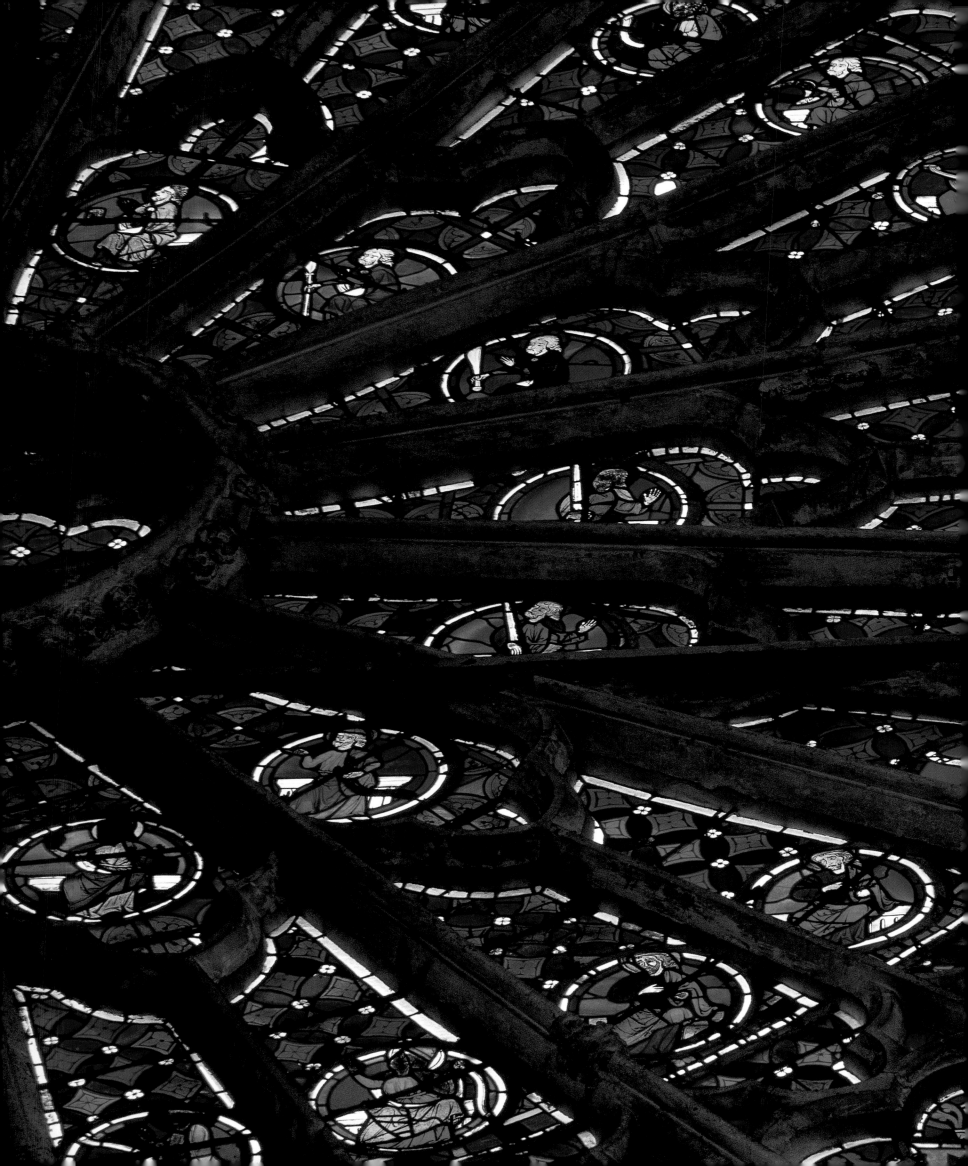

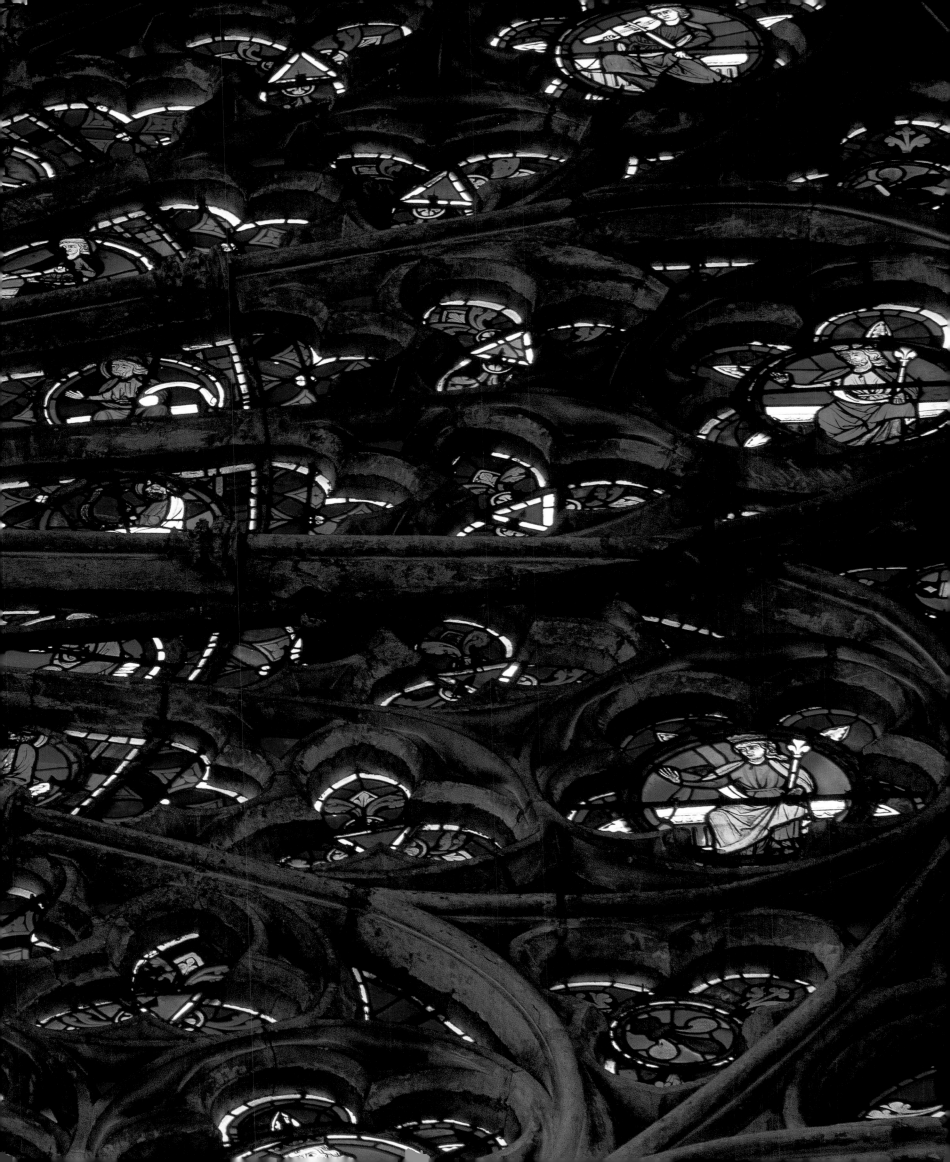

THE NOTRE-DAME TRANSEPT ROSES

And so we arrive at the true superstars of rose window design, the north and south transept windows at Notre-Dame. Widely seen as the highest expression of the Rayonnant, they are vast, nearly fifteen metres (fifty feet) in diameter. Of the two, the north rose, begun by Jean de Chelles in around 1245, achieves the highest ratio of glass to stone (and one of the most intricate designs) of any rose window of any time. Based on the number sixteen the window begins with a lobed oculus at the centre (which contains the Virgin and Child) from which grow the sixteen elongated and tapering panels that contain prophets. Their shape is then repeated, with a minor modification, in the next layer, where the thirty-two subdivisions contain the Old Testament kings. But by the time this layer is achieved, the outermost tips of the panels have become widely separated from each other, so that in order to achieve consistency of rhythm in the tracery a small five-fold opening is inserted between them. The composition is completed with a final layer of thirty-two large trefoils (and two sets of thirty-two little triangular openings between the trefoils) that run round the perimeter. The rose is then integrated with the square that contains it by a system that fills the four spandrels (though only the lower pair are glazed) with a variety of trefoils, sexfoils and triangular openings so that the entire composition is filled with the same thickness and shape of tracery, the hallmark of Rayonnant architecture.

The south rose was constructed some ten years later, in around 1260, with some significant differences. The new master, Pierre de Montreuil, used geometry based on the number twelve rather than sixteen and squeezed in an extra layer of alternating trefoils and quatrefoils (before the outermost circle of trefoils) by reducing the size of the first two layers. The glass is partially original – some martyrs and angels have survived – although two rebuildings mean that much has been lost.

OPPOSITE An early 19th-century engraving of the interior of Notre-Dame, looking towards the north rose

ABOVE RIGHT Viollet-le-Duc's analysis of the south rose, which he rebuilt in the 19th century, in the process rotating the window by fifteen degrees

OVERLEAF The spectacular transept windows of Notre-Dame, Paris. On the left, the north rose, begun around 1245 and glazed from c. 1255. Most panels are original, if repaired. On the right, the south rose, built originally by Pierre de Montreuil in 1260, then rebuilt in 1726, then yet again by Viollet-le-Duc. The subject matter mixes original panels with a number of 12th- and 13th-century panels from the atelier of a 18th-century glazier[3]

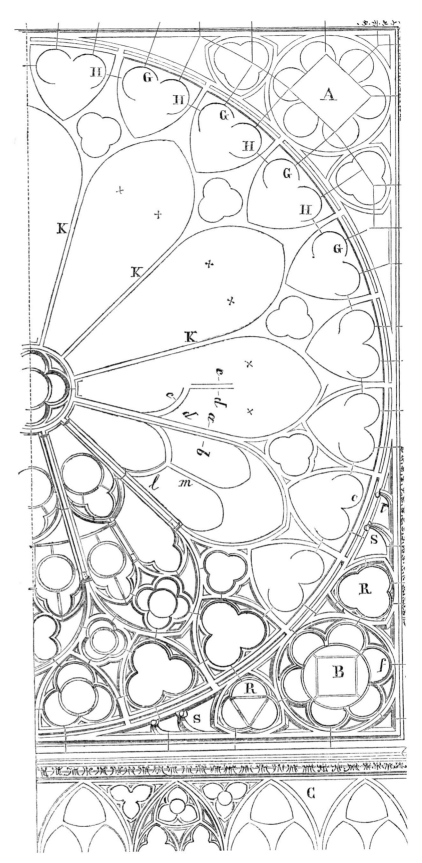

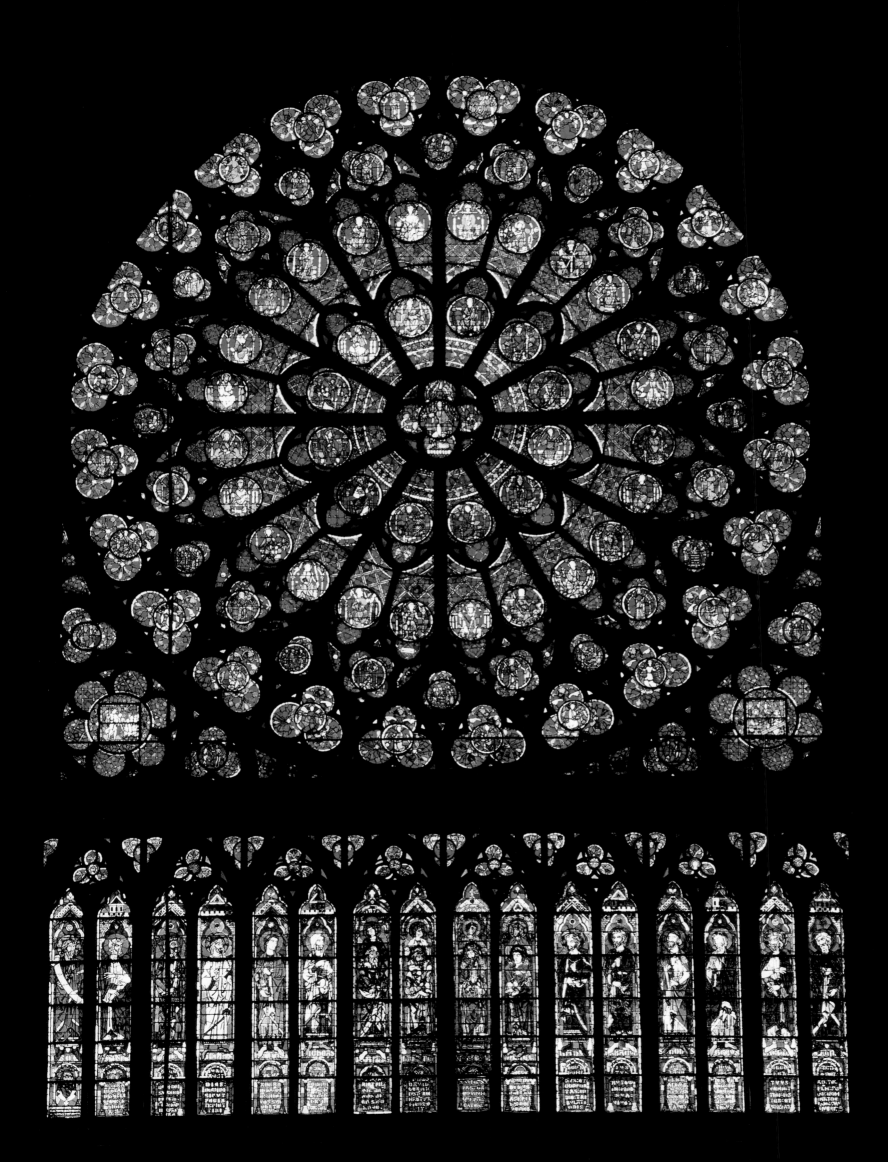

THE LEGACY OF THE NOTRE-DAME ROSES

The characteristic, even archetypal, Rayonnant rose windows of St Denis and Notre-Dame proved to be immensely popular. In part we might speculate that this was due to their associations with royalty – Notre-Dame, the Sainte-Chapelle and St Denis are all prominent royal sites – though in truth the style was sufficiently elegant and up-to-the-minute to be appealing on its own terms. So, not too long after the south transept at Notre-Dame we find copies, or interpretations, at the cathedrals of Carcassonne, Rouen, Tours, Clermont-Ferrand, Amiens and Reims, to name just a few. The latest was probably the north rose at Troyes Cathedral, which, incredibly, was still following Notre-Dame in the 15th century. However, the thinness that made these roses so desirable posed certain structural risks, and at least a couple – for example, Tours – needed reinforcement soon after construction.[4]

While France was the prime innovator in 13th-century Gothic architecture, other countries were quick to take up the rose window. Ideas and styles could travel by many different means. Architects and craftsmen, for example, could be highly mobile: the most famous example is Villard de Honnecourt, but there were many other similar cases. Thus, it is not surprising to find Notre-Dame influenced roses in northeastern Spain (at Sant Cugat, or Santa Maria del Pi in Barcelona), or to find Rayonnant rose windows in Germany (at Ebrach Abbey, or even Minden).

Two of the earliest applications of the Notre-Dame style can be found in England. The first example was at Westminster Abbey, perhaps the most 'French' of all English churches. Under Henry III, doubtless inspired by the example of Louis IX, the Abbey was worked on intensively, to create Henry's version of St Denis, the Sainte-Chapelle and Notre-Dame combined. The architect, Henry of Reyns, began with the north side (since this was the main ceremonial portal), and by around 1260 had completed both transepts. Sadly neither of the roses that we see today is original. The north rose was rebuilt and reglazed in the 18th century, to an unusual design by Sir James Thornhill (and was rebuilt again in the 19th century), but happily 17th-century engravings give us a reasonable idea of how it originally looked. The chief influences apparent in this original design, aside from Notre-Dame north, are St Denis or possibly the Amiens transepts (which, too, have been replaced). Westminster's south rose has also been rebuilt – or at least remodelled – this time by Sir George Gilbert Scott, in 1849.[5]

The other important church in London was Old St Paul's Cathedral. Before the entire structure of Old St Paul's was demolished after the Great Fire of London in 1666, there was a fine rose window at the east end – another of those rare examples of eastern roses – some twelve metres (forty feet) in diameter, over seven lancet windows. Again, happily, it was recorded by Wenceslaus Hollar before its destruction, and using his engravings

ABOVE LEFT Later followers of Notre-Dame, such as this window at Tours Cathedral, used ever thinner tracery, to the point that buttressing was needed to prevent total collapse (north rose, Tours Cathedral, c. 1300, buttress c. 1371)

OPPOSITE Later Rayonnant roses employed large areas of simpler, though not necessarily less effective, glazing, such as this diaper pattern. The central part was restored by Viollet-le-Duc to reinforce the theme of the Virgin as Queen of Heaven and the angels (north rose, Carcassonne Cathedral, c. 1300–20)

has been dated to around 1270–80. Stylistically it, too, seems to derive from the Notre-Dame transepts, though the closer one looks at the external view the more one begins to think of the Curvilinear style of the 14th century! The twelve petals seem to terminate in ogee arches, while a counterpoint of semicircles defines the other twelve, each trefoil being offset with respect to its neighbour. If the exterior drawing is accurate, then we have to see the St Paul's window as being one of the first examples of the Curvilinear in England. The rose at St Paul's was certainly popular, as is evident from the passage in Chaucer's 'Miller's Tale', where a character is described as having 'Powles wyndowes corven in his schoos'![6]

In other parts of Europe, however, more idiosyncratic interpretations of Rayonnant were emerging. An excellent example of late Rayonnant is the west façade of Strasbourg (see pp. 108–109), begun in 1277, where the play of horizontals and verticals is far busier that at Notre-Dame. Amid this riot of geometric forms the rose window is set within a square complete with four blind spandrels. A close examination of the façade reveals that much of the thin, elegant tracery is in fact standing proud of the main body of the surface by a few feet. A similar feature can be discerned on the front of St Lorenz, Nuremberg (discussed and illustrated in Chapter 3), where the unusual rose has enormous embellishments on its exterior surface. The effect at Strasbourg is to give the rose a sun-like aura.

After the spectacular collapse of the choir of Beauvais Cathedral in 1284 – the tallest Gothic cathedral ever built – the Rayonnant tailed off. However, the rose had already shown a remarkable adaptability to new forms of architecture, and by the late 13th century it was clearly considered a vital part of any great church. While the days of great unified glazing programmes, as seen at Chartres, had certainly drawn to a close, the true potential of tracery as an expressive medium was still in its infancy.

OPPOSITE The Notre-Dame type of rose found many adherents, each with a subtle innovation. Clockwise, from top left: Clermont-Ferrand, *c.* 1320, glass modern; Carcassonne south, *c.* 1320; the lozenge-shaped south rose, Tours Cathedral, late 13th/early 14th century; Sant Cugat, Sant Cugat del Vallès, 1337–50, glass later

RIGHT As with Westminster Abbey, the design of the east rose at Old St Paul's Cathedral, London, looked to France for its inspiration, particularly the south rose of Notre-Dame, with twelve divisions (engraving of east end of Old St Paul's by Wenceslaus Hollar, rose *c.* 1270–80)

OVERLEAF LEFT AND RIGHT The rose of the west façade at Strasbourg simplifies the Paris design. Some tracery stands proud of the main surface, bringing the surface to life as the sun moves during the afternoon (west façade of Strasbourg Cathedral, 1277–1318, rose *c.* 1290)

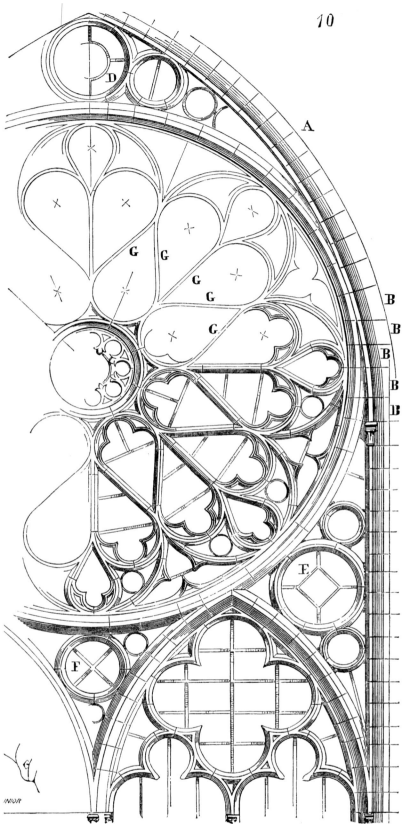

ABOVE LEFT AND RIGHT Today the groundbreaking church of St Nicaise in Reims is known to us primarily through an engraving made by De Son in around 1620 (left). The façade, which was designed in around 1231, is the first to integrate the rose and the lancets into what is effectively one large window. Viollet-le-Duc's reconstruction of the St Nicaise rose (right) was probably based on this engraving, but still allows us to appreciate the animated design of the tracery. There is discussion over the date of the rose itself.

AN ALTERNATIVE TO NOTRE-DAME: REIMS CATHEDRAL AND ST NICAISE

While many rose windows of the later 13th century and beyond emulated the Notre-Dame transept type, a slightly different development was emerging not far away in Reims. Reims Cathedral, which was begun soon after 1210, belongs essentially to the High Gothic period, but due to its drawn-out construction incorporates many later elements. It has no less than four rose windows, one in each of the transepts and two, one above the other, in the west façade (see pp. 114–15). The transept roses are the earliest, dating to between 1231 and 1241 (see pp. 112–13). The spokes radiate outwards from a series of arches that are tangential to the central hub, creating a 'shield' shape when viewed from the inside. The same kind of design, though with subdivisions, can be seen in the later north rose of *c.* 1260 at the cathedral of Châlons-sur-Marne (now Châlons-en-Champagne), and in the north rose at Burgos, in Spain (see p. 117).[8]

The other unmissable innovation in the Reims transept roses is the curious fillet inserted above each rose. This shape reconciles the circle of the rose with the vault, but also marks the further integration of the rose into the façade – or, rather, the gradual erosion of the masonry of the façade in favour of glass. The prototype for this must have been the west façade of Reims's other major church, St Nicaise. Sadly demolished in the early 19th century, this extraordinary church, built from around 1231, is known today primarily through a 17th-century engraving (Viollet-le-Duc later created a reconstruction, probably based on this engraving). The engraving serves well enough to show us how the architect, Hugh Libigier, pulled the lancets and the rose together – and filled every gap between the two elements – to create a totally unified composition. The effect is reminiscent of a clearstorey window, and it may be that, in turn, the format was derived from Reims Cathedral's apse clearstorey.

The cathedral of Châlons-sur-Marne (today called Châlons-en-Champagne) was begun in 1230, about the time that the Reims transept roses were being built. This rose develops the Reims roses by increasing the number of spokes and introducing a layer of small circles just outside the central hub. In its appropriation of lancet window forms it also seems to offer a prototype for roses such as Nuremberg Cathedral (north rose, Châlons-sur-Marne Cathedral, after 1256)

The transept roses at Reims Cathedral have both suffered over the years. The earlier, the south rose (left), dates from the 1230s, but the glass was destroyed in a storm in 1580. It was reglazed in 1581, but was again destroyed in the First World War to be replaced with Jacques Simon's glass of 1937, with Christ in Glory surrounded by angels and the twelve apostles. The north rose (right) dates from c. 1240, but was restored in the 17th century. It shows scenes from Genesis in the inner layer, with animals, fish and angels in the outer layer. At the centre is the Virgin and Child.[9]

There are two west roses at Reims, one in the tympanum of the central portal (c. 1255), the other, larger, in the centre of the façade. The main rose (right) depicts the Assumption of the Virgin Mary, and dates from 1260 onwards, though the date of the glasswork is unclear. Twelve metres (39 feet) across, it has three main layers, with the twelve apostles, then twenty-four angels, surrounding the ascending Virgin at the centre. In the spandrels Christ, between sun and moon, carries the soul of his mother to heaven. The window was releaded in the 18th century (when the panels got mixed up) and badly damaged by hail in 1886. After the First World War only about one quarter of the glass was original. It was again heavily restored in 1925. The lower rose contains glass by Jacques Simon (Reims west façade and rose c. 1255–60, original glass c. 1290?)

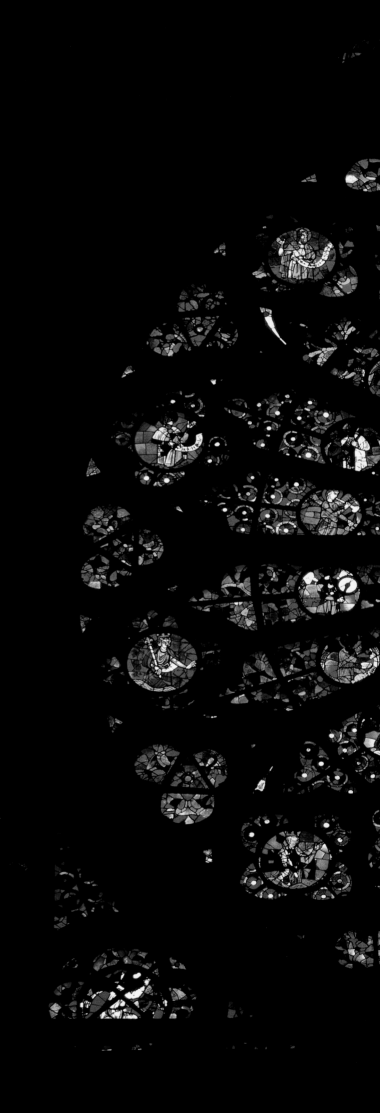

OPPOSITE The six rose/lancet windows at Minden
Cathedral, of which this is one, draw on Notre-Dame-type
tracery and the innovations of St Nicaise and Reims while
creating something entirely new (rose from south aisle
of Minden Cathedral, c. 1260)

ABOVE The south rose at Burgos Cathedral in Spain is,
unusually, based on the number ten. The cathedral itself,
begun in 1221 and consecrated in 1260, employed a
number of French architects, and the form of this rose
clearly echoes the Reims transept and Châlons-sur-
Marne north rose. The glass, which was much damaged
by Napoleon's troops, shows scenes from the Passion
(south rose, Burgos Cathedral, c. 1280)

SOUTHERN ROSES IN ITALY AND SPAIN

As the rose window form grew in popularity, it soon developed new species and sub-species, and was, in general, subject to regional variation and interpretation. In the cases of Spain and Italy, both regions embraced the rose window quite early on, but each had specific ideas about how it should look.

Although the Cistercians had introduced the Gothic style into Italy at Fossanova (it has a large 13th-century rose window to prove it) in the late 12th century, generally the northern European style of architecture was not eagerly embraced south of the Alps. The most Gothic-looking rose from the 13th century can be found on the façade of the eastern end at S. Francesco in Assisi (see p. 120), though even here the architect obviously felt bound to the local Romanesque style. This rose – or rather giant wheel-window – is a wonder to behold: of particular delight is the mosaic inlay, which glitters in the sunshine. Straight away it is obvious that this rose is designed to be seen from outside.

The same is true of nearly all roses and wheel windows throughout Italy, and this emphasis on the exterior marks a decisive shift away from the French Gothic model where ultimately the rose is designed to impress and awe the devout *inside* the church. Often the rose is 'squared off' with sculpture, typically the symbols of the Evangelists, which sit at the corners. In central Italy, meanwhile, there are several 13th-century wheels that are surrounded by Romanesque sculpture, sometimes recycled.[10]

Other notable wheel windows can be found in Tuscania at S. Pietro and S. Maria Maggiore, again in Assisi at S. Chiara, S. Rufino and S. Pietro, and, in the south of the country, at Trani, Troia, Bari, Ruvo, Bitetto, Bitonto and Matera, as well as at Trapani and Palermo (see p. 156). These Sicilian roses often have intriguing tracery that interweaves the ends of the petals in an exotic and refined manner. At Troia, the window is infilled with perforated sheets of thin marble, highly reminiscent of Islamic designs.

Such Islamic influence is a commonplace in parts of Spain, particularly the south. The wonderful series of churches in Cordoba, built or rebuilt to commemorate the reconquest of that city from the Moors by Fernando III in 1236, boast some magnificent roses: perhaps the most memorable – and certainly the most Islamic-influenced – is that at San Lorenzo, which looks like a giant sunflower; others, such as the one at San Miguel, seem to be very close to Italian wheel windows, though again with a Moorish flavour. In northwestern Spain, meanwhile, we find two spectacular and unusual windows at the monastery of Armenteira – again showing some Moorish influence in the shapes – and San Martín, in Noia, Galicia. However, other parts of Spain, notably the northeast, proved more receptive to French ideas, as we can see in the 'twin' windows of Santa Maria del Pi, in Barcelona, and Sant Cugat, both of which were based on Notre-Dame. Similarly two of the roses at the key cathedrals of Burgos and León imitate French designs – Reims and Chartres, respectively.[11]

ABOVE LEFT This rose is unusual in two ways: first, it has eleven divisions; second, the rose is filled not with glass but with delicately perforated sheets of marble. It combines Romanesque, Pisan and Islamic influences, the patterns in the marble sheets being unmistakably Islamic in inspiration (west rose, Troia Cathedral, façade c. 1096, rose c. 1200)

OPPOSITE Typically Italian, the rose at S. Chiara in Assisi, combines Romanesque colonnettes and solidity with delicate interlacing around the edge. It feels like a more elegant version of the Cistercian roses found in 12th-century Britain (west rose, S. Chiara, Assisi, façade built c. 1257–65)

OPPOSITE PAGE Italian roses of the 13th century show considerable variation while retaining an essentially Italian character. The most unusual by far is that at Trani, which is a genuine one-off. Clockwise from top left: east rose, S. Francesco, Assisi, before 1250; S. Chiara, Assisi, glass modern; S. Rufino, Assisi, before 1250, possibly before 1230; north rose, Trani Cathedral, c. 1200

THIS PAGE Spanish roses share certain characteristics with Italian roses – the influence of the Romanesque and an Islamic flavour – but were also more influenced by developments in France. Clockwise from left: west rose, Armenteira Monastery, 13th century; façade, San Martín, Noia, 14th century; west rose, San Francisco, Cordoba, after 1236

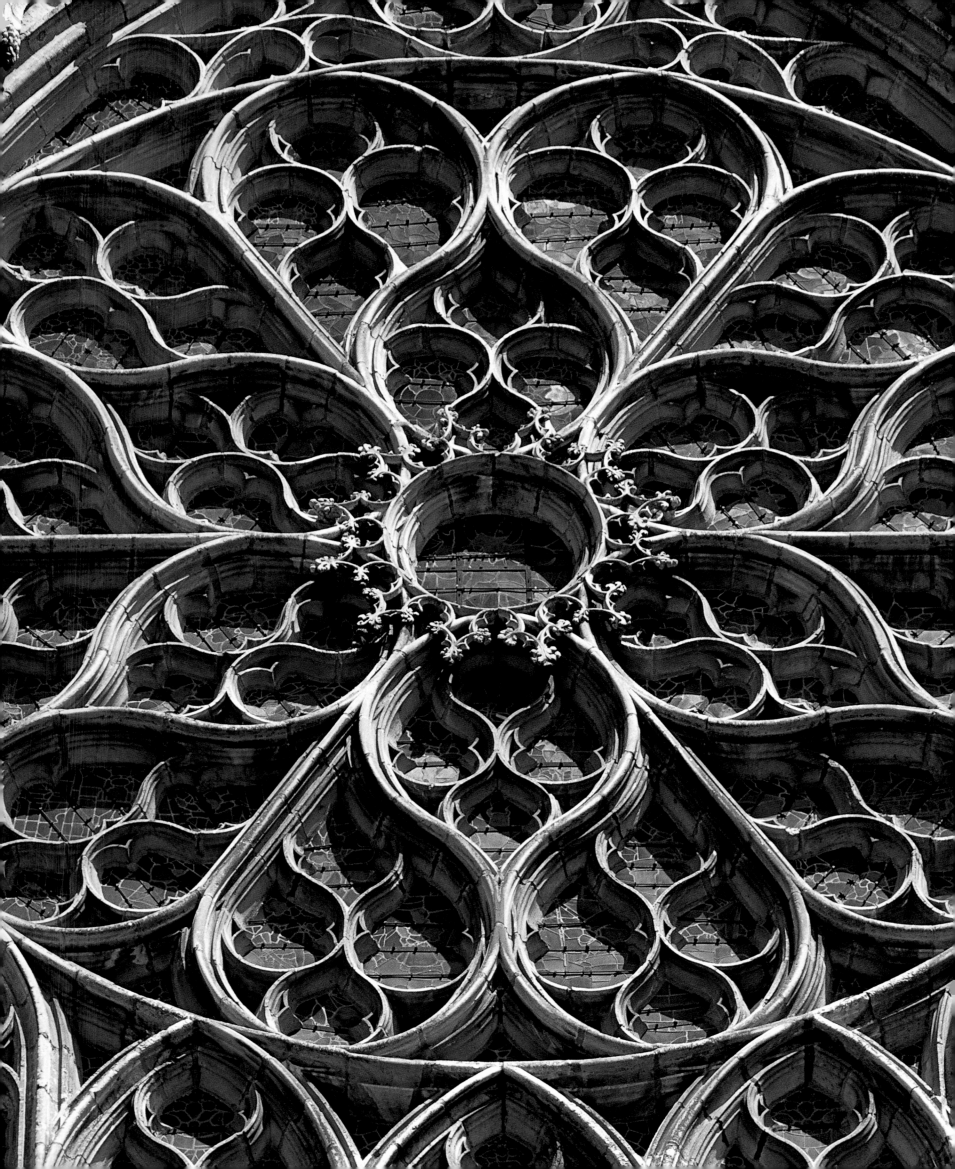

CHAPTER 3
EXPERIMENTS IN FORM: FROM CURVILINEAR TO FLAMBOYANT

It has often been said that after the late 13th century, Gothic architecture was concerned more with decoration than scale. Why this might be is open to debate, but undoubtedly plague, financial depression and seemingly endless war between England and France each had a hand. However, while reductions in scale meant that the grand Rayonnant style of the Notre-Dame transept roses eventually fell out of favour, the change in architecture if anything seemed to spur on rose window designers to ever greater feats of imagination. This chapter looks at a number of different paths that each originated around 1300, and which culminated in the astonishing organic forms of the 15th and 16th centuries. The two principal styles that emerged over this period were the Curvilinear, essentially an English development, and its close relation, the Flamboyant. Both depart from the linear, radiating tracery typical of the Rayonnant in favour of a flowing, graceful tracery reminiscent of foliage or flames (the term 'Flamboyant' comes from the French for 'flaming' – see p. 254–7). These styles originated in the 14th century, before taking off in the 15th, and reaching a zenith in the early 16th. As will be seen, however, dating can become very difficult in this period, as stylistic currents merge. We begin, however, with signs of impatience with the Notre-Dame style.

THE END OF THE RAYONNANT

If we look at the mid-14th century rose at St Lorenz, Nuremberg (see p. 124), we can readily discern the development of a new type, a fresh use of Rayonnant devices. While the tracery radiates from the centre, it does so in pairs of parallel lines which turn, quite unexpectedly, into lancet windows. Some of these lancets point inwards, while others point outwards, setting up a highly unusual rhythm. It is a moment of startling originality. This approach probably appeared for the first time, on a more modest scale, some eighty years earlier at the abbey church of St Germain in Auxerre (see p. 125). Soon after, in the early 1270s, it appeared again at Sées Cathedral in Normandy (see p. 125) where the crystalline effect of the elegant Rayonnant tracery and lightly coloured glass – about one-third original – gives the impression of a snowflake. Other examples can be seen above the Calende portal in the south transept of Rouen Cathedral (see p. 125), on the north side of the western transept at Saint-Quentin Cathedral, and, most spectacularly, in the north transept of Amiens Cathedral (see pp. 126–7). There, the five-pointed star at the centre – which in itself is something of a puzzle – grows into radially disposed lancets. However, the tracery was especially thin, and soon after completion a double buttress was added to prevent the rose from collapsing.

In spite of its energy and beauty, however, this Rayonnant-influenced style found only limited adoption – mostly around Paris and the Ile-de-France – and had a relatively a short life.[1] By the time of the Nuremberg rose, which is certainly the most inventive and risk-taking of the group, the style had largely fallen out of favour, and it is telling that the other late examples, the stunning south side roses at St Katherine, Oppenheim, are also to be found in Germany, away from the style's birthplace. Where this type of design does appear, however, it provides a welcome relief from the ubiquitous Notre-Dame-inspired designs bounded by squares.

The south rose of Beauvais Cathedral is one of the masterpieces of the celebrated late Flamboyant architect, Martin Chambiges (south transept, Beauvais Cathedral, designed before 1532, built 1540s)

123

OPPOSITE West rose, St Lorenz, Nuremberg, central portion of façade built 1353–62

ABOVE These windows took as their building block a typical 13th-century lancet window, with two lights and a rosette. The impression is that of a windmill or even a snowflake. Clockwise from top left: north rose, St Germain, Auxerre, c. 1270; north rose, Sées Cathedral, early 1270s; south rose (above the Calende portal), Rouen Cathedral, c. 1280; the interior of the west rose of St Lorenz, Nuremberg, glass 19th century

THIS SPREAD The north transept window at Amiens is an extraordinary design with its pentagram and fifteen divisions; it dates from the early 14th century, and probably replaced an earlier Notre-Dame style rose.[2] The twin reinforcements in the rose were added in the 14th century. The glass is largely modern (north rose, Amiens Cathedral, early 14th century)

pp. 128–9 These two roses can be found in the south side of St Katherine, Oppenheim. The five-fold window has some glass that dates from 1332–3, though the glass of the three-fold window, which is related to the Nuremberg west rose, is modern (nave windows, St Katherine, Oppenheim, tracery 1320s, glass 1330s)

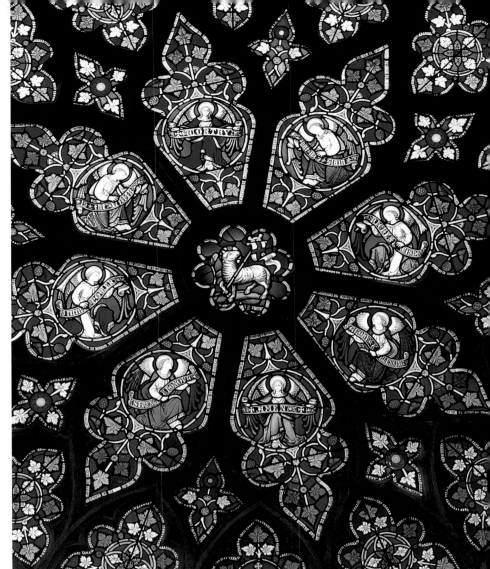

TOWARDS THE FLAMBOYANT

In spite of the innovations in England, it was a number of decades before the Flamboyant style arrived – or evolved – in France.[4] The rose on the south side of the west end at St Georges, Sélestat (see p. 228), which dates from about 1330, is still very much in a 13th-century style, although the division into ten segments is something of a novelty. The glazing, however, is clearly 14th century, with its use of red and green glass, 'silver' stain (actually yellow) and delicately painted faces. Not too far away, at Niederhaslach in the Alsace region, there is a fine rose window of a decade later that is on the border of being Flamboyant. It shows a complex intertwining of Rayonnant forms such as spherical triangles, trefoils and quatrefoils, and dates from 1340–50 (though is filled with later glass). It also shares the undulating forms of the slightly earlier window in St Anselm's Chapel at Canterbury Cathedral, or the more-or-less contemporary west rose at Exeter Cathedral (see p. 268), both in England, and perhaps represents a French take on the Curvilinear.

Other roses experimented with established Rayonnant forms to generate fresh designs. The rose on the west façade of Bourges is set above a pair of lancets, each of which contains smaller roses above three lancets (see p. 134). The glass dates from around 1390 and while the stonework is in most respects essentially Rayonnant with its graded tracery, trefoils and quatrefoils, the rose is lozenge shaped rather than round. Similar lozenge shapes can be found at Tours, and in the spectacular 15th-century blind tracery 'rose' in the gable over a door at Pont-Croix (see p. 18). Other roses use the Rayonnant vocabulary of shapes with more surprising results: a good example is St Pierre in Caen, dating to 1325–50, which conjures undulating tracery from simple circles. Other designers obviously found it more difficult to innovate: the eleven-metre (thirty-six-foot) rose at the west end of Metz Cathedral (see pp. 136–7), glazed in around 1385, is still completely Rayonnant-inspired. Yet at exactly the same time, something very different was happening at Lyon Cathedral.

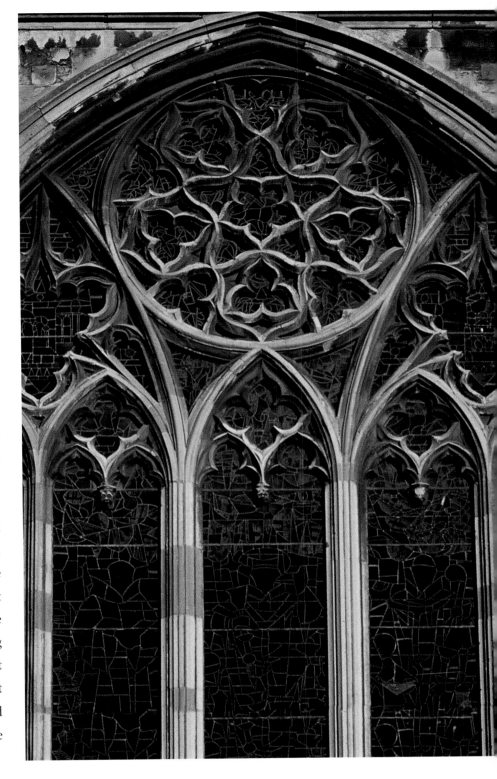

OPPOSITE The design of the Niederhaslach window no longer radiates from the centre; instead the movement is around the periphery (St Florent, Niederhaslach, c. 1340–50)

ABOVE RIGHT This window at Canterbury Cathedral shares the approach of the Niederhaslach window, though it is further embellished with ogees (St Anselm's Chapel window, Canterbury Cathedral, 1336)

OPPOSITE The west rose at Bourges is unusual for its lozenge shape, again a move away from Rayonnant forms. The two rosettes below contain coats of arms of patrons, held by angels, including those of Pope Nicholas V (west window, Bourges Cathedral, c. 1390, glass after 1452)

ABOVE This rose at St Pierre in Caen begins with six large circles, each of which contains three more circles. This anticipates the early Flamboyant window at Lyon – see p. 138 (St Pierre, Caen, mid-14th century, glass 20th century)

OVERLEAF LEFT AND RIGHT The rose at Metz marks a resistance to change, relying exclusively on Rayonnant forms at the end of the 14th century (west rose, Metz Cathedral, 1385–92)

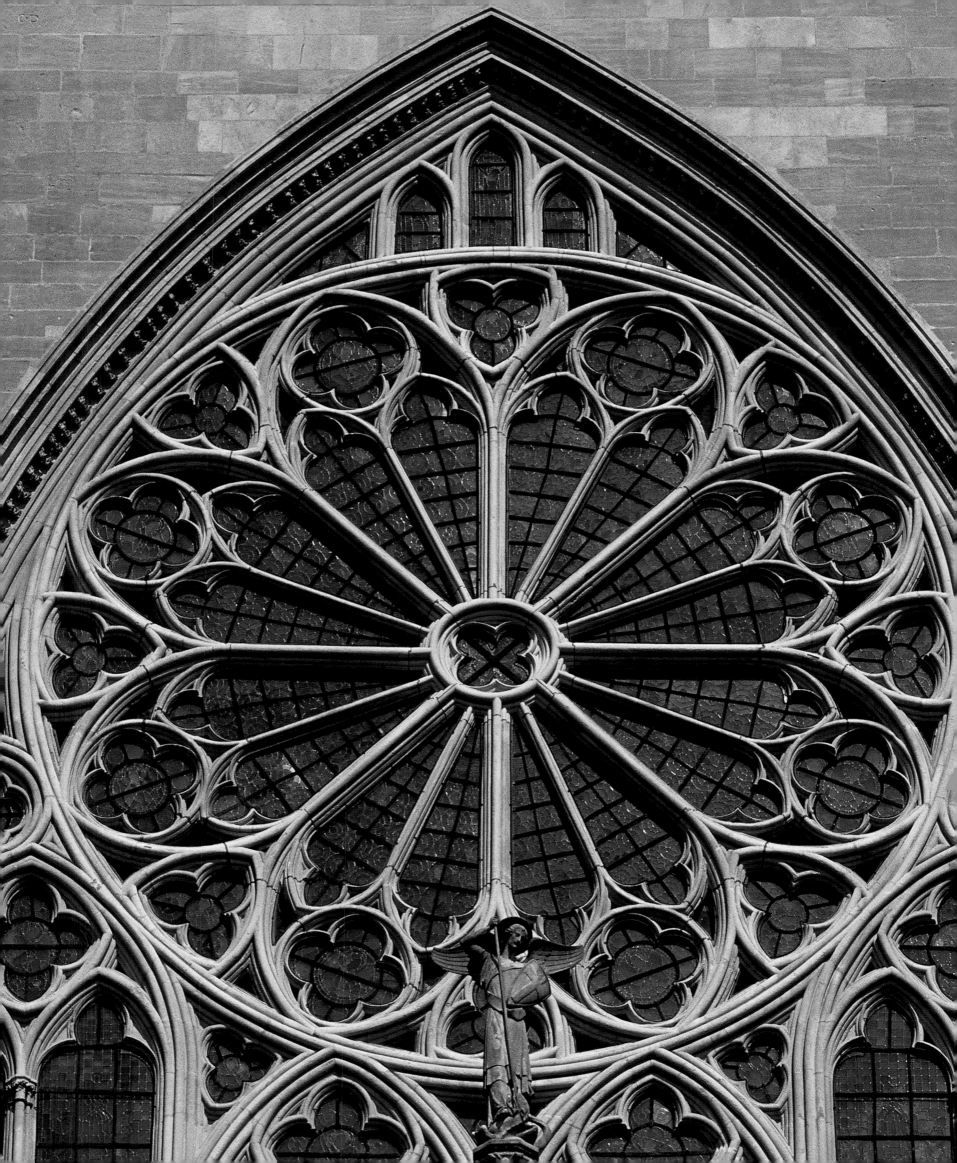

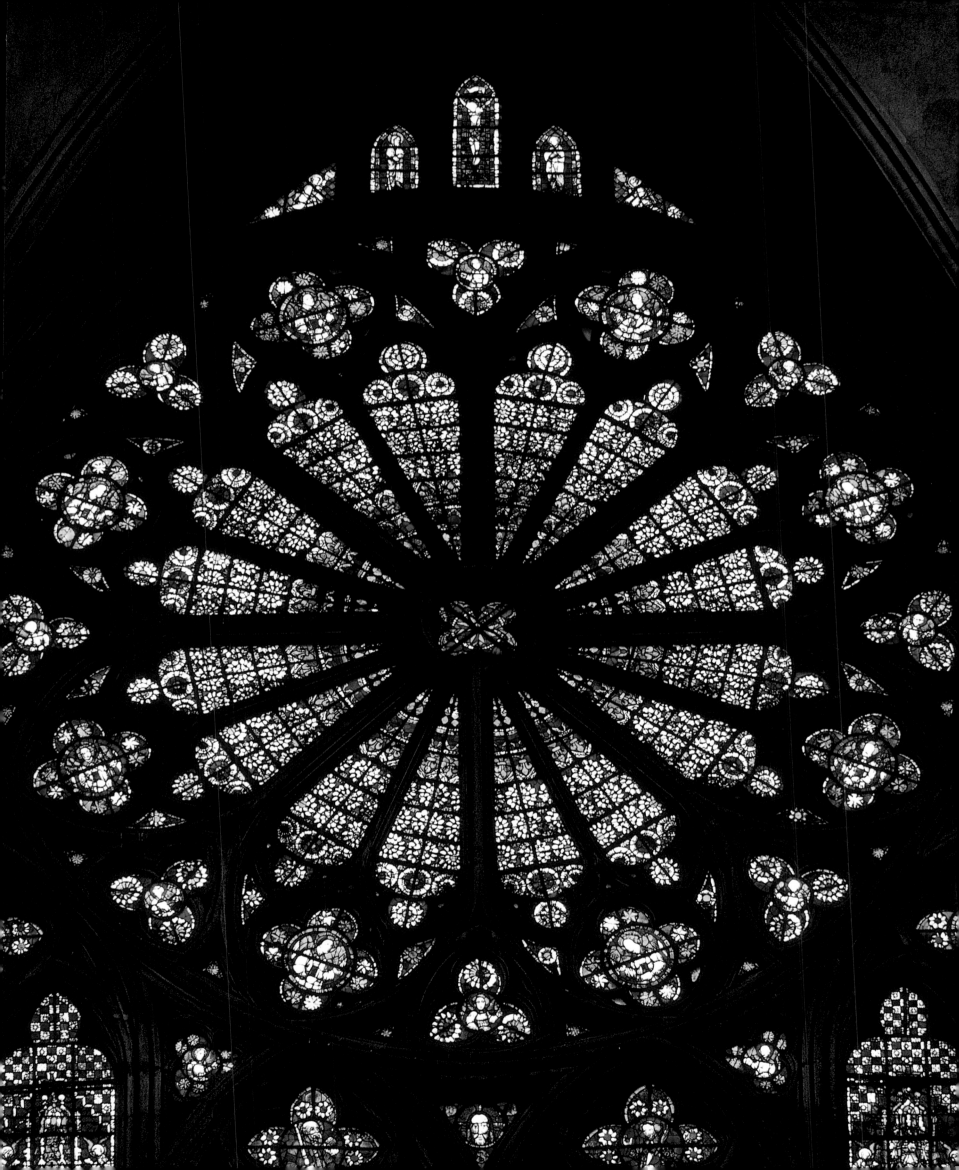

THE EARLY FLAMBOYANT ROSE IN FRANCE

If we need to nominate the first Flamboyant rose window, the best candidate would be the one on the west façade of Lyon Cathedral, which dates to 1392–3 and was glazed in 1394. Although the petals are formed from large, graceful Flamboyant curves, the glazier Henri de Nivelle obviously struggled to cope with these exotic new shapes, and has instead reverted to the traditional roundel form – a sure sign that we are looking at a transitional rose. The essential form of this rose is simple, being composed of six large circles around a hub – similar to St Pierre in Caen (see p. 135). Just like St Pierre, each of the large circles is filled with three smaller circles, though at Lyon only nominally, since they are then used to generate flowing tracery (see p. 255 for a discussion of the geometry).

Lyon aside, concrete dates are few and far between at this early stage. Those that can be reliably dated are therefore here used as 'anchors' against which the many other undated roses can be compared. One such datable rose is that in the south transept of St Ouen at Rouen (see p. 216), which is from before 1441, the date of the death of its architect, Alexandre de Berneval. The design, which shows considerable advances on Lyon, is closely related to the west rose at St Jacques in Dieppe. The north rose at St Ouen (see pp. 198–9), which is probably earlier than the south, is a mystery, the whole window being dominated by a huge five-pointed star.

The other anchor in the 15th century is the magnificent rose in the Sainte-Chapelle (see pp. 140–41), which replaced an earlier Rayonnant one. A profusion of interweaving mouchettes (in three different sizes) and thin soufflets or daggers, this window was built in 1485 and shows how far the Flamboyant had already come. The tendency towards exotic shapes seen at the Sainte-Chapelle is continued at the charming ruined rose at the Royal Abbey at Lieu-Restauré (see p. 259), which probably dates from a little later. The century ends with the south rose at Amiens Cathedral (see pp. 142–3), an essay in elegance set within a *c.* 1300 Wheel of Fortune.

OPPOSITE Perhaps the first Flamboyant rose window, realized by Henri de Nivelle and with a diameter of 6.2 metres (20 feet), this features scenes from the lives of St Stephen in the interior circle and St John Baptist in the exterior[5] (west rose, Lyon Cathedral, *c.* 1390)

ABOVE RIGHT A superb early Flamboyant window reminiscent of the south rose St Ouen, Rouen, where the Rayonnant trefoils and quatrefoils are enclosed by scaled tracery and adopt the weaving double curves of the Flamboyant (west rose St Jacques, Dieppe, early 15th century)

OVERLEAF The west end of the Sainte-Chapelle was rebuilt mid-15th century and the rose dates from *c.* 1485. The subject is St John's Revelation – see p. 239 for a guide to the scenes (Sainte-Chapelle, Paris, *c.* 1485)

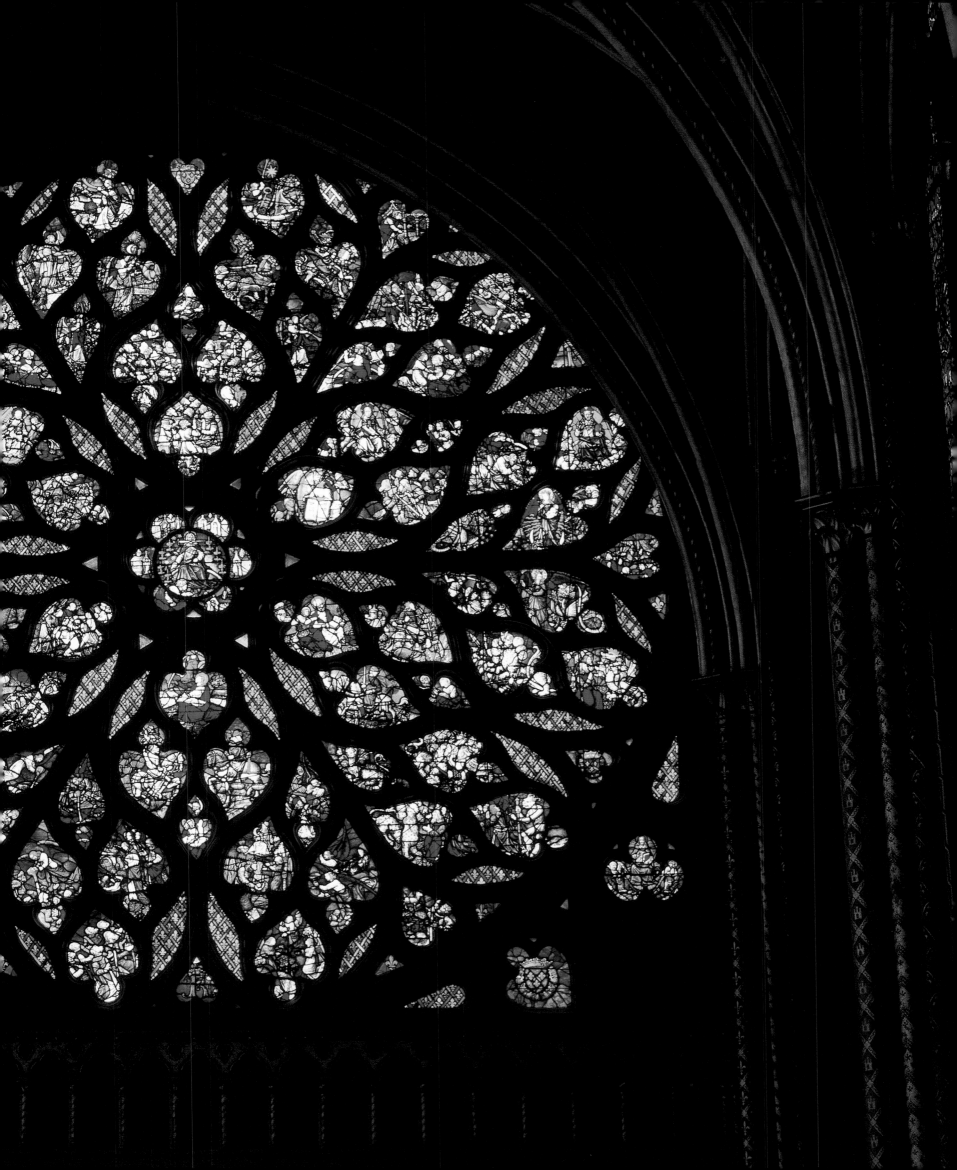

The south rose at Amiens Cathedral, which dates to around 1500, was fitted within an existing Wheel of Fortune arch with seventeen figures, dating to *c.* 1300; the glass shows an array of angels, and geometric motifs (south rose, Amiens Cathedral, *c.* 1500)

The Spirit of the Rose: Flamboyant Invention

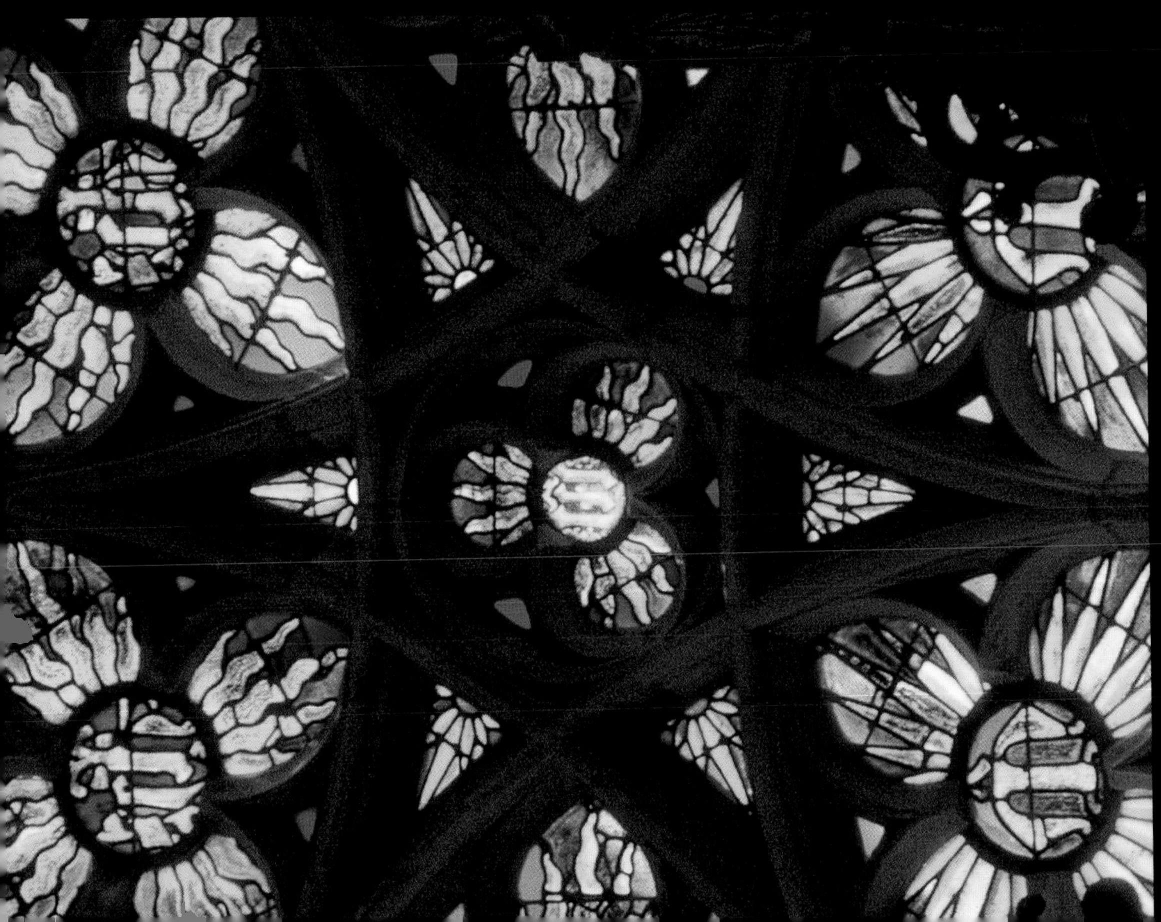

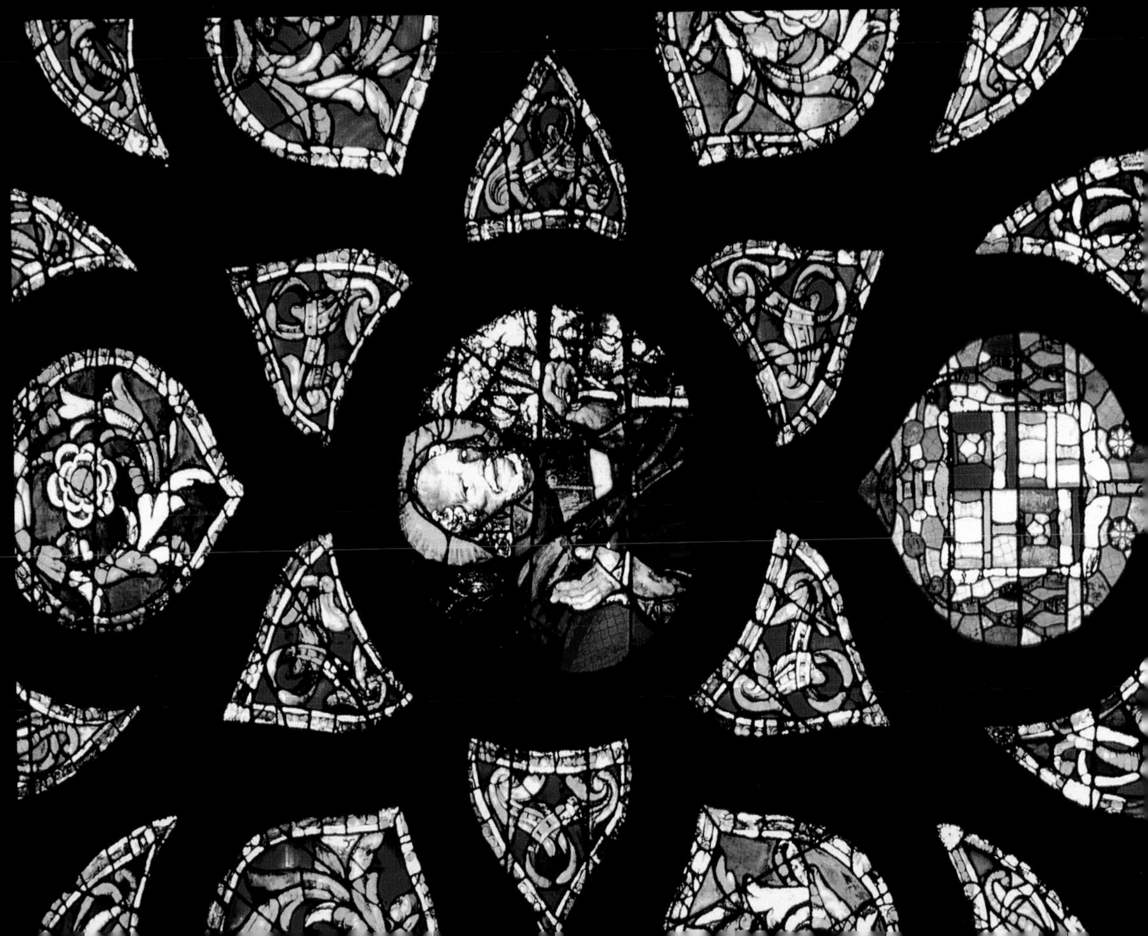

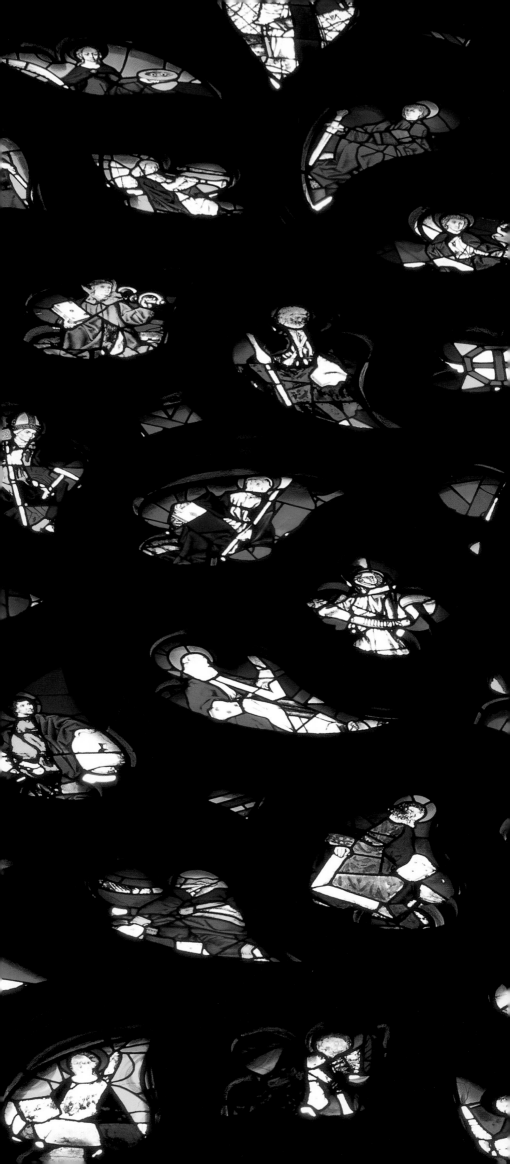

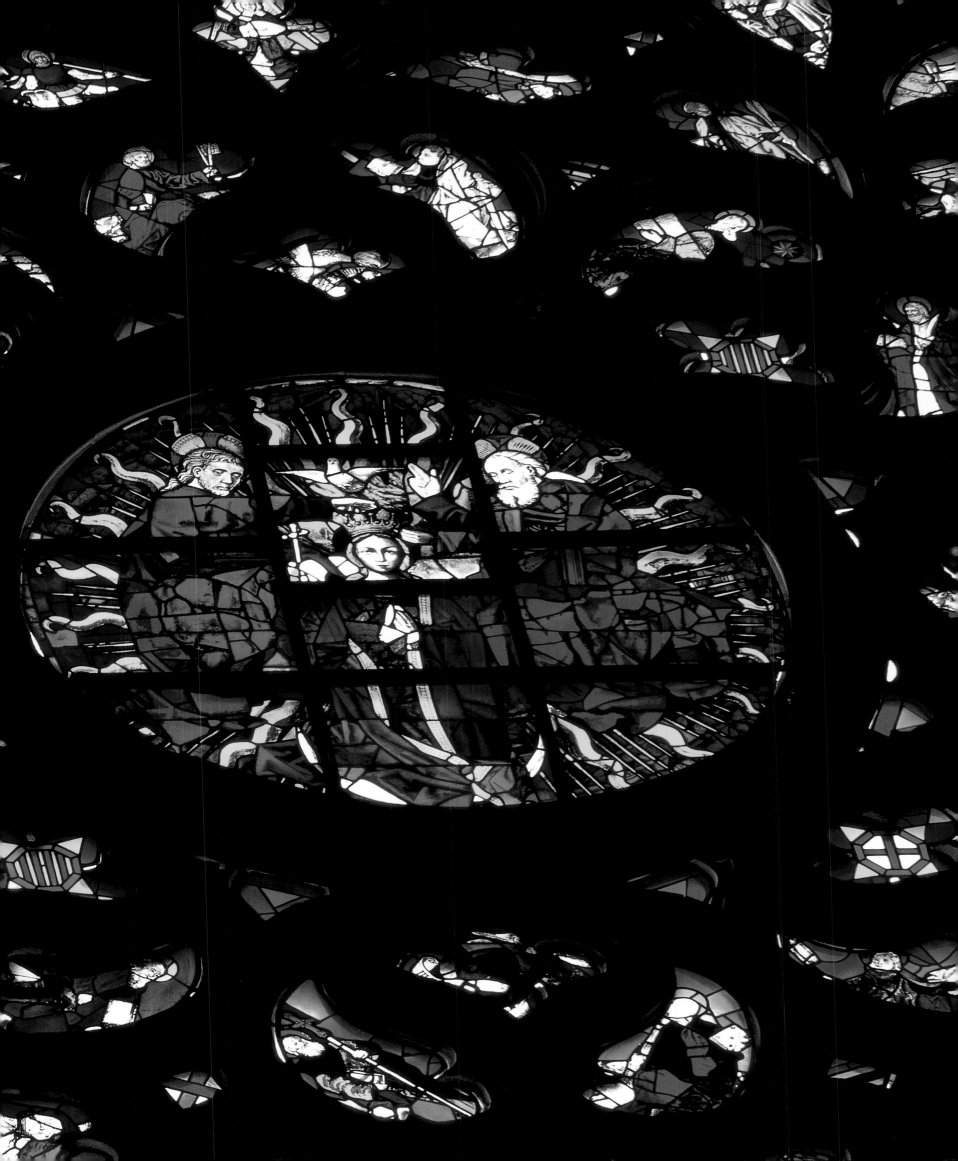

MARTIN CHAMBIGES: *SUPREMUS ARTIFEX*

With the turn of the 16th century a figure appears who applied the Flamboyant in all its glory to the façades he worked on. Born in Paris around 1460, Martin Chambiges was probably the most famous master mason of his day in France: the chapter of Troyes Cathedral referred to him as *supremus artifex*, and his expertise commanded fees far in excess of those of local masons. Involved in all manner of building projects, he is best known for his façades with their prominent and elaborate rose windows, and today his work can be seen at the cathedrals of Sens (see p. 244), Troyes, Senlis and Beauvais (where he died in 1532). It has been suggested that he was also responsible for the rose window at the Sainte-Chapelle, although more likely he was simply aware of the design – his earliest rose, the south window at Sens that he executed in 1494, echoes certain aspects of it, though the tracery is heavier.

It is often said that Chambiges used the same basic design for all of his rose windows, and there is some truth in this. The clear odd one out is Sens north, which is based on the number five rather than six. At Senlis the transept rose windows are almost identical to one another in structure, and at Beauvais (where his designs were not executed until a number of years after his death), the differences are only slight. The inflexibility of his designs must have placed a strain on the glaziers, who had to respond to the shapes they were presented with. Sometimes the effects can be engaging – witness the Beauvais south window, which shows the Creation, teeming with lifeforms (see pp. 214–15). In other cases, however, the glaziers were overwhelmed by the sheer scale of the project: in the north rose of Sens the figures to the left and right sides mirror each other (see p. 34), meaning only half as many cartoons needed to be drawn up. While his style enjoyed some influence – see the window at St Etienne in Beauvais, from around 1520 – essentially it died with its author. It is interesting to note that his architect son, Pierre, was better known for châteaux in the new Italian, Classical style.

Perhaps Chambiges's masterpiece, the south window at Beauvais Cathedral measures 21 by 8.8 metres (69 feet by 29 feet). The rose contains scenes from Genesis, notably the Creation, while the two galleries beneath are filled with New Testament saints (interior of south façade, Beauvais Cathedral, designed before 1532, glass c. 1550)

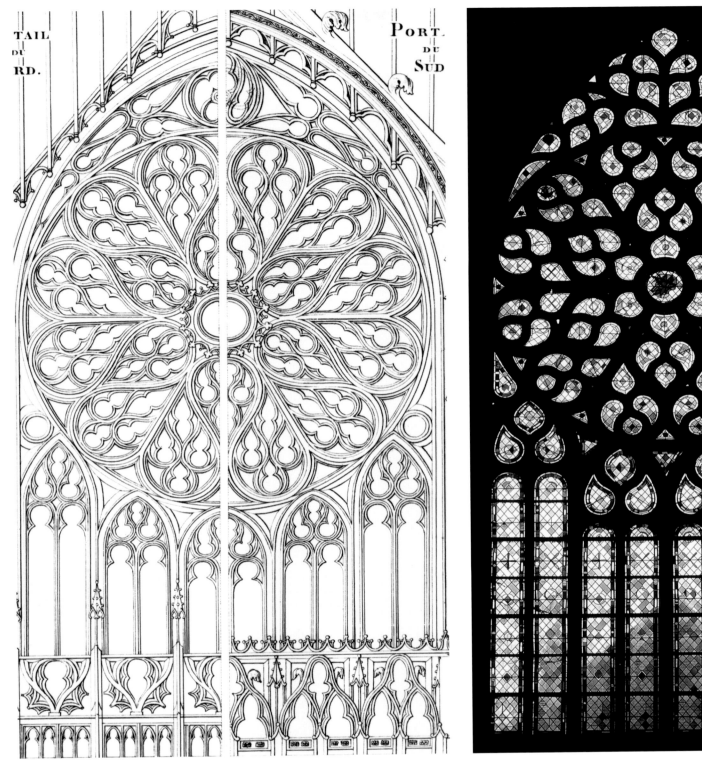

ABOVE Chambiges tended not to vary his designs much, as this comparison between north and south roses at Beauvais shows

ABOVE RIGHT Four hundred years after its original Wheel of Fortune (see p. 56), St Etienne in Beauvais gained this Chambiges-inspired giant. It differs from Chambiges's design in that the mouchettes are fatter and simpler, and 'swim' towards the centre rather than away from it (east rose, St Etienne, Beauvais, c. 1520)

LATE FLAMBOYANT WINDOWS IN FRANCE

The Chambiges type of rose, in its comparative sobriety and sense of restraint is only one side of rose window design in the 16th century, however. The other side sees the rose become, perhaps for the first time, a vehicle for almost individualistic expression. In these roses we find inventiveness, playfulness and often downright eccentricity. We also find an increasingly complex geometry, which seems to dispense with a strictly 'medieval' approach, based on squares and circles, in favour of a more liberal approach that values the exotic over the rational. This complex underlying geometry is then wilfully obscured by elaborate, almost over-the-top, tracery, reflecting the more general shift in late Gothic architecture towards surface decoration. We are now a long way from the simple demonstrations of form seen in the 13th century.

None of this, of course, is necessarily a bad thing, and many late Flamboyant roses are masterpieces by any standard. The rose at Bazas Cathedral, completed by 1535, for example, builds on a

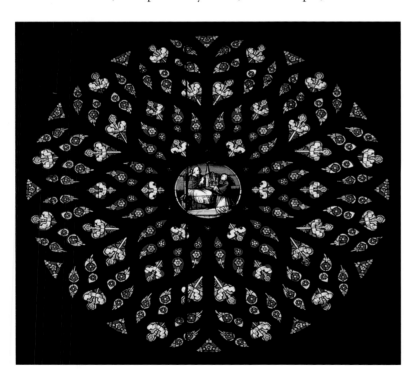

Chambiges-type rose, but uses differently shaped openings for the 'inner' and 'outer' petals; it also increases the number of lights. As a result it loses some of the structural blandness seen at Beauvais and Sens, where the large, rounded openings cater better for a grand, canvas-like glazing programme. St Martin in Harbonnières (see p. 152) has less divisions than Bazas, but creates fantastical new shapes by interweaving thin lines of tracery in a lace-like effect. This sort of effect is also seen at Vincennes, where sinuous lines of tracery gracefully arc and weave around each other (see p. 152). As with many later Flamboyant roses, one feels that they have been designed to be seen from the outside as much as the inside.

Such is the emphasis on originality in the later Flamboyant, it is rare to find two roses of the same design.[6] Even the spectacular helicoidal spiral in the Chapel of the Bourbons in Lyon Cathedral – one of some seven rose windows at that church – is not quite unique since the two small spiral designs on the façade of Bayonne Cathedral date from around the same time, as does the spiral at the west end of St Etienne, Fécamp.[7] Other roses that deserve to be mentioned include the three at Rodez Cathedral; the two at St Germain l'Auxerrois in Paris that still contain much original glass and date from the first quarter of the 16th century; and the north rose at Auxerre Cathedral, which has spectacular glass (see p. 223). And then there is Cognac (see p. 267), where the huge rose is cruelly imposed onto a Romanesque façade, Notre-Dame de la Dalbade at Toulouse, Lavaur Cathedral, St Maclou in Pontoise, the Abbey of Saint-Leu-d'Esserent (see p. 192), Blénod-lès-Toul (see p. 192), and Notre-Dame in Montferrand (see p. 152).

It is difficult not to sense in these windows the death throes of the Gothic style. Irrespective of their invention, there is often a lack of inspiration or vitality, as if the vocabulary of forms has been stretched to its limit. Before long France, and the rest of northern Europe, would embrace the ideals of the Italian Renaissance – and Britain and north Germany would embrace Protestantism.

ABOVE LEFT The imagery of this fine rose at Bazas is confined to the panel in the centre, the smaller openings better suited to decorative elements (west rose, Bazas Cathedral, c. 1535)

OPPOSITE Perhaps surprisingly, spirals appear only rarely in rose windows. In this case, was it merely a virtuosic display, or does the shape have symbolic value? (Chapel of the Bourbons, Lyon Cathedral, late 15th century)

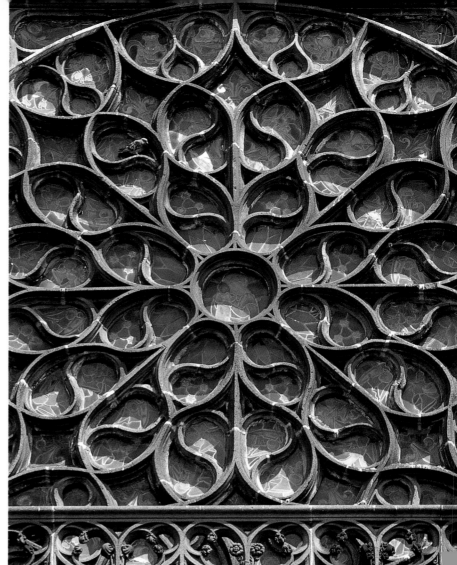

OPPOSITE In the 16th century, tracery tended to grow more and more complex, departing from traditional Gothic forms. Clockwise from top left: west rose, St Martin, Harbonnières, late 15th century; west rose, Notre-Dame, Montferrand, early 16th century (with fine 19th-century glass by a local glazier depicting a Tree of Jesse); Chapel of the Château, Vincennes, 16th century, partially destroyed by a hurricane in 1788; Vernon, Notre-Dame, late 15th/early 16th century.

ABOVE Even without their glass these late Flamboyant windows impress with their robust designs (Saint-Nicholas-de-Port, before 1560)

ITALY

Outside France the development of rose window design in the late 13th to 16th centuries very much follows the taste of the country concerned. In Italy, where the Anglo-French Early and High Gothic styles had had a rather lukewarm reception, the wheel window rolled on throughout the 14th century, often with very little fundamental change in design, as, for example, on the façade of Todi, begun in 1292. At Cremona the wheel on the main façade, which dates to 1274, becomes more rose-like as alternating spokes interweave with their neighbours on the perimeter. On the north façade of the same church we find a similar design with thirteen spokes – highly unusual, but presumably deliberate.

Interweaving spokes are the focal point of a number of later roses/wheels in Sicily, notably at the Chiesa dell'Annunciazione, Trapani (see p. 268), and S. Agostino, Palermo (see p. 156). In both of these windows the interweaving petals employ extremely broad tracery such that the openings in the stone become very restricted resulting in a plane of rather heavy filigree. At Palermo the interweaving starts from short radial spokes meaning that each is linked to a spoke not two away but four away.

At the Or San Michele in Florence, begun in 1337 and completed by Andrea da Cione (alias Orcagna) in 1359, a new tendency can be seen. Exotic tracery at the tops of the windows incorporates small wheel windows with spiral spokes in order to match the richness that surrounds it (see p. 156). A similar design can also be found in the tympanum of the Lower Church at Assisi and at Fermo. This filigree carving in the petals is also the focal point of the beautiful window on the façade of Otranto Cathedral in the south of Italy where the spokes of the wheel give rise to exotic tracery-filled onion shapes (see p. 156). Orcagna also worked, briefly, on the façade of Orvieto Cathedral (see p. 27) where there is a delicate rose in which the spokes give birth to ogee arches, which contain trefoils, circles and spherical triangles in a design reminiscent of French Rayonnant.

Perhaps the most important exception to Italy's generally independent and idiosyncratic approach is Milan Cathedral (see pp. 156–7). This magnificent but problematic church, which was begun in 1386, was designed almost by committee, drawing on the expertise of first Italian, then later French, and finally German, architects. There are three rose windows in the apse, integrated into large, elegant lancet windows. The tracery shows some French Flamboyant influence – remarkably early – with mouchettes chasing each other around the perimeter, though there is no single precedent for these sophisticated creations.

OPPOSITE, CLOCKWISE FROM TOP LEFT Central east window,
Milan Cathedral, early 15th century; west rose,
Otranto Cathedral, 15th century; rosette, Or San Michele,
Florence, mid-14th century; west rose, S. Agostino,
Palermo, late 14th century

ABOVE Side east window, Milan Cathedral, early
15th century

GERMANY AND SPAIN

While the Gothic style was popular across Europe, different regions developed their own variations. Both Germany and Spain were more receptive to Gothic architecture than Italy, but the results were very different to one another, and it is interesting to compare the two.

Very broadly speaking, the rose in Germany becomes a decorative element, used to embellish the outsides of buildings. This is first seen at churches such as the Cistercian Abbey in Chorin, where the façade was completed by 1319. The rose remains in its axial position, but is blind (and was always so), and built from brick. A little later, another blind rose appears in the huge gable of the Marienkirche in Prenzlau, near Berlin (see p. 161). There it is surrounded by an astonishing array of similarly blind rose window-inspired designs, a riot of cusped oculi, spherical triangles, lozenges and lancets. At Prenzlau, the tracery actually stands slightly proud of the wall, an innovation first seen at Strasbourg Cathedral in the late 13th century (see pp. 108–109). This effect was taken to its logical, and spectacular, conclusion in the freestanding structures of St Katherine, Brandenburg (see p. 160) and Tangermünde Town Hall (see p. 161). In both of these the rose is held up, emblematic yet robbed of its glass – and thus, largely, its meaning. It is difficult to understand today what value these adornments had in the eyes of their creators, but this approach was popular in eastern Germany, with other notable examples appearing in the gates of Neubrandenburg, and Stralund Town Hall. What is particularly interesting is that these are the first occasions on which the rose window – albeit as a decorative element – has been used in secular architecture. Certainly any liturgical function that the rose might have originally had has been lost completely.

In Spain, the rose generally retains its place on the axis and much of its importance. However, it also largely fails to move on significantly from the forms of the 13th century – like Germany, there is

ABOVE LEFT The nave of Palma Cathedral is dominated by this huge, hovering, six-pointed star, some 11.3 metres (37 feet) in diameter. The rose has suffered greatly over the years: it fell in 1581, was repaired in 1857, then in 1904, then again damaged in the Spanish Civil War. Beyond the nave, in the eastern chapel is the rose window reglazed by Antoni Gaudí in 1904 (east nave rose, Palma Cathedral, window c. 1370, glass 16th century and modern)

OPPOSITE Although not a window, this circular design with rose-like tracery on the west façade of Chorin Abbey shows the Cistercians were still interested in such designs well into the 14th century (west façade, Cistercian Abbey, Chorin, completed by 1319)

little evidence of the Flamboyant, but instead a recycling and reworking of old Rayonnant (and Romanesque) motifs. Nonetheless, the Spanish approach to rose window construction in the 14th century onwards often displays some remarkable originality. At Palma Cathedral, on the island of Mallorca (see p. 158), the rebuilt east rose of *c*. 1370 in the crossing is in the form of a six-pointed star, and must be related to the six-pointed star in the rose at Valencia Cathedral. Right the other side of Spain, at Betanzos, in Galicia, is the late 14th-century San Francisco, which has a rose window at the east end and two more on the south façade, one above the other, all with high-relief carved surrounds. The tracery of the main south rose is unusual in that it is comprised of twelve petal-shaped loops, each apparently carved from a single piece of stone, and arranged around the central lobed oculus. Like many smaller Spanish roses it has a rather heavy and rough-hewn feel.

Much later we encounter one of the marvels of Spanish architecture, the façade of San Pablo in Valladolid, intensely decorated and with a richly traceried rose which at first glance might appear Flamboyant but which is actually a network of quatrefoils. Although the church was begun in 1276 it was Simon of Cologne who created this riot of sculpture in the late 1470s. He was also responsible for the nearby San Gregorio college, both façades being executed in the so-called 'Isabelline' style that combined late Gothic and Mudéjar traditions. At Toledo Cathedral the early 15th-century west window resists both Rayonnant linearity and Flamboyant exuberance, finding a third way through imaginative use of trefoils, quatrefoils, cinqfoils and other classic early Gothic shapes.

There is one notable exception to the general resistance to Flamboyant: the rose at Santa Maria del Mar in Barcelona. Northeastern Spain had always been most susceptible to French influence, and the rose at Santa Maria del Mar shows the influence of the Sainte-Chapelle. Curiously, like the Flamboyant rose in that building, the one at Santa Maria del Mar replaced an earlier rose.

TOP ROW In eastern Germany the rose is seized upon as a decorative motif, typically unglazed. From left to right: roses on the south gable, St Katherine, Brandenburg, 1387–1411; Town Hall, Tangermünde, *c*. 1420–30; west façade, Marienkirche, Prenzlau, church after 1325, but rebuilt 1972–6

BOTTOM ROW In Spain there is less sense of a national style than might be found in France, Germany or even Italy. From left to right: west façade, San Pablo, Valladolid, late 15th century[8] (façade *c*. 1463); west rose, Toledo Cathedral, 15th century[9] (glass 1418–1561); San Francisco, Betanzos, church begun 1387 (the sculptured pig is the patron's emblem)

CHAPTER 4
DECLINE AND REVIVAL: POST-MEDIEVAL ROSES

At the risk of oversimplification it may be said that the mid-16th century marks the end of the Gothic 'style' and the beginning of the Renaissance – in architectural matters at least. For admirers of Gothic art and philosophy, it also marks the point when the spiritual inspiration of architecture, driven by Humanism, assumed a more abstract character, when the perfection of geometry (for instance, the circle) was no longer seen as an attribute of the divine.

We might expect that the rose window, so closely tied to the Gothic, would have shared the style's fate, but this is not entirely the case, and rose windows in other guises can be found through the 16th, 17th and 18th centuries. Why the rose was able to outlive its parent style is open to debate – perhaps it had just become part of a broader church vocabulary, independent of fashion. And of course earlier roses still needed to be replaced as they were damaged or else collapsed. Efforts to reconcile the rose window with Classical architecture, however, are not entirely successful, as if there were a fundamental clash of cultures, and the results can lack the aspiration and inspiration of their predecessors. This period also saw the widespread destruction of roses, through neglect and vandalism. France, with the largest number of rose windows, suffered particularly in the Revolution of 1789 and its aftermath, losing many important churches and with them roses. In the 20th century, meanwhile, northeastern France became a battleground twice, with important monuments such as the cathedrals at Reims and Soissons being particularly badly damaged.

However, the 19th century also saw the first real attempts to record and conserve Europe's Gothic heritage, as well as a renaissance of the rose window as part of the wider Gothic Revival. This movement, driven by architects and designers such as A. W. N. Pugin in England and Viollet-le-Duc in France,[1] often placed the rose window at the heart of ecclesiastical architecture, while the 20th century sees the rose reinvented as a vehicle for individualistic artistic expression, or as a spectacle in its own right, a giant blaze of colour. As ever the story of the rose is more easily told in several parallel histories rather than one linear one, and so we begin this final section with some astonishing Renaissance oculi.

RENAISSANCE GLASS IN THE OCULUS

Among the most impressive examples of late medieval or early Renaissance glasswork in Europe are the rose windows or oculi found in Italy and, less often, Spain. Examples of glass-filled oculi, in which the composition is supported by ironwork (called ferramenta) rather than stone tracery, go back at least to the north window of Canterbury Cathedral in around 1180. Around one hundred years later we encounter the east window of Siena (see p. 17), in which ironwork neatly divides the circle into nine sections allowing a clear narrative designed by Duccio (and possibly Cimabue as well).[2]

The first signs of something less medieval come in 1365 at S. Maria Novella in Florence. The giant oculus on the west façade is filled with a single composition, the Coronation of the Virgin Mary. This magnificent window paved the way for other oculi filled with single-scene pictures, in Italy but also in Spain. There, the cathedrals of Seville and Girona used a similar approach in the mid-16th

The Coronation of the Virgin by Andrea di Buonaiuto
(Florence, Santa Maria Novella, 1365)

century. Seville combines Flamboyant carving with Renaissance-style glasswork in the rose windows that are found on all three façades, although only one of these – at the west end – is radial, with twelve spokes. The fantastic carving on the inner and outer surfaces of the north and south roses is unlikely to be missed by the visitor. The scene in the glass of the north rose is the Ascension dating from 1539 and is by Arnao de Flandres, who also did the Assumption of the Virgin in the south oculus two years earlier. On the west front, aside from the large spoked window, there are three smaller round windows all by Vicente Menardo: north-west is the Visitation (1566–8); south-west, the Annunciation (1560–67); centre west are the four Evangelists (1577 but restored 1831, as the glass indicates). At Girona, meanwhile, the big oculus over the crossing has the Resurrection in one scene, with twenty-four radial beams of light that, ironically, seem to mimic a rose window. Other glazed oculi in the building include a large 17th-century composition with St Michael, and two marvellous kaleidoscopic 'flowers' (see p. 190).

The most stunning examples of Renaissance oculi, however, can be found in the drum of the dome of Florence Cathedral. These windows depict key scenes from the life of Christ, and are particularly rare in that they are stained-glass windows designed by well-known Renaissance artists; in fact the list of designers is a roll-call of early 15th-century Florentine talent. Lorenzo Ghiberti designed three: the Presentation of Christ in the Temple, Christ in Gethsemane and the Ascension (all around 1443–5). Andrea del Castagno was responsible for the Deposition (1444), while Paolo Uccello designed the Resurrection and Nativity panels (1443), and the Coronation of the Virgin is by Donatello (1438). The eighth window (the Annunciation by Uccello) was lost in a storm in the 19th century. In the same cathedral on the west front are three more glazed oculi designed by Ghiberti of which the Annunciation in the centre is the best, glazed in c. 1405 by Niccolo Tedesco. Ghiberti also did a number of other windows in the cathedral.

OPPOSITE While the Assumption of the Virgin oculus by Arnao de Flandres is eyecatching, and grand, it is the fantastical stonework around the oculus – inside and out – that grabs the viewer's attention (south oculus, Seville Cathedral, 1536–7)

ABOVE RIGHT The Ascension in the north oculus at Seville is a slightly later work also by Arnao de Flandres (north oculus, Seville Cathedral, glass 1539)

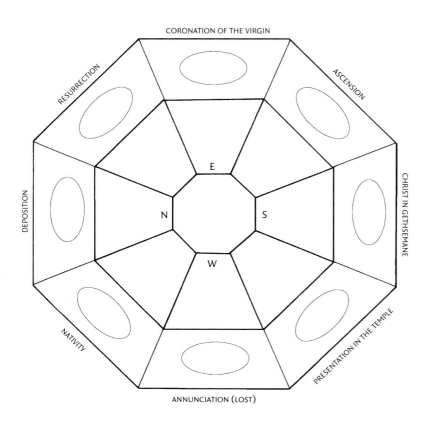

CORONATION OF THE VIRGIN

RESURRECTION

ASCENSION

DEPOSITION

CHRIST IN GETHSEMANE

E

N   S

W

NATIVITY

PRESENTATION IN THE TEMPLE

ANNUNCIATION (LOST)

The oculi in the dome of Florence Cathedral are among the masterpieces of Renaissance glass painting, and represent the culmination of the Italian love of oculi. Together they illustrate the life of Christ, along with the Coronation of the Virgin. There were originally eight windows: the seventh window, not illustrated here, shows the Presentation in the Temple, and is by Ghiberti; the eighth, the Annunciation by Uccello, was lost to a storm in the 19th century

ABOVE A diagram of the disposition of the panels around the drum of the dome in Florence Cathedral.

THIS SPREAD, CLOCKWISE FROM TOP LEFT Christ in Gethsemane, designed by Ghiberti, made by the local glazier Bernardo di Francesco, 1443–5; the Nativity, by Uccello, 1443; the Ascension by Ghiberti, glass by Bernardo di Francesco, 1443–5; the Resurrection by Uccello, 1443; the Coronation of the Virgin by Donatello, made by a glazier from Pisa, 1438; the Deposition by Andrea del Castagno, 1444

pp. 168–9 Detail of the Deposition

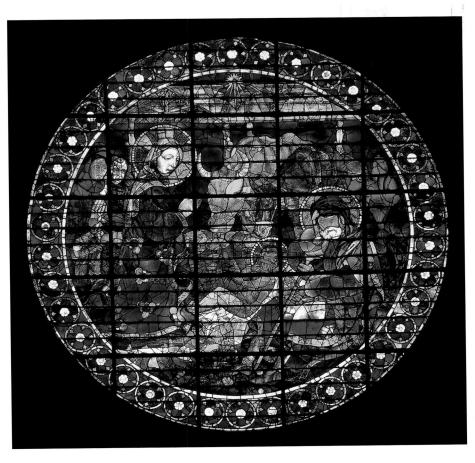

BETWEEN FLAMBOYANT AND REVIVAL

It is difficult to generalize the history of the rose window in the later 16th, 17th and 18th centuries. Looking at four examples from the second half of the 16th century, we can see four different directions. At the west rose at Evreux Cathedral (see p. 175) we find an attempt to rationalize the Flamboyant rose into lines and circles; at St Remi in Dieppe (see p. 174) a great step backwards, to an early 13th-century type of rose set within a square, all in overheavy tracery. At Ivry-la-Bataille (see p. 175) and Othis, meanwhile, we find attempts to reconcile the fundamentally Gothic nature of the rose with the demands of Classical architecture, with pleasing results. Ivry-la-Bataille reduces the rose to a series of circles, a moderately popular approach which can found be found elsewhere in the Ile-de-France at Ennery (six circles around a central circle) and Epiais-Rhus (with five). The 'Classical' rose in the village of Othis just outside Paris, takes more of a risk in employing scroll-like forms in place of Gothic tracery.[3] Dating from 1573 – a carved plaque tells us so – this is an example of great inventiveness, and the viewer can pass some agreeable moments visually exploring its ingenious arabesques.

In Italy at this date we find the continuation of the two traditions of the giant oculus – good examples can be found in Apulia, in the very south, at Lecce, Squinzano and Minervino – and the wheel window. The wheel windows tend to be rather fantastical, building on a noble heritage of Italian invention. Acquaviva Cathedral (see p. 174), for example, employs spokes that might have been turned on a lathe. The fine filigree tracery in between them gives the whole a lace-like quality, faintly reminiscent of the early 13th-century marble screens at Troia (see p. 118). Just down the road, anyone waiting for a train at Gravina will be entertained by the extraordinary façade of the church of the Madonna delle Grazie of 1602 that looks onto the platform. The small rose there forms part of the body of a huge eagle that spreads across the entire upper half of the church, the arms of the builder, Bishop Vincenzo Giustienti.

Moving into the 17th century, we find a rare rose in London at St Katherine Cree (built 1628–31), which was probably inspired by the east window at nearby Old St Paul's (see p. 107) – albeit on a smaller scale with a single 'layer' of petals. If Old St Paul's was indeed the source of inspiration, then the curvilinear tips of the petals may well confirm Hollar's print. The glass at St Katherine Cree is partially original, though it was renewed in the 18th century. The building itself is a curious mixture of Classical and Gothic forms, constructed at a time of religious tension in England. A similar mixing of styles is also found at the exactly contemporary St Eustache in Paris. The transept roses differ to one another, the south made almost entirely of straight lines, the north formed from heart shapes (see p. 179). South of Paris, in Pithiviers, meanwhile, there was an attempt at a genuinely new rose window design (see p. 176), in the mould of Othis. The tracery is now formed entirely from Baroque motifs, yet it is hard to imagine what 17th-century architect was so keen to maintain the rose window form, let alone studiously update it.

Over on Mallorca at the end of the century we find another Baroque-inspired rose at Sant Francesc in Palma (see p. 174). This peculiar creation takes the approach seen at Acquaviva to a logical conclusion, filling in almost all of the lights and decorating the surface with a sort of blind tracery. More conventional – though certainly spectacular – are the north and south roses at Orléans Cathedral (see p. 172), which date from 1687–9. The tracery is somewhat conservative, but the glasswork more than compensates, incorporating the royal fleur-de-lis symbol – indeed, it is tempting to read the sunburst form of the rose as referring to the 'Sun King', Louis XIV who reigned for much of the 17th century in France.

18th-century roses are something of a rarity, and judging by the very few surviving examples – see the rose at Toussaint Abbey in Angers, p. 177 – this century can reasonably be considered the low point in the rose window's history.

OPPOSITE This exotic late Renaissance rose is dated 1573. There is nothing like it anywhere else in France! (Nativité-de-la-Sainte-Vierge, Othis, 1573)

OVERLEAF LEFT The large roses in the transepts of Orléans Cathedral were part of the rebuild under Louis XIII and Louis XIV. The glass dates from 1687–9. This, the north rose, includes Louis XIV's motto, NEC PLURIBUS IMPAR: 'Without Equal' (north rose, Orléans Cathedral, glass 1687–9)

OVERLEAF RIGHT Perhaps this late rose window was chosen to remind the congregation that St Catherine – to whom the church is dedicated – was martyred on a wheel. Certainly there are no other roses in England of this date. The decorative glass is partially original (St Katherine Cree, London, c. 1630)

THIS DO IN REMEMBRANCE OF ME

Roses in the later 16th and 17th centuries tend to be more rational or functional, sweeping away much of the sometimes overwrought Flamboyant decoration.

TOP ROW, LEFT TO RIGHT St Remi, Dieppe, later 16th century; Sant Francesc, Palma de Mallorca, late 17th century; interior, Ivry-la-Bataille, glass 19th century; exterior, Ivry-la-Bataille, late 17th century

BOTTOM ROW, LEFT TO RIGHT Madonna delle Grazie, Gravina, 1602; Acquaviva Cathedral, 16th century; west rose, Evreux Cathedral, 16th century

OPPOSITE Baroque scrolls embellish this rather
enchanting late 17th-century rose (St Salomon-
St Gregoire, Pithiviers, late 17th century)

ABOVE Toussaint Abbey, Angers, was destroyed soon
after its completion: today it is a sculpture gallery.
The 18th-century rose survived, allowing us a glimpse
of how the Age of Reason viewed the rose

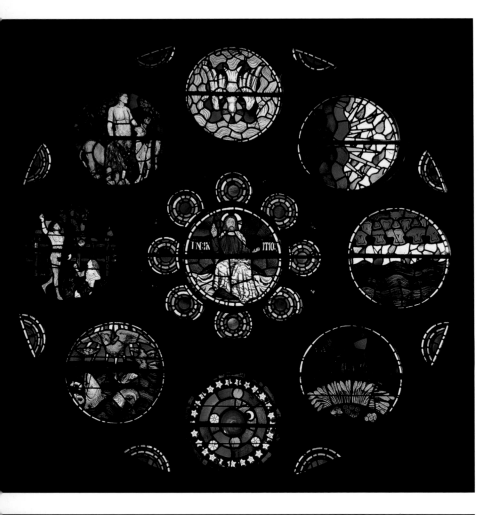

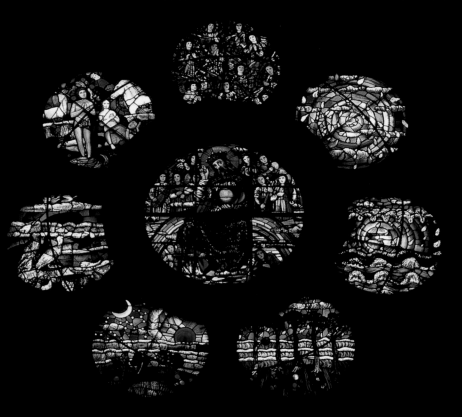

REVIVAL AND INVENTION IN THE 19TH CENTURY

While the 18th century was the low point of rose window production, its love of documenting and categorizing the past saw the birth of antiquarianism and thus sowed the seeds of the 19th-century 'Gothic Revival'. This primarily affected England and France – and later North America – where thousands of new churches sprang up, particularly in the expanding cities. For commentators such as John Ruskin, or Viollet-le-Duc, the Gothic Revival represented a return to 'truth' in religious architecture. The rose window, as a key phrase in the Gothic vocabulary, was vigorously restored in these new churches, as can be seen at Truro Cathedral and the west end of Bristol Cathedral (see p. 180), two major 19th-century ecclesiastical projects. Many other examples exist throughout Britain and France, but while the stone and glasswork is often highly accomplished, somehow there is something missing: perhaps this is due to the generally mass-produced 19th-century glass, but perhaps also it is that the designs do not take any risks.[4] Of the handful that aspire to something beyond watery pastiche, St Luke's Caversham Road, London (see p. 181), stands out.

The two most exciting roses from this period, however, belong to the Arts and Crafts movement. Designed by Sir Edward Burne-Jones, and Philip Webb with William Morris, at Waltham Abbey and Selsley respectively, they successfully combine pared-down form and didactic content. Both depict the classic cycle of the Creation, which reveals itself around the central figure of God, and both designs teem with life, a reminder of the importance of the natural world at the time of the Industrial Revolution. The emphasis in these windows is on craftsmanship and appropriateness to setting, as Morris and Burne-Jones saw it in the medieval tradition. Indeed it might be said that the practitioners of the Arts and Crafts approach were more interested in reviving medieval work practices than specific medieval forms, and perhaps in this respect they get closer to the original spirit of the rose.

OPPOSITE The north rose at St Eustache, which was built in the 1630s was reglazed in the 19th century (north rose, St Eustache, Paris)

LEFT ABOVE Designed by Philip Webb for Morris & Co., and including figures by William Morris, this window shows: at the top, the Spirit; above left, Adam with the animals; above right, 'Let there be light'; to the left, Adam and Eve; to the right, the separation of the firmament from the waters; below left, the creation of birds and fish; below right, the creation of dry land; at the bottom, the earth (All Saints, Selsley, 1862–4)

LEFT BELOW Along with the Creation window at Selsley, this is one of the most successful of all 19th-century roses. God is surrounded by the days of Creation (Creation window by Sir Edward Burne-Jones, Waltham Abbey, 1860–61)

OPPOSITE Though the glass is 19th century, the designer, John Hardman, has studiously given the angels genuine medieval instruments (west rose, Bristol Cathedral, 1877)

ABOVE The forms in this rose are less obviously 'Gothic' than many 19th-century windows. The glass was designed by Sir Henry Holliday, and made in the celebrated studio of Heaton, Butler & Bayne (St Luke, Caversham Road, late 19th century)

THE ROSE WINDOW SINCE 1900

Twentieth-century attitudes to the rose window built on those of the 19th century, but often with an added emphasis on the abstract. From the late 19th century the rose had become popular in North America, and we find one of the most prolific practitioners, stained-glass artist Charles J. Connick, producing eye-catching and esoteric designs for a number of important ecclesiastical projects there, including the giant at the cathedral of St John the Divine in New York. In Europe at the turn of the century, the most significant rose windows were those planned for the Sagrada Família, Antoni Gaudí's masterpiece in Barcelona (see pp. 186–7). Though work on the temple is ongoing, some windows have already been glazed using the designs of Joan Vila-Grau.

Undoubtedly the most original rose of the 20th century, however, is that designed by Henri Matisse for the Union Church in Pocantico Hills – in fact the last work completed by Matisse before his death in 1954. It represents a perfect harmony between form and glass, building on the beautiful organic forms typical of his late *papier collé* works. The abstraction seen in the Matisse window is symptomatic of rose windows over the past fifty years, as audiences gradually lose an acquaintance with traditional religious iconography, and a premium is placed on striking visual effects. This approach reaches its zenith in the west window at Washington Cathedral by Rowan le Compte, which incorporates prisms amid conventional stained-glass pieces to throw the light in all directions. Like the Morris and Burne-Jones roses it depicts the Creation – specifically the creation of light – a common theme in modern windows, and there is no doubting the popularity of this powerful window. Even today, it seems, it is still possible to create a 'new' rose window. The fifteen-petalled rose at Chester Cathedral (see p. 189), built in 2003, is placed within a spherical triangle, the brickwork radiating from the centre. Subtle, quietly sophisticated and elegant, it shows an admirable awareness of a centuries-old tradition.

ABOVE RIGHT Charles Connick, St John's Episcopal Church, North Adams (Mass.), 1939

BELOW RIGHT Charles Connick, west window, Cathedral of St John the Divine, New York, early 20th century

OPPOSITE This design by Henri Matisse was created in memory of Abby Aldrich Rockefeller who had helped found New York's MoMA. Matisse died soon after completing the cartoons, and the glass was made by Paul Bony the following year (Union Church, Pocantico Hills, N. Y., 1954)

pp. 184–5 *The Creation* by Rowan le Compte and Dieter Goldkuhle, Washington Cathedral, 1976

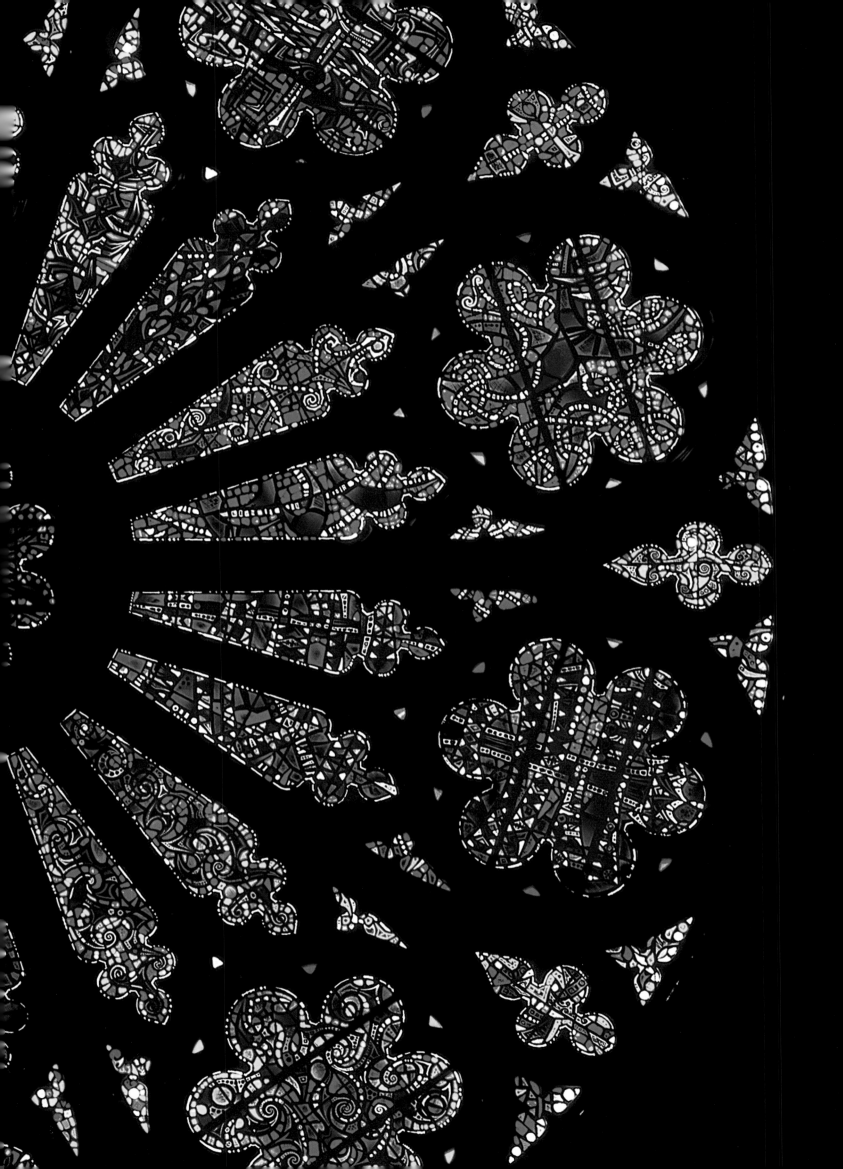

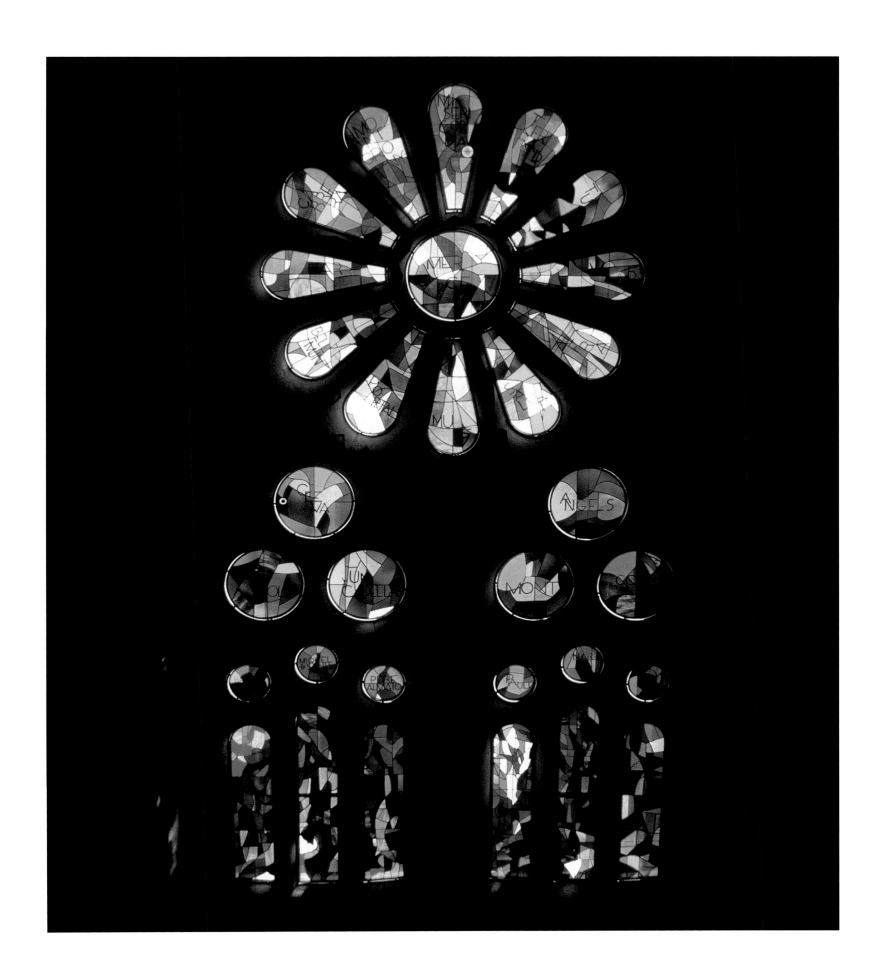

OPPOSITE The western rose window in 1983 before it was glazed (Sagrada Família, Barcelona, early 20th century)

ABOVE Some of the windows in the Sagrada Família have been designed by the respected Catalan stained-glass artist and historian, Joan Vila-Grau (side window, Sagrada Família, Barcelona, 1999)

ABOVE This design by Rosalind Grimshaw from 2004 is
the pre-cartoon drawing to give an overall idea of a
window. Inspired by the Psalms of David, song and even
dance, this window combines the sacred with the secular,
appropriate for its proposed location in a choir school

OPPOSITE With imagination, and an appreciation of
history it is possible to create a fresh rose window
even in the 21st-century (rose window by Andrew Arrol,
Choir School, Chester Cathedral, 2003)

Few rose windows retain their original glazing, which is perhaps just what makes famous examples such as Chartres so special. Glass has most often been lost due to storms or hail, but also due to vandalism and structural failure. Medieval masons did not hesitate to replace original glass with glass in an up-to-date style, and so it is not unfitting that windows damaged – sometimes entirely destroyed – in the 20th century should be entirely reglazed in a contemporary style.

Indeed, some of these new schemes are breathtaking, responding to the tracery forms in innovative and intuitive ways: a good example is the stunning window at St Albans by the renowned stained-glass artist Alan Younger. At Girona Cathedral a combination of new and old glass creates beautiful flowers, true kaleidoscopes of colour, while other compositions, such as that at Crema Cathedral, are more daring, yet give a rather static rose great life and movement. At Réthel, the rigid, geometrical Sées-type rose has been refilled with appropriately cubist-inspired, angular glass, while others such as Saint-Leu-d'Esserent allow the strong forms of the tracery to show through. Purists may find such treatment anachronistic, but when done well the new glass gives the rose a new sense of purpose. Perhaps the most striking example is that at Vernon, where a 16th-century Flamboyant window is given 'flaming' glass – a witty reference, full of symbolism and spiritual intent. And so today, the rose window retains all its power to impress and amaze, to intrigue and to inspire.

CLOCKWISE FROM TOP LEFT St Nicholas, Réthel, glass by Jacques Simon; one of two eastern side oculi, Girona Cathedral (glass 15th, 19th and 20th centuries); Saint-Malo Cathedral, glass designed by Jean le Moal, realized by Bernard Allain (1968); north rose, St Albans Cathedral, glass by Alan Younger (1989); St Wulfran, Abbeville (20th-century glass); east rose, Gisors, St Gervais & St Protais, glass by Jacques Bony (1979–80)

CHAPTER 5
CYCLES OF MEANING: ICONOGRAPHY AND ENLIGHTENMENT

'Meaning' is always elusive in art and rose windows are certainly no exception. Their scale, richness, prominent placing and obvious expense force us to ask why they were constructed, what was their purpose. Perhaps this question is anachronistic: to lay viewers in the Middle Ages, as far as we can tell, there was no self-conscious search for meaning beyond the imagery that taught them the truths of the Christian faith. But for their creators these windows clearly meant more. 'They are great in themselves but signify greater things still',[1] says the Life of St Hugh, referring to the rose windows at Lincoln Cathedral. And in the early 20th century Emile Mâle, the great expert on French Gothic art and iconography, insisted that 'medieval art was, before all things, a symbolic art in which form is used merely as the vehicle of spiritual meaning.' 'Everything in medieval symbology has hidden meanings: that is, showing men one thing and inviting them to see in it the figure of another.'[2]

Rose windows clearly go far beyond merely letting in light and displaying edifying scenes. Indeed, even when they have lost their glass – which, alas, is too often the case after centuries of war, neglect, vandalism and storms – they express a whole range of ideas fundamental to the medieval view of the world: number, geometry, hierarchy, concepts of cycles, or even of the universe. How much time must have been spent poring over the designs, adjusting and refining! This chapter examines the ways in which we can look at rose windows, dealing first with the meaning of the form, then moving on to the specific meaning of the glass in the window, and the great iconographic programmes that even today intrigue us in their complexity and subtlety.

OPPOSITE Christ as the Logos in a rosette high in the north transept at Chartres: he sits enthroned above a rainbow with a book – symbolizing the Word – on his knee, holding the world in his left hand[3] (clearstorey rosette, north transept, Chartres Cathedral, c. 1235)

ABOVE RIGHT The figure of Philosophy from the north rose at Laon has her head in the clouds. Although it is a 19th-century replacement window, it is based on the figure of Philosophy on the west front of Notre-Dame. The book in her hand symbolizes the Wisdom of the Word, while the ladder symbolizes the stages of study needed to achieve it (north rose, Laon Cathedral, glass 19th century)

THE SYMBOL OF THE CIRCLE

All-important in rose window and oculus symbolism is the circle, symbolizing not only the spiritual but also that which is infinite: the universe or the cosmos, including everything created and uncreated. To St Augustine the circle was itself a symbol of virtue – in the words of Richard Krautheimer, Augustine saw it as 'pre-eminent among all other geometrical figures and comparable to virtue because of the conformity and concordance of its essentials';[4] Augustine himself is supposed to have written that 'the nature of God is a sphere whose circumference is nowhere and whose centre is everywhere'.[5] The portrayal of God wielding a large pair of compasses, as used by medieval architects, symbolizes this very idea – a marvellous example survives in glass at Malvern Priory.

Others, meanwhile, have seen the rose as a form of intuitive mandala or meditation diagram, a symbol whereby the macrocosm of the universe and microcosm of human life are brought into harmony in the mind of the individual, thereby imparting meaning. And perhaps it is not too far fetched to see in the layers of concentric circles of the rose window the medieval conception of the universe in miniature, with the earth at the centre of the spheres. Since Plato the universe had been conceived of as being a series of spheres, while later, more elaborate, models contained not just planets but also angels, the elements and even moral qualities, each with their own spheres. The angels were an essential component organized in a hierarchy of nine 'levels', with the seraphim being the closest to God. This hierarchy was originally delineated by John Scotus Eriugena and was much studied at St Denis by Suger and his fellow monks.[6] They also feature in Dante's depiction of the cosmos in his *Paradiso*. The hierarchy itself does not actually figure in any of the early rose windows – through they are sometimes depicted in sculpture in the portals beneath, as at Chartres. It does, however, appear partially in the north rose at St Ouen in Rouen, some two hundred years later.

OPPOSITE God the Creator in a window at Malvern Priory. 'When he prepared the heavens I was there: when he set a compass upon the face of the depth...when he appointed the foundations of the earth' (Proverbs 8: 27–29). The idea that certain ratios represent perfection – as in architecture and music – goes back to St Augustine. In the Middle Ages geometry was accorded almost divine status, and the architect, with his compasses, was imitating his divine master (Malvern Priory, second half of 15th century)

RIGHT The rose window joins light to infinity (St Nicholas, Outines, 1936)

OVERLEAF The angelic hierarchy in all its awe-inspiring splendour (north rose, St Ouen, Rouen, early 15th century)

THE DESIRE FOR ORDER AND HIERARCHY

The medieval mind was to a very large extent concerned with order. Thomas Aquinas articulated commonly held beliefs when he said that: 'The divine nature keeps all things in their proper order, without confusion, in such a manner that all are linked together in a concrete coherence, each retaining its specific purity'.[7] Rose windows, with their circular form, neat subdivisons and large dimensions were the perfect vehicle for demonstrations of this 'coherence', and it seems reasonable to assume that their early popularity stemmed in large part from their ability to unify complex, tiered information. One could express not only the cyclical view of

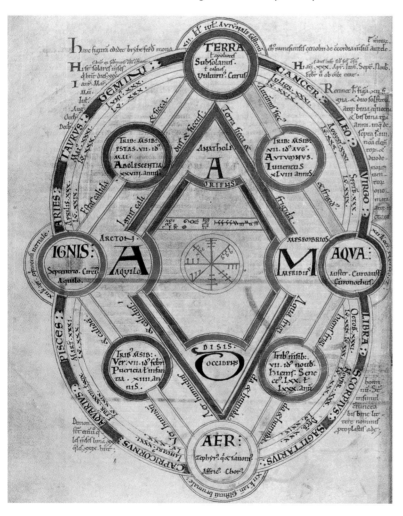

the world and of history, but also the fundamentals of the Christian faith such as polar opposites (for example, vices and virtues) and radiating hierarchies. In addition, every rose has a centre, a focus, where the most important imagery – often Christ or the Virgin – invariably gets concentrated. At Chartres, Christ is at the centre of all of the rose windows as the source of all spiritual 'energy'. The 15th-century German Cardinal Nicholas of Cusa expresses this idea as follows:

> The universal power of the macrocosm that moves itself
> and all things is perpetual because it is a round and circular
> movement, having all movement in itself, just as the pattern
> of the circle includes all patterns within itself, and man is the
> microcosm corresponding to this and deriving all knowledge
> from the central point, which is Christ.[8]

The desire for order, at least in the 13th century, engulfed the entire church. Chartres is perhaps the best example today of a unified iconographic programme, but originally there must have been many others. At Chartres the roses assume pride of place in a grand iconographic scheme which also involves sculpture, the church plan and other stained glass. The content of the roses reinforced the three 'ecclesiastical directions' of north, south and west, which were traditionally associated with the past, present and future respectively. So, in the north rose at Chartres we find the Old Testament leading up to the Virgin Mary, through whom Christ was incarnated – this is symbolized by twelve Old Testament prophets and twelve kings around the Virgin Mary with the infant Christ. In the south rose, facing the sun, the light of the world, is Christ as the light of the present world, surrounded by the twenty-four Elders of the Apocalypse. And in the west, the direction of the future, the setting sun, we find the Last Judgment at the end of time.[9] Christ presides over the trial of souls, with the elect being led off to heaven, while sinners are dragged off to hell.

ABOVE LEFT The medieval systematization of knowledge can be readily appreciated in diagrams such as this from Byrhtferth of Ramsey's *Computus*; adapted from Bede's *De Temporibus*, it is a schematic representation of the elements (Earth, Fire, Air and Water) with the seasons, months, direction and signs of the zodiac representing the macrocosm, the microcosm of humanity represented by the four ages of man and the four humours (Byrhtferth's original *c.* 988–96, this copy *c.* 1110)

OPPOSITE God, in this 16th-century window at Hengrave Hall, creates the universe by the Word, portrayed here as a series of concentric circles. The signs of the zodiac appear on the exterior, the sun (in a red sphere) and the earth at the centre. The glass was probably made in Troyes, France (Hengrave Hall, Suffolk, early 16th century)

WHEELS OF TIME AND FORTUNE

Many early rose windows take the form of a wheel, an almost universal symbol of time, its turning evoking the cyclical nature and the seemingly endless repetition of night and day, year after year. The spokes of the wheel hint at a symbolic image of the sun with its rays emerging from the central disc and, with the sun's passage through the sky marking out time, time and light are inevitably related. Solar symbols are found in the pre-Christian, Nordic and Celtic worlds as well as in the East, where they symbolize life and death. These symbols express the idea of continuity, while the related Chi-Rho monogram typically appears with the Alpha and Omega letters, signifying eternity. The twelve-fold form of many roses, meanwhile, accommodates images of the labours of the month or the signs of the zodiac, calendars of day and night.

It was St Jerome (AD 340–420), as Helen Dow has pointed out, who echoed Virgil's *Aeneid* when he spoke of *rota in rota, annum in anno* (the wheel within the wheel is the circulation of the year).[10] Nowhere is this better illustrated than in the wheel on the façade of Orvieto Cathedral (see p. 27) where Christ's head is at the centre of the wheel within the wheel (surrounded by a square made up of fifty-two faces, perhaps symbolizing weeks), while Jerome and the other three Church Fathers sit in the corners.[11] Moreover, it was Jerome who saw in the same imagery the New Testament being born of the Old: *rota in rota, lex in legem, vetus in novum* (the wheel within the wheel, the law within the law, the old within the new).[12]

And it was Jerome, too, who drew parallels between the four seasons, the four rivers of Paradise, the four elements, the four quarters of the world and other 'quaternities', and the 'four living creatures' – equated by Jerome with the four Evangelists – described in Ezekiel's vision in the Old Testament. This vision is of particular importance in our interpretation of rose windows, since the creatures 'went together with [a] wheel'. Ezekiel (1:16–20) also speaks about 'a wheel in the middle of a wheel':

The appearance of the wheels and their work was like unto the colour of a beryl: and they four had one likeness: and their appearance and their work was as it were a wheel in the middle of a wheel... Whithersoever the spirit was to go, they went, thither was their spirit to go; and the wheels were lifted up over against them: for the spirit of the living creature was in the wheels.

We find such depictions of 'a wheel within the middle of a wheel' in Italy (for example, at Assisi, Spoleto Cathedral, Tuscania, Lugnano, Castel San Felice) and Spain (for example, Betanzos and Las Huelgas at Burgos). Whether these roses deliberately refer to Ezekiel's vision is unclear, but the appearance of the Evangelist symbols in the corners makes such a reading irresistible.

OPPOSITE The east rose of St Etienne, Brie-Comte-Robert, shows Christ at the centre surrounded by the twelve apostles with traditional attributes, then the labours of the months, symbolizing time (east rose, St Etienne, Brie-Comte-Robert, 1225–35, restored 1889 and 2003)

ABOVE RIGHT The wheel within the wheel, surrounded by the symbols of the Evangelists, brings to mind Ezekiel's vision (S. Felice di Narco, near Spoleto, late 12th/early 13th century)

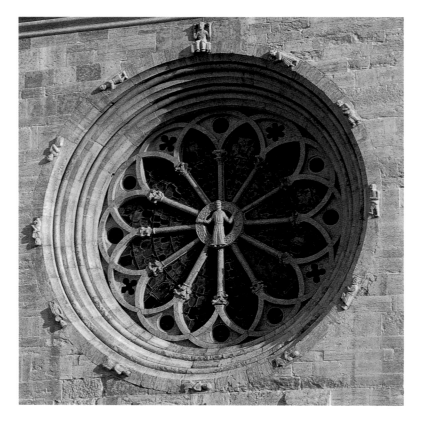

Other roses make more concrete allusions to their wheel status. Wheels of Fortune can be found at St Etienne in Beauvais, Trent Cathedral, S. Zeno in Verona, Basel, and on the south façade of Amiens. Emile Mâle, in *The Gothic Image*, draws our attention to the 12th-century writer Honorius of Autun, who echoes Boethius in describing fate and fortune thus:

> Philosophers tell us of a woman fastened to a wheel which turns perpetually, so that they say she is sometimes rising and sometimes falling with its movement. What is this wheel? It is the glory of the world which is carried round in perpetual motion. The woman fastened to the wheel is Fortune, whose head alternately rises and falls because those who have been raised by their power and riches are often precipitated into poverty and misery.[13]

The 8th-century German monk Walafrid Strabo echoes this: 'he who clings suspended to the fleeting globe now rises, now falls; thus the earth's wheel drags him on'.[14] These wheels have an obvious didactic aim, reminding the viewer of the transience of earthly power, wealth and status, as figures are dragged round the perimeter as though through life, only to descend into oblivion. This is spelled out in two inscriptions in the centre of the wheel window at Verona: on the outside, 'Behold, I, Fortuna, rule mortals all alike. I raise them up and cast them down: I give good and bad to all'; and on the inside of the church, 'I clothe the naked and strip those provided with raiment; if anyone relies on me, he will end up scorned'.[15] The figures on the perimeter of the window are clothed and naked accordingly.

Sadly none of the Wheel of Fortune windows that survive have retained their original glass, which quite possibly could have offered an equally didactic antidote to random fortune. While Fortune is not a specifically Christian figure – rather, a powerful popular image – in medieval theological terms the power of Fate could be transcended in the 'Psychomachia', or battle in the soul, by exercising the moral and intellectual virtues. Personifications of these virtues appear in rose windows at Notre-Dame (west – see p. 91), Braine (south, since removed) and Auxerre choir (see p. 226). At the centre of the north rose at Laon Cathedral we find the figure of Wisdom or Philosophy, surrounded by the Liberal Arts (see p. 70). And it is interesting to note that the Wheel of Fortune illustrated in the 12th-century Corpus Christi manuscript is captioned: 'The men bound to Fortuna's wheel in the centre of the composition must turn with it, whereas Sapienta offers them liberation through Virtue in the words of Proverbs 8, 12–17.'[16] The figure of Fortune to the left of the wheel says: 'All things in this world are put into motion by accident'; Sapienta (Wisdom), to the right, counters: 'Nothing in this world is made by accident.' The wheel offers both a warning and the path to salvation.

ABOVE LEFT Twelve figures move anti-clockwise on this Wheel of Fortune, while the personification of Fortune stands at the centre. The west façade of this church has a rose window with the Virgin Mary at the summit and with the Evangelists rising towards her, as if to contrast with this Wheel of Fortune (north façade, Trent Cathedral, early 13th century)

OPPOSITE The Wheel of Fortune was a perennially popular theme in the Middle Ages, in many different media, perhaps reflecting on the instability of society. Clockwise, from top left: south rose, Amiens Cathedral, figures c. 1300, window c. 1500; a 12th-century Wheel of Fortune (Corpus Christi ms. 66); St Etienne, Beauvais, c. 1150; a Wheel of Fortune as sketched in Villard de Honnecourt's book, c. 1235

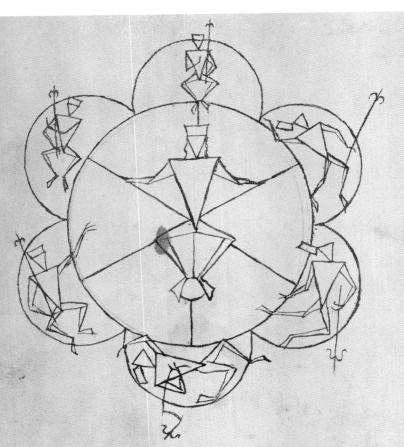

On prent kaus z tieule mulue de paiens z fereskume. autre tant
del une cu del autre z un poi plus del tieule de paiens tant come
ses color vainke les autres. destemprez ce ensemut doile de linuise
sen poez faire un vassel pur euge tenir.

On prent mine. kaus volere z orpiement se lemer on en euge bol
lant z cile · ist unnemous est bon ne vail ostier·

THE SIGNS OF THE ZODIAC

Just as the appearance of Fortune in a Christian context may surprise us, so too, initially, is it jarring to find zodiac signs in rose windows. Nonetheless, they appear in the west rose of Notre-Dame, the south rose of Angers, in the rose at Lausanne, and also at Braine (though these were removed in the early 19th century). What precisely these signs meant to medieval viewers is difficult to say but we have to bear in mind that in medieval times there was no distinction between astronomy and astrology. The stars at night must have been far more tangible then, playing a larger role in people's lives, giving rhythm to the year, and so too the zodiac in medieval art often refers to the passage of time. In the Lausanne and Notre-Dame roses we find the signs of the zodiac alongside the labours of the months, creating a kind of calendar in stained glass and stone (at Brie-Comte-Robert, p. 202, the labours are coupled with the twelve apostles). At Paris there is also a further pairing with virtues and vices, suggesting that the zodiac, as a representation of fortune, fate, or time, might also have a moral dimension.

The glass from Braine, which dates to around 1200, is particularly interesting. Some of the panels depicting the zodiac were reset in 1890 into a clearstorey light in the choir of Soissons Cathedral (the other signs are copies of originals now lost or sold).[17] Since the Abbey at Braine was vandalized in the early 19th century, we cannot be entirely sure of the original programme, but Caviness has proposed that the zodiac signs were originally placed in south rose with the Liberal Arts (including Astronomy) and the four seasons. The whole, then, would have been a cycle of time and morality.

There is one final interesting point worth making in relation to the signs of the zodiac. The word zodiac originates from the Greek *zodiakos kyklos*, 'wheel of animal figures', referring to the grouping of the stars in the night sky into twelve constellations that suggested animal-like shapes. The usual interpretation of the four sacred creatures that often surround Christ, and that appear at the corners of early wheel windows, is the four Evangelists, the typological transformations of the creatures that Ezekiel saw in the wheel.[18] These four creatures also relate to the four 'fixed' signs of the zodiac – Leo (the lion of St Mark), fire; Taurus (the bull of St Luke), earth; Aquarius (the man of St Matthew), air; Scorpio (the eagle of St John, an alternative symbol for this sign), water – although this derivation, however attractive, is less secure.

OPPOSITE At Angers the signs of the zodiac fill the large roundels in the upper half of the window (the Elders of the Apocalypse holding phials and lutes filling the lower set), while Christ sits at the centre. Virgo is depicted as St Margaret, alluding to Margaret of Anjou of the Angevin court (south rose, Angers Cathedral, tracery 13th century, glass 1452)

ABOVE RIGHT The difficult history of these zodiac panels, originally from the south rose at Braine Abbey but now at Soissons Cathedral, means some detective work is needed to unravel the original programme. Madeleine Caviness suggests that they were originally paired with Liberal Arts and the four seasons (Soissons Cathedral, most panels copies made by Gaudin in 1890)

LAUSANNE: THE *IMAGO MUNDI*

Almost everything discussed so far comes together in one spectacular window at Lausanne Cathedral. Dating to around 1220–35 (though possibly planned as early as 1205), this acts as a summation of, a definitive statement on, the medieval universe, known and unknown. Round, like the universe itself, when seen from the

outside (see p. 251), inside the design fragments into clusters of roundels arranged into an astonishingly inventive and beautiful pattern. The centre, which today contains a scene of the Creation, originally contained a personification of the Year – *Annus* – surrounded by the Sun and the Moon, Light and Dark (this arrangement is also found in the Zwiefalten manuscript of a few decades earlier). Moving outwards to the four semicircular clusters, we encounter the four seasons, each surrounded by three months. The months are represented by labours: May carries his falcon to a hunt, while September harvests grapes, and January, with his two heads, looks at the year past while toasting the year ahead. In between these groups are four larger groups, of five roundels each, which each contain an element (Air, Water, Fire, Earth), surrounded by three signs of the zodiac and a prophecy figure. Two of these prophecy figures have since been replaced by the Sun and the Moon originally in the centre. In between each of these larger groups are the four rivers of Paradise, accompanied by the fantastic creatures so popular with the early medieval encyclopedists such as Isidorus of Seville. Finally, in the clusters of three small roundels around the perimeter, are the eight winds of heaven.

What is curious about this window is the almost total lack of conventional Christian iconography. Its creator was clearly influenced by the world of Late Antiquity – only the four rivers of Paradise might be construed as referring to the four Evangelists. Instead we sense an attempt to catalogue and systematize the entire range of human experiences. Needless to say the wealth of iconography in this window means that it has attracted more scholarship than almost any other rose window[19] (and it obviously enjoyed some fame in its day, since it was one of only two roses sketched by Villard de Honnecourt). The difference between the Lausanne and Chartres roses is pronounced, Chartres dispensing with such pagan iconography in favour of overwhelming statements of the Church's beliefs, power and heritage.

ABOVE LEFT The rose at Lausanne has a precedent in diagrams such as this Cycle of the Year from a 12th-century manuscript from Kloster Zwiefalten, Swabia. It shows the Year surrounded by the Sun, Moon, Night and Day, while the signs of the zodiac and labours of the months appear in the next two circles; the four seasons inside the corners of the rectangle and the four stages of the day outside complete the cycle (c. 1140)

OPPOSITE The Lausanne rose window represents an *Imago Mundi*, a summation of all knowledge on the universe. The glass was designed and made by Pierre d'Arras, and restored by E. Hosch in 1894–8, when some missing panels were replaced or improvised. The rose measures just over 8 metres (26 feet) across (Lausanne Cathedral, tracery c. 1205, glass, c. 1230)

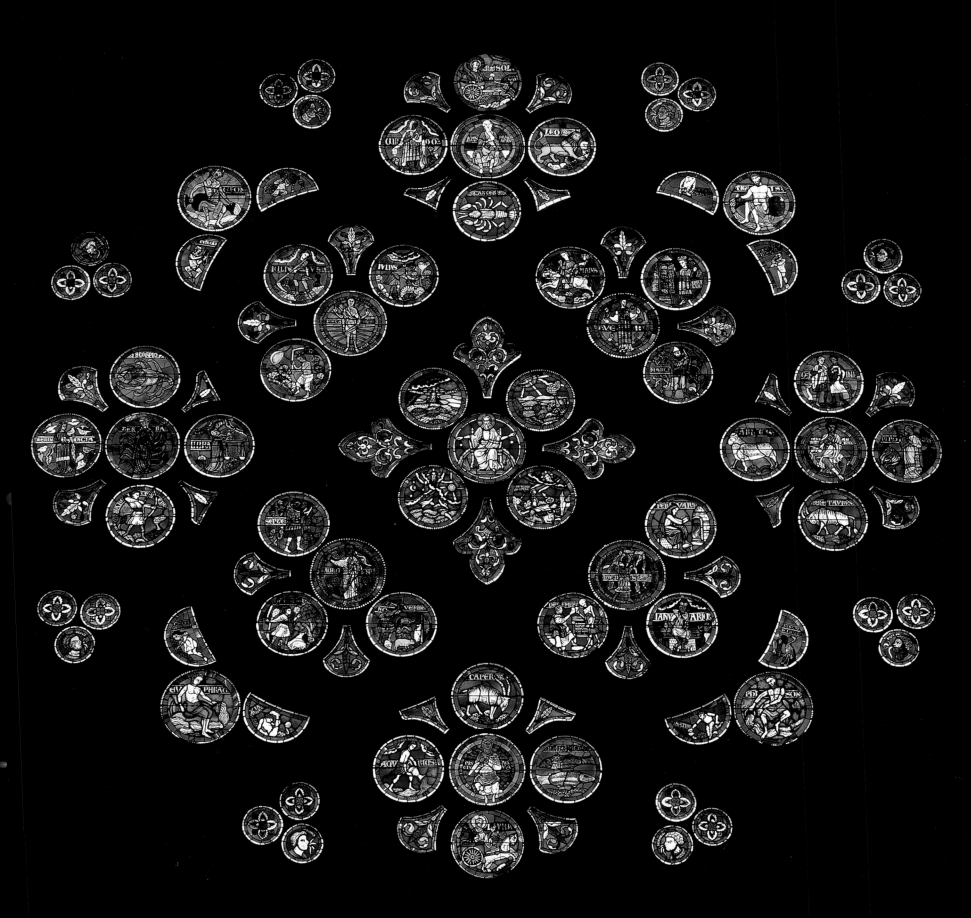

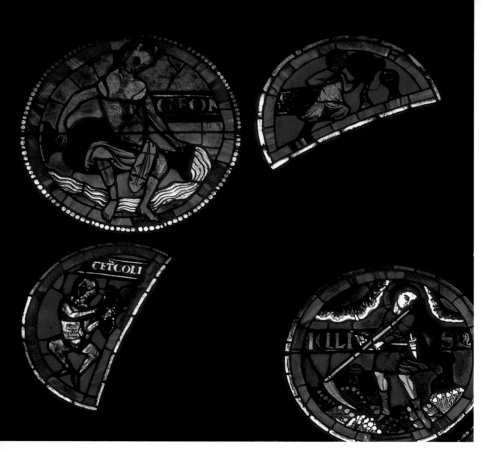
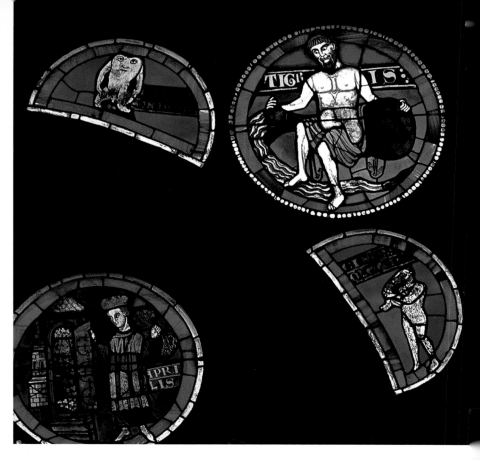

ABOVE, CLOCKWISE FROM TOP LEFT The Geon [42] with
Ethiopians [46] and Gangaridae [47], above July [14];
the river Tigris [43] with Acephali [48] and Cynocephali
[49] above April [11]; December [19], January [20]
and February [21] around Winter [9]; September [16],
October [17] and November [18] around Autumn [8].

OPPOSITE Cancer [29], Leo [30] and Virgo [31] surround
Fire [25], with the Sun [38] above

LAUSANNE: THE *IMAGO MUNDI*

This is the present-day disposition of the Lausanne rose. Panels marked with an asterisk are replacements of 1909.

1 God the Father*

In the small square

2 light and dark* **3** land and sea* **4** Fish and birds* **5** Animals and men*

In the four semicircles

6 Spring, a man surrounded by flowers and leaves and holding a flower **7** Summer, red rays warming the blue sky **8** Autumn, amid the red and white grapes **9** Winter, dressed in white and hooded, weathers a storm of icicles **10** March, wearing a cotton turban-like hat, pruning the vines **11** April, wearing a toque, flowers in hand, opens the door to his garden **12** May, on a white horse, carries his falcon to the hunt **13** June, incorrectly labelled IULIUS, cuts the hay **14** July, reaps the harvest with a sickle **15** August, stripped to the waist, threshes the harvest under a baking sun **16** September, harvesting the grapes **17** October, tending his pigs while they eat acorns (and hunt for truffles?) **18** November, the month of cattle and pig slaughter **19** December, raising his glass to death, symbolizes the year that has gone* **20** January, a double-headed Janus figure, with one half holding up his cup to the bountiful year ahead, the other looking at the year that has passed **21** February, warming his hands*

The elements and the zodiac, formative and beyond time

22 Earth, a woman surrounded with ears of corn **23** Water, breastfeeding a fish **24** Air, doing likewise to a dragon **25** Fire, feeding a salamander **26–37** The signs of the zodiac portrayed in usual medieval style; 27, 29, 34 and 36 are replacements **38** The sun with a fiery halo being drawn across the sky in a chariot **39** The moon being drawn likewise but with only two horses **40** Aeromancy, surrounded by seven doves by whom she foretells the future **41** Pyromancy, foretelling the future from the flames of the fire

Paradise and the lands of myth

The four rivers of Paradise portrayed as bearded men pouring their waters across the four corners of the earth:
42 The Geon (Nile) **43** The Tigris **44** The Phison (Ganges) **45** The Euphrates **46** Ethiopians, with four eyes to help the accuracy of their archery **47** Gangaridae, inhabitants of the Ganges who supposedly lived off the sweet smell of fruit - and died in the presence of any foul odour **48** Acephali, creatures with no heads and with eyes in their bodies **49** Cynocephali, dog-headed men, thought to live in India **50** Pygmies, also thought to inhabit India, here fighting a crane **51** A Satyr, a small hook-nosed creature with horns and goat-like feet **52** Sciapodes, creatures that lived in the desert and had only one foot, which they used as a sunshade* **53** Cephi, elusive creatures detectable only by their human-like footprints

The eight winds of the cosmos

54 Auster, the south wind **55** Euroauster, the south-south-east wind **56** Subsolanus, the eastern wind of the Levant **57** Vulturnus, the south-east wind **58** Septentrion, the north wind **59** Corus, the north-west summer wind **60** Zephyr, the west wind **61** Austerozephyr, the south-west wind

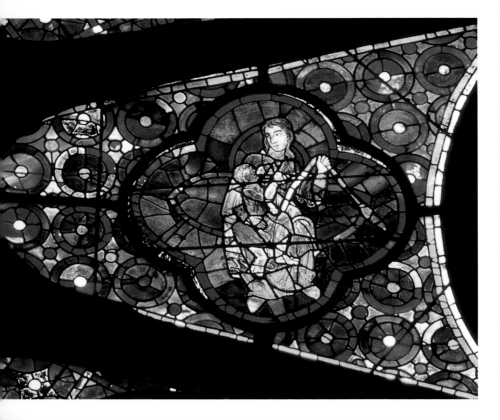

THE CREATION

Rose windows have always been suited to large narrative cycles, and one of the grandest of these is God's creation of the universe. The theme is fitting, since the rose window itself has always been a highly conscious act of creativity, as well as being a demonstration of geometrical prowess, and, like Creation itself, circular. However, the form of the rose window also allows the highly important story of the Fall of Man – through eating the fruit of the Tree of Knowledge – to be told in a clear, concise, way. This cycle appears in bold and luminous images in the north rose at Reims Cathedral, which shows the Fall as well as the hardship of Adam and Eve after the expulsion from the Garden of Eden. The overriding importance of the Fall from a Christian point of view was that it could only be redeemed by Christ's sacrifice on the cross. This point is made clearly enough in the south rose at Lyon Cathedral, which juxtaposes Adam and Eve being expelled from the Garden of Eden (an angel ushers them out, while they cover their genitals with bright green leaves) with Christ liberating souls from hell.

It is interesting to compare these early windows with a much later approach, in the 16th-century south rose at Beauvais Cathedral (see pp. 214–15). This glorious window, the creation of Martin Chambiges and the glazier Nicholas le Prince, depicts the Creation and the early history of mankind and the Israelites, including the stories of the building of the Tower of Babel, Abraham and Isaac, and Moses leading the Israelites from captivity in Egypt. By this time the approach to glazing had changed radically – no longer was the glazier confined to small, didactic roundels, but instead could treat the entire web of glass as a canvas. The window teems with life, with the birds, animals, fish and trees and plants of Creation, so that this feels more like a celebration of God's world than a heavy, didactic reminder of mankind's Fall into sin. It is interesting to note, in passing, that the Creation is also a popular theme in modern roses.

LEFT, ABOVE AND BELOW The north rose at Reims tells the story of the Fall of mankind in the Garden of Eden. In the panel at the top, Eve feeds her son Seth; in the two panels below we see Adam and Eve in the Garden, and then, after the Expulsion, Adam delving while Eve spins. The top panel is from around 1241, while the lower two are restorations of 1872 (north rose, Reims Cathedral)

OPPOSITE In the south rose at Lyon the Fall of Man – when Adam and Eve tasted the Forbidden Fruit – is paired with the Redemption through Christ. Here we see Eve offering the apple to Adam, and the Expulsion from the Garden of Eden (south rose, Lyon Cathedral, 1235–40, with much 19th-century restoration)

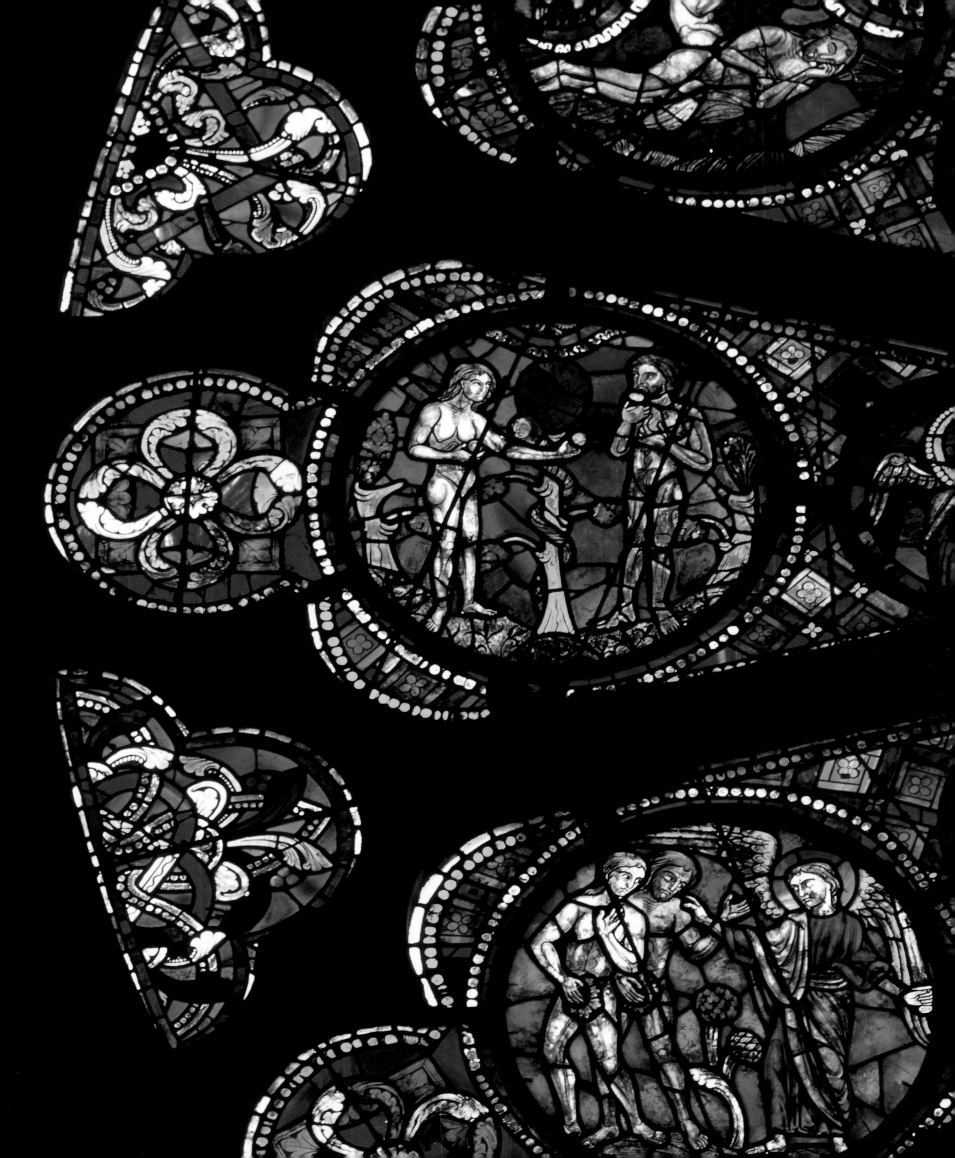

BEAUVAIS CATHEDRAL: THE CREATION

The whole composition of the south rose and lancets is 21 metres by 8.8 metres (69 feet by 29 feet). Glazed by Nicholas le Prince in around 1551–2, the rose portrays the Creation together with scenes from Genesis, though there is some restoration. The structure of the rose window is based on Martin Chambiges's 'regular' design that can also be seen at Senlis, Troyes and Sens, although it may have been built after his death in 1532.

The overall composition uses the circle to express the idea of the Fall. At the summit of the rose is the heavenly realm, populated by angels. Just below is the earthly paradise where Adam and Eve can be seen before their expulsion from the earthly paradise. Their successors lead humanity to the folly of trying to reach heaven by building an enormous tower at Babel; this represents the lowest point in human faith at the bottom of the window. Thereafter the return to faith begins with the proposed sacrifice of Isaac by Abraham. Abraham's successors can be seen struggling towards the Promised Land and in the desert find their faith rewarded by manna descending from heaven. Here are the groupings of panels in detail:

1 At the centre God the Father
2 The sun moon and stars
3 The creation of birds
4 The creation of trees and plants represented as a pristine forest
5 The creation of animals
6 The creation of fish
7 The four winds of heaven
8 & 19 The celestial Paradise in the angelic realm
9 The earthly paradise: Adam relaxing under a tree while Eve, watched by the snake, offers the forbidden fruit
10 Adam and Eve being driven out of Paradise by an angel with a flaming sword
11 Adam tilling the ground while Eve spins
12 The Flood with a dove bringing three ears of wheat to the ark on the waters
13 The Tower of Babel
14 Abraham about to sacrifice Isaac – an angel intercedes
15 The benediction of Isaac – Rebecca waiting behind
16 Joseph being lowered into the pit by his brother Reuben
17 The burning bush; Moses learns how he will deliver the Israelites into the Land of Canaan
18 Manna, in flakes white as snow and large as saucers, falls from heaven to the Israelites in the desert

Within this 'Fall and Return' cycle there are some other subtle relationships. God is at the centre and therefore always next-door to any event – a panel away – whether the people concerned are aware of it or not. His creatures and creations also provide the backdrop for the various dramas. Angels and manna emerge from the neighbouring panels of heaven.

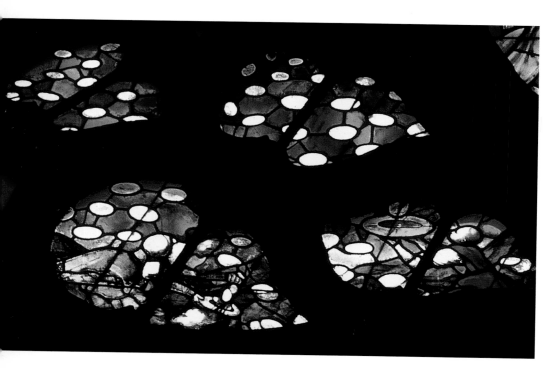

ABOVE The Children of Israel in the desert seeing the manna descending from heaven [18]

OPPOSITE, CLOCKWISE FROM TOP LEFT Four angels from the hierarchy, with two prominent purple-clad seraphim [19]; the creation of animals in the main petal beneath God [5]; building the Tower of Babel in the lowermost window [13]; Abraham about to sacrifice the kneeling Isaac as an angel intercedes from on high [14]

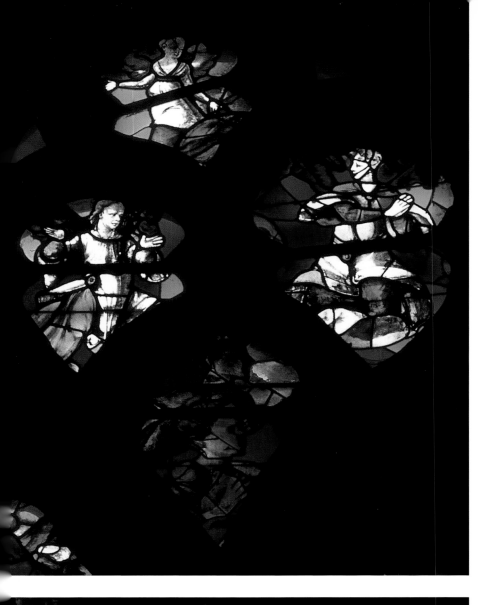

THE TREE OF JESSE

The Tree of Jesse, the vital link between the Old and New Testaments, was an extraordinarily important theme in 12th- and 13th-century art. It was depicted in manuscripts, metalwork and sculpture, as well as in a spectacular 12th-century lancet under the west rose at Chartres, but there are no surviving Trees of Jesse in rose windows until the 15th century. This late appearance reflects the change in approach to rose-window design over the intervening two hundred years: perhaps the glaziers were not able to cope with such a linear programme in the 13th century? Certainly the subject was more easily dealt with by the 'painterly' approach of the 15th century that saw the rose as a large canvas, suitable for a single scene. But crucially it was the organic growth of Flamboyant roses, the leaflike shapes of the openings, that probably prompted an interest in the Tree of Jesse as a subject.

Jesse was the father of King David, and the first few verses of the Gospel of Matthew relate the lineage from Abraham, via Jesse, to Joseph, the husband of the Virgin Mary. This was later conflated with Isaiah 11:1–2: 'And there shall come forth a rod out of the stem of Jesse, and a Branch shall grow out of his roots. And the spirit of the LORD shall rest upon him, the spirit of wisdom and understanding, the spirit of counsel and might, the spirit of knowledge and of the fear of the LORD.' Typically this lineage, the 'stem', is depicted as sprouting from the sleeping Jesse's loin – we see this at the centre of the rose at St Ouen, Rouen – and leads to the 'rod' of Christ.

Another intriguing treatment of the subject can be found at Nogent-le-Roi, where the tree originates in the lancets beneath the rose (these are today filled with prophets in 19th-century glass, but quite possibly were originally filled with a large sleeping Jesse figure), then creeps up into the rose, to the Virgin and Child who occupy the centre. The kings of the Tree of Jesse peak out from the surrounding foliage, David at the summit with his harp.

OPPOSITE The patriarch Jesse sleeps at the centre of the tree, surrounded by twelve prophets and the kings of Judah. Christ carrying the Cross, accompanied by the Virgin, appears at the top of the window (south rose, St Ouen, Rouen, first half of 15th century)

ABOVE RIGHT The Virgin and Child at the centre of this Tree of Jesse are immediately surrounded by angels with musical instruments then by kings, the ancestors of Christ, amid the foliage. Jesse would have appeared in the lancets below (St Sulpice, Nogent-le-Roi, 16th century, with much restoration)

CHRIST

The circle represents perfection and in the Christian faith Christ represents the perfection that human life should aspire to. At the heart of Christianity lies the sacrifice of Christ. There are surprisingly few depictions of the Crucifixion in rose windows, perhaps because this is a subject reserved for other media. However, it does appear in the centre of the spectacular north rose at Sées Cathedral, where it is surrounded by six curiously small narrative scenes depicting the story after the Crucifixion, including, at the bottom left hand corner, the Resurrection. More often, however, we are reminded of Christ's sacrifice in Last Judgment scenes, when angels hold the instruments of the Passion – the nails, the cross, the lance – as we can see in the rose at Mantes (see pp. 74–5).

Christ appears in many guises in rose windows. Perhaps most often he appears as the Judge at the end of time, as he is described in Revelation. At other times he appears as the Logos, the creative force, as seen in three clearstorey rosettes at Chartres (see p. 194). There he holds a book, symbolizing the Word, and sits on a rainbow (another vision taken from the Revelation of St John). As we have already seen, when accompanied by the Alpha and Omega he also represents time, a constant theme in rose windows, it seems. However, he also appears as the head of the church, a 'type' for priests or even kings, something that the clergy were often keen to reinforce in the minds of laymen.

Furthermore, it can be speculated that Christ is implied in every rose window, wheel and oculus that has the four Evangelists' symbols at the corners of the square containing the rose or wheel (as at St Denis, St Gabriel, Tarascon, Assisi); in some instances his face or figure actually appears carved into the central boss, as at Ostuni and Orvieto. But more commonly he is to be found in the centre of the glass: the scheme at Chartres highlights his multifaceted nature, by portraying him as a child in the north, in glory in the south, and at the Last Judgment in the west.

OPPOSITE The north rose in Sées Cathedral contains six scenes from the Resurrection surrounding the Crucifixion: the three visible here are 'Noli me tangere'; the Three Marys at the Tomb; and the Resurrection (north rose, Sées Cathedral, early 1270s)

ABOVE RIGHT The Christ trumeau of the south portal at Chartres, with the north rose behind

OVERLEAF The Childhood of Christ and the Glorification of the Virgin fill the north rose at Soissons. Clockwise, from the top, the scenes are: Annunciation; Visitation; Nativity; Annunciation to the Shepherds; Presentation in the Temple; Flight into Egypt; Massacre of the Holy Innocents; Magi before Herod; Adoration of Magi; the Magi travelling; death of the Virgin; the Coronation at the summit (north rose, Soissons Cathedral, 13th century, with restoration)

THE VIRGIN

The rise of the cult of the Virgin coincided precisely with the birth of the High Gothic cathedral (and the rose window), and it is no surprise that the cathedrals of Chartres, Paris, Amiens and Reims are all dedicated to Notre-Dame. She appears in a number of guises – as the mother of Christ, of course, as we have just seen at Soissons, but also as an intercessor, as the Queen of Heaven, as a personification of the Church, even as Philosophy (as seen at Laon). The Virgin features at the centre of the northern rose windows of Chartres and Paris and in the west at Reims (where there is a spectacular Coronation sculpture on the exterior – see p. 224), and probably in the original north rose window at Amiens. Frequently she seems to be presented as a role model; certainly later iconography of the Virgin – for example, the Litany of the Virgin in the north rose at Auxerre Cathedral, where the curling banderoles cut across the flowing tracery – spells out clearly her attributes and qualities. The period also saw the rise in importance of the Assumption of the Virgin, which was duly depicted in sculpture and glass: it is the focus of the west rose at Reims, accompanied by the twelve apostles and a great heavenly choir, some carrying trumpets.

In the east rose window at Laon, the Virgin Mary holds out a rose to all mankind as it faces the rising sun, which prompts an interesting speculation on the specific link between the Virgin and the rose window. As we discussed in the Introduction, the first documented use of the term 'rose window' comes in the 17th century. However, the rose as a flower was always closely associated with the Virgin – she is referred to as a 'rose without thorns', and in the later medieval period she is often depicted in rose gardens or surrounded by garlands of roses. Possibly it was felt from early on that the decorative qualities of the rose window were appropriate and fitting somehow for the Queen of Heaven. It is from this time that the rosary originates, named after a rose garden (*rosarium*). A rosary itself, of course, functions as a sort of prayer wheel.[20]

ABOVE LEFT The Virgin at the centre of the east rose at Laon holds a rose, symbolizing the Word made flesh, as foretold by Isaiah and communicated to the world by St John, both of whom appear in neighbouring panels. The face of the Virgin has been restored (Virgin, east rose, Laon Cathedral, *c.* 1210-1215)

OPPOSITE The Virgin Immaculate sits at the centre while the Trinity occupy the topmost lights. The scenes around the Virgin depict aspects of the Litany of Loreto, which was composed in the late 15th century. Each item in the Litany is announced in the inscribed banderoles and illustrated: the Ivory Tower, the Ark of the Covenant, the Lily, the Jericho Rose, the Rose of Sharon, and others (north rose, Auxerre Cathedral, *c.* 1528 and late 16th century)

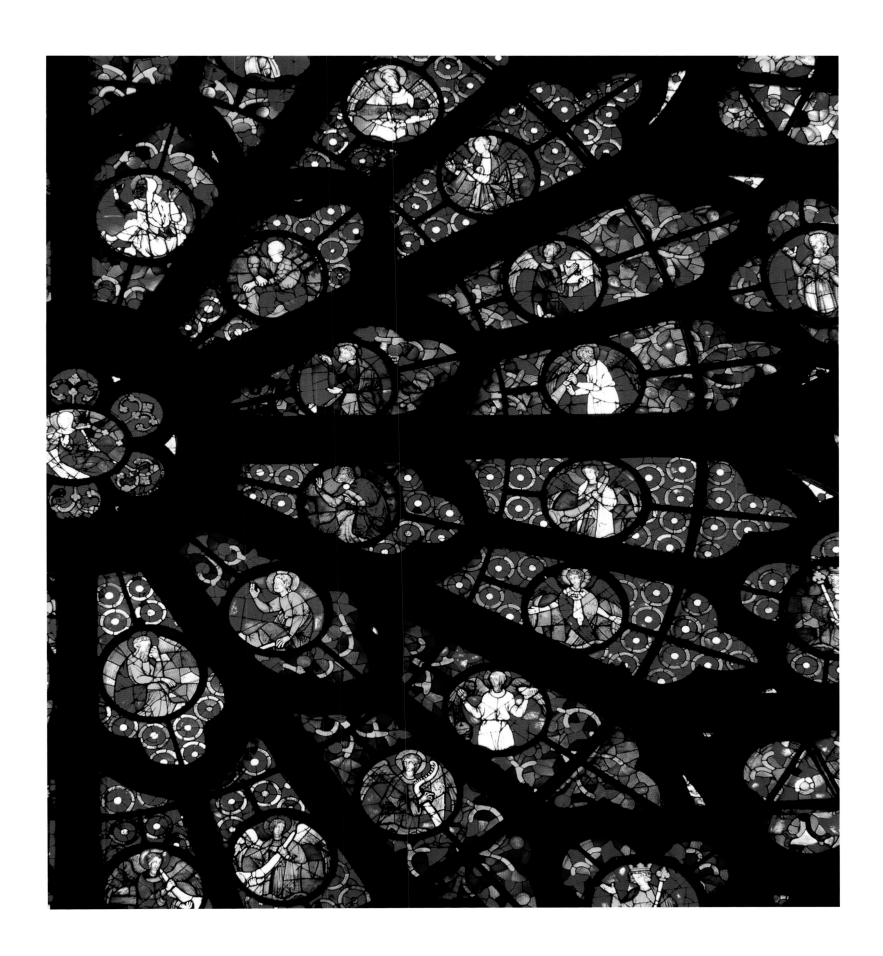

The west façade at Reims is an extended hymn to the
Virgin, inside and out, the sculpture and glass clearly
conceived as two parts of the same programme. The
Coronation of the Virgin appears in the pignon (gable)
above the central portal, while the glass in the rose behind
depicts the Assumption of the Virgin, surrounded by the
heavenly choir and the twelve apostles (west façade,
Reims Cathedral, second half of 13th century, glass
possibly 1299, with much restoration in 1909 and 1925)

THE INSTRUCTIVE ROSE

One of the most hotly contested questions in the study of medieval art is that of audience – for whom were these works made? In the case of rose windows there is no single answer; or, rather, the answer is that they were designed to function on many different levels and to appeal to a range of viewers. So, an erudite audience of priests, monks and scholars might appreciate a particular typological parallel or allusion, whereas a broader audience of pilgrims and laymen could at very least appreciate the complexity and splendour of the windows. They may not have been literate, but they would certainly have understood the import of a Last Judgment, or have been overawed by the sight of Christ in Majesty. One thing that is certain is that rose windows are very much about display, and therefore it is not surprising that many of them have specific messages of an improving or moral nature.

The north rose at Laon is an interesting example of a rose aimed at a rather narrow, elite, audience. Depicting Philosophy surrounded by the Seven Liberal Arts, it reflects the medieval curriculum, as well as celebrating Classical learning (though the resemblance between Philosophy and depictions of the Virgin elsewhere in the cathedral suggests an attempt to reconcile Antique with Christian iconography). The seven arts were taught in the cathedral schools of both Laon and, more famously, Chartres, and included music, arithmetic, geometry, astronomy, dialectic, logic and grammar; in the Laon rose they are joined by medicine. All are personified as women carrying symbolic attributes. As ever, number was important, the Seven Liberal Arts recalling the biblical Seven Pillars by which Wisdom 'hath builded her house' (Proverbs, 9:1).

At Auxerre we find a rosette with a more immediate moral message. It depicts – and even spells out in writing, though it is doubtful whether many could have read it – the vices and virtues. At the top is 'Sobrietas' (sobriety) and descending to the left is

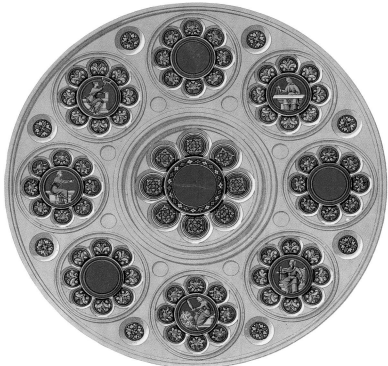

OPPOSITE A small rosette in the choir of Auxerre Cathedral illustrates eight of the Virtues (Auxerre Cathedral, first half of 13th century)

ABOVE RIGHT The Liberal Arts in the archivolts of the west porch at Chartres: Music is represented by Pythagoras below, while Grammar is exemplified by Donatius or Priscian (west porch, Chartres Cathedral, c. 1150)

RIGHT Only around half of the lights in Laon north are original. The Liberal Arts as they were in c. 1840, with only five panels present. Originally the glass dated from 1200–1205. A nearby explosion in 1870 caused even more damage. Six of the panels today contain significant remains: Grammar, Dialectic, Astronomy, Arithmetic, Medicine, Music

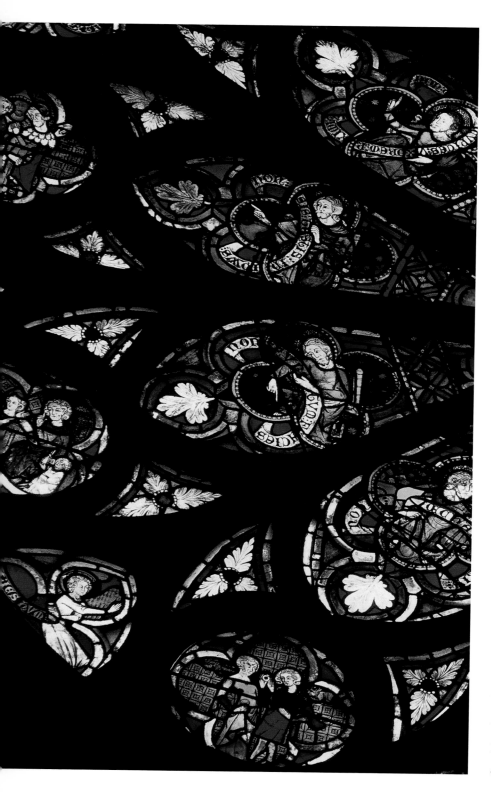

'Sapiencia' (knowledge), 'Concordia' (peace), 'Justicia' (justice), 'Paciencia' (patience) at the bottom, then 'Humilitas' (humility), 'Castitas' (chastity) and 'Largitas' (generosity). Around the perimeter are the vices, of which 'Avaricia' (avarice) can be seen in the top right corner, and 'Superbia' (pride) bottom right by humility. Such overt moralizing can also be found in the depiction of the Ten Commandments in the rose at St Georges in Sélestat. In this window each of the ten petals contains a figure representing Christ holding a banderole upon which a commandment is written, while the neighbouring quatrefoil contains an illustration of the commandment being broken. These must have had great popular appeal at the time, combining high ideals with earthy humour – for example, the judge having his purse stolen while delivering his verdict – in a way that characterizes much medieval art. Most interesting perhaps is that the format of the window seems to have responded to the desired programme, being divided into ten rather than the conventional twelve.

As the Middle Ages progressed, saints came to play an increasingly important role in the Catholic church. As humans who had endured hardship, and often martyrdom, they were held up as role models for priest and layperson alike. The small rose of around 1225 at the church of St Vincent at Saint-Germain-lès-Corbeil, spells out wonderfully the trials and qualities of six important saints including St Martin dividing his cloak – a classic symbol of charity – St John the Baptist being beheaded, and St Lawrence being burned on a gridiron. At the centre we find the *Agnus Dei*, the Lamb of God, a symbol of Christ, reminding the viewer that these saints' sacrifices have not been in vain – and, of course, that their sacrifice was prefigured by Christ's own. The viewer is taught that by leading a virtuous and Christian life they, too, can become close to God, and will be spared the horrors of hell at the time of the Last Judgment, when their souls would be weighed for purity of content (see p. 234).

ABOVE LEFT This is a unique representation in a rose window of the Ten Commandments. Christ appears in each petal holding a banner proclaiming each commandment, while in the neighbouring quatrefoil is the commandment being broken. At the bottom here is 'Thou shalt not commit adultery', with a couple being encouraged by a pair of devils; above is 'Thou shalt not steal' with a couple before a judge who is being robbed of his money bag! (St Georges, Sélestat, c. 1330 and 1847)

OPPOSITE Six scenes of saints surrounding the *Agnus Dei* – Lamb of God – at the centre. Clockwise, from top left: the execution of St John the Baptist (with Salomé watching?); St Lawrence being roasted on a gridiron; the Mass of St Giles; the martyrdom of St Margaret; St Martin on horseback, dividing his cloak; the martyrdom of St Catherine (St Vincent, Saint-Germain-lès-Corbeil, c. 1225)

THE LAST JUDGMENT

The location of the Last Judgment in west windows is fairly consistent in the late 12th and early 13th centuries: we find it in this position at Chartres, Laon and Mantes. Since the west rose would have been the most visible – and since the Last Judgment was surely one of the most persuasive images – it is a logical siting. In fact the west end had become associated with the Last Judgment in the early 12th century, with many late Romanesque portals featuring sculptured versions: again, partly for reasons of public display, partly because the west is the direction of the setting sun, and thus the future. There are a number of exceptions: at Donnemarie the Last Judgment appears in the east rose, while at Lincoln Cathedral and at Angers it appears in the north (and possibly again in the south rose at Lincoln).

The Last Judgment is referred to throughout the New Testament – for example in Matthew, 24:30: '...and they shall see the Son of man coming in the clouds of heaven with power and great glory. And he shall send his angels with a great sound of a trumpet, and they shall gather together his elect from the four winds, from the one end of heaven to the other'. The Last Judgment was to be preceded by a series of apocalyptic events as described in The Revelation of St John (which are illustrated in the Sainte-Chapelle rose – see pp. 238–9). Then the world would witness the Second Coming of Christ: as the Nicene Creed, repeated at mass, describes it, 'He shall come again with glory to judge both the living and the dead'. Such apocalyptic imagery brought out the best in rose window designers, who clearly enjoyed dreaming up the demons of hell, as well as the hosts of angels. One of the most breathtaking is the late Flamboyant rose at Evreux Cathedral: there flaming seraphim dominate the centre, while around angels with trumpets wake the dead. Beyond them are rings of solemn prophets, popes and priests, the full weight of the Church conspiring to fill the viewer with awe and wonder.

OPPOSITE A 13th-century depiction of the Last Judgment (Ste Radegonde, Poitiers, c. 1269)

ABOVE RIGHT Angels carry souls into heaven at the Last Judgment (Mantes Cathedral, c. 1220)

OVERLEAF The Last Judgment at Evreux has a particularly Apocalyptic feel. A pair of trumpeting angels, as well as saints and martyrs, surround the flaming seraphim at the centre. In the next layer are Christ, the Virgin and various of the elect, including the apostles. In the outer layer are Old and New Testament figures, including Moses and St Veronica. At the bottom the dead rise from their tombs and divide: some go to Christ, others are led off by terrifying devils (north rose, Evreux Cathedral, early 16th century)

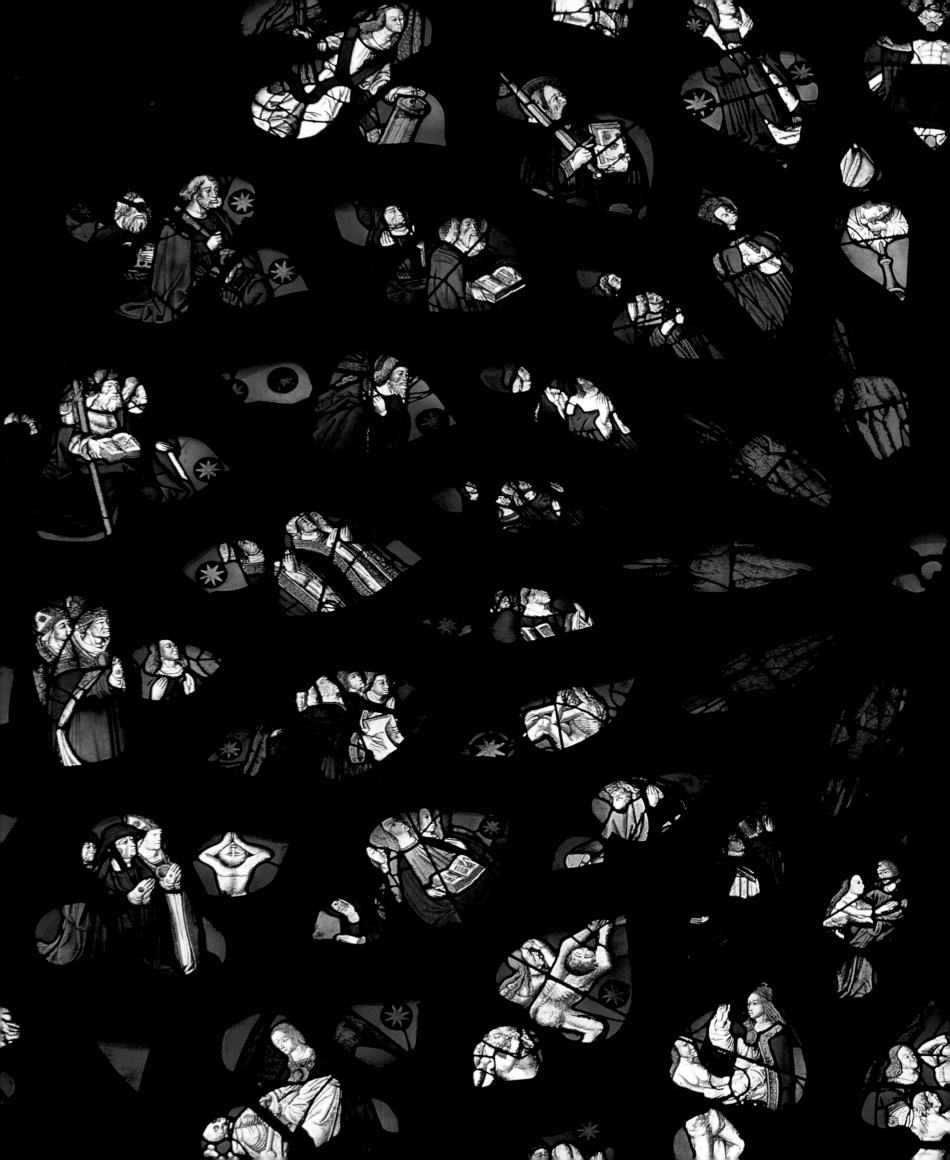

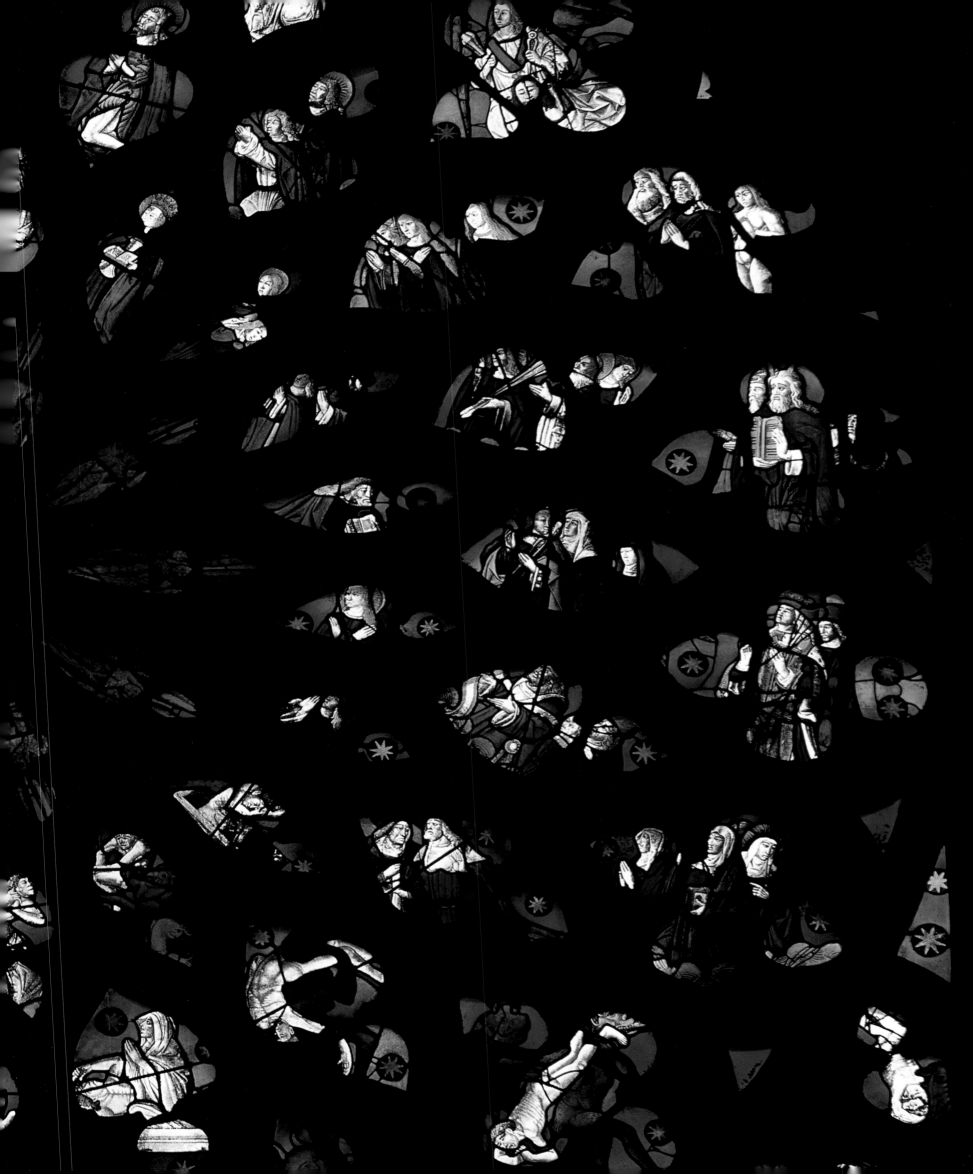

ABOVE, CLOCKWISE FROM TOP LEFT Two souls in the Mouth of Hell (turn the page upside down for a full appreciation!) [31]; two apostles [10]; souls rising from the grave [29]; St Michael weighing two souls, with the devil trying to cheat the scales [7]

OPPOSITE The three panels on the right [9, 10, 11] each contain two apostles, while the two rosettes on the left contain souls rising from graves [33] and the elect [34]

CHARTRES WEST ROSE: THE LAST JUDGMENT

The subject of this rose is Last Judgement as described by Hildegard of Bingen but in a composition that was to become a kind of standard representation. This rose measures around 12 metres (39 feet) or 13.5 metres (44 feet) with the complete surround . It is made from 84 elements of Berchere limestone that forms the structure, such that each of the main openings is surrounded by seven pieces of stone. The glazier here also did the Joseph window in the north aisle (and Prodigal Son at Sens just before).

At the centre is Christ, surrounded by:
1 Abraham holding a number of souls in a sheet (the 'Bosom of Abraham'), flanked by two six-winged seraphim [**2** & **12**], while in six panels [**3**, **4**, **5**, **9**, **10**, **11**] are the twelve apostles, two in each panel. At the bottom of this inner circle is St Michael weighing a souls (in **7** with a devil trying to cheat by putting his foot on the scales), while in **8** an angel leads the elect to heaven and a devil [in **6**] takes his haul off to hell (note a figure among them clutching a money bag – this could be Judas, with his forty pieces of silver, or alternatively a usurer). In the small circles closest to Christ are the four sacred creatures and angels.

In the outer circle hell is portrayed in the two lower panels, one as the Mouth of Hell [**31**] the other with devils manipulating various souls [**30**]; The wounds of the Passion (cross and spear in **36** and **25**); angels blow trumpets in **26** and **35**, the elect look on in **34** and **27**, while souls emerge from their graves in **28**, **29**, **32**, **33**.

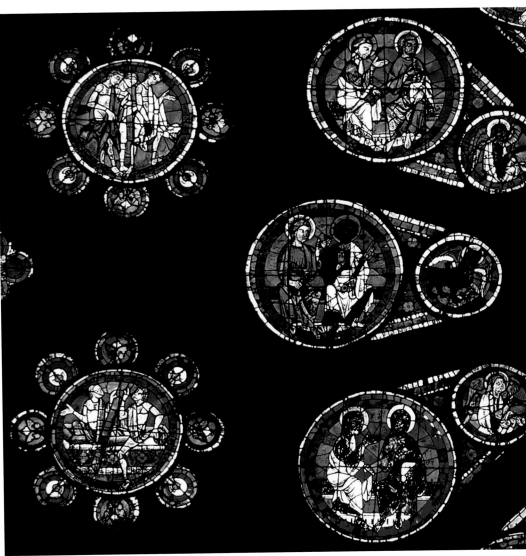

THE NEW JERUSALEM

Pierre le Chantre, who died in 1197, wrote 'the vision of the New Jerusalem far from being the future destruction of the world represents at the same time the present and the future – that is to say, an image of that which is and that which is to come.'[21] For many years the Gothic cathedral was seen as an image of the Heavenly Jerusalem as described in Revelation, largely because of its stained glass. Perhaps this was due to the exaggerated importance attached to the influence of the writings of Pseudo-Dionysius on Suger at St Denis, but today the tendency is to see Gothic churches and cathedrals more as *Ecclesia Universalis* – a manifestation of the Universal Church.

There is, however, one superb rendition of the Heavenly Jerusalem in the north rose window at the cathedral of Châlons-sur-Marne (today Châlons-en-Champagne). The iconography of this rose puzzled people for many years until Meredith Lillich suggested that it might be a portrayal of the New Jerusalem, couched in the hidden meaning of medieval symbolism.[22] At the centre is a Majestas Domini, or Christ resurrected, surround by the four Evangelist symbols. The first circle has the dead rising from their tombs among angels; the circular panels then depict the childhood of Christ which also extends into the next layer at the inner ends of the long main openings. These openings themselves are mainly filled with a foliage design of vine and ivy, symbolic of the Tree of Life, while all round the rim are the happy heads of the elect. The childhood of Christ stands for the first coming of Christ, whereas the faithful who rise at the Last Judgment will join the happy elect at Christ's second coming amid the leaves of the Tree of Life.

In Revelation the city is generally implied as being square and with twelve gates, but circular dispositions can also be found in medieval literature (for example, the Liber Floridus of 1260, a copy of which could originally be found at Reims). Precious stones are evoked by other colours in the glass, although green is the most important – as well as being the most noble and beautiful colour according to Hildegard of Bingen and Hugh St Victor – since it was the colour of Paradise and Resurrection. In fact, every rose window can be seen as a kind of archetypal New Jerusalem, particularly when it is built on the number twelve, with its coloured glass, descending, as it were, from the vaults of heaven 'Like a bride adorned for her husband' (Revelation 21:2). To fully understand rose windows, sometimes we need to make a leap of imagination, to look at the stone and the glass together, to make all the subtle interconnections.

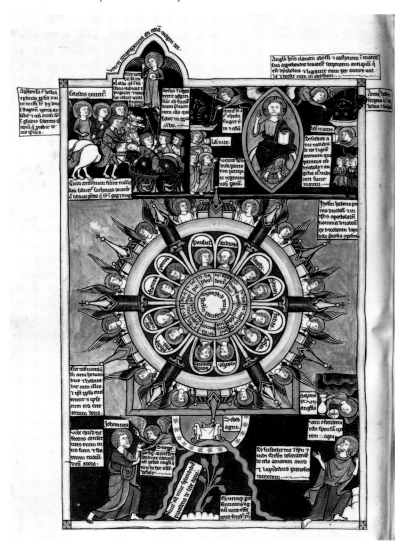

ABOVE LEFT This New Jerusalem, in the Liber Floridus manuscript of c. 1260, is shown in circular form rather than square, as suggested in Revelation. The manuscript used to belong to the diocese of Reims, and is almost exactly contemporary with the Châlons north rose window

OPPOSITE Among the dense foliage of this extraordinary window, we can see episodes from the Life of Christ: the Annunciation, Visitation, Nativity, Adoration Shepherds, the Magi ahead of Herod, Magi travelling, Adoration of Magi, Circumcision (north rose, Châlons-sur-Marne Cathedral, second half of 13th century)

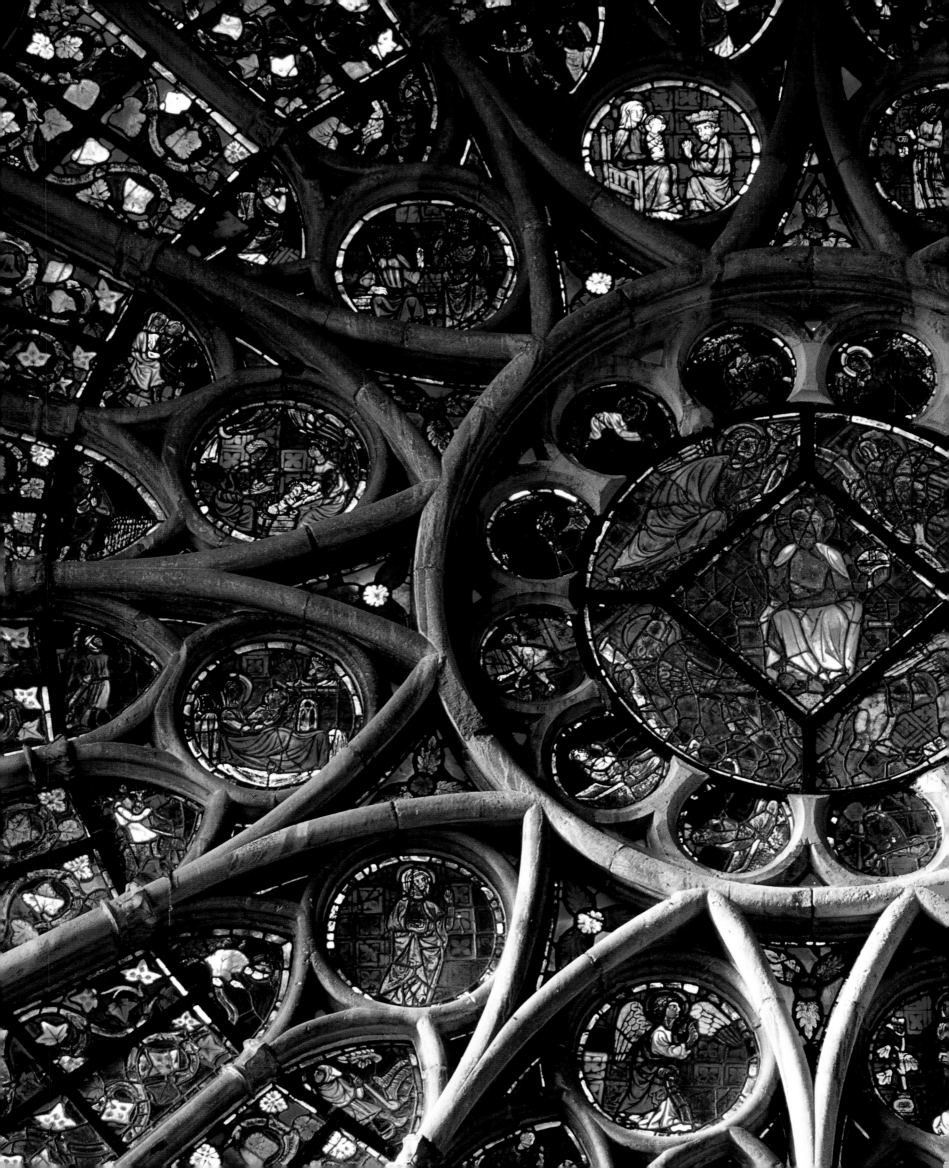

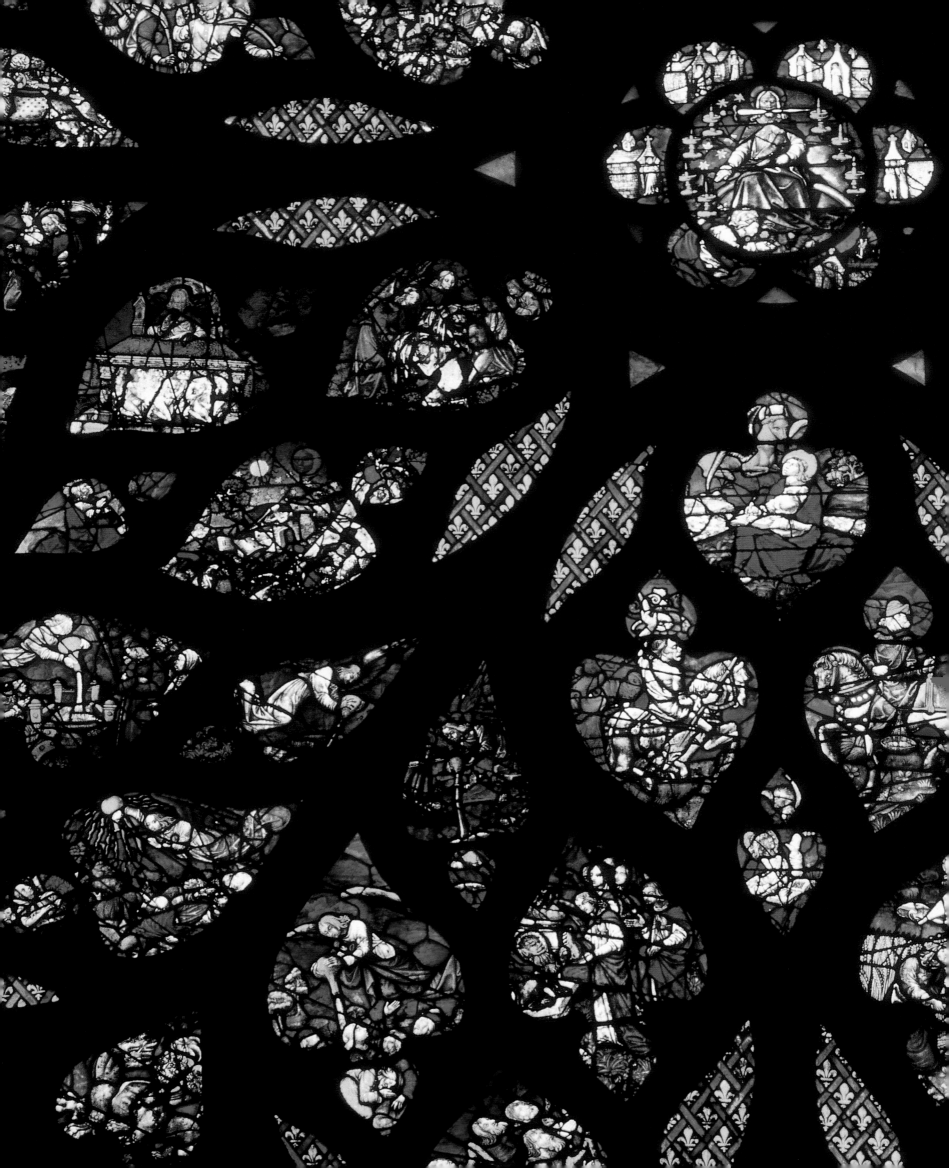

THE SAINTE-CHAPELLE: REVELATION

The theme of the 15th-century rose at the Sainte-Chapelle is the Book of Revelation, depicted here from chapter 1 right up to the New Jerusalem of chapter 21. Of the eighty-five major panels, nine are 19th-century restorations (marked with an asterisk) and a further nine are fairly extensively restored (double asterisk). The numbering of the panels in the diagram follows the order of the description in Revelation.

1 At the centre is Christ enthroned on a rainbow surrounded by seven golden candlesticks and the seven churches of Asia. In His mouth is the sharp two-edged sword. His hair is white as snow-white wool, His eyes flame like fire and His face like the sun in full strength. Above His right hand are the seven stars (1.11–16)

2 Some of the twenty-four Elders with musical instruments (4:4–10)

3 Twenty-four Elders together with the angel of St Matthew and the lion of St Mark (4:10)

4 God on his throne with the closed book of seven seals (5:1)

5 More Elders, the bull of St Luke and the eagle of St John (5:5)

6 The book is given to the lamb (5:6)

7 The lamb with seven horns and seven eyes opens the book. Note the four Evangelists' symbols (5:7)

8 The Elders, with harps and phials of perfume, prostrate themselves (5:8–10)

9 Angels chanting (5:8–12)

10 Opening of the first seal, with the angel of Matthew (6:1)

11 A man on a white horse with a bow and crown (6:2)

12 Opening of the second seal, with St Mark (6:3)

13 A man on another horse (not red, as in the text) with a sword to take peace from the earth (6:4)

14 Opening of the third seal, with the bull of St Luke (6:5)

15 Another horseman (his horse not black as in the text) carrying the scales to measure the wheat and barley (6:5)

16 Opening of the fourth seal, with the eagle of St John (6:7)

17 The pale horse with the grotesque figure of Death, armed with a javelin and vipers. He is emerging from the huge green Mouth of Hell with its red eye. Beneath the horse in the mouth can be seen the 'Venetian' two-toned glass representing the flames (6:8)

18 Opening of the fifth seal (6:9)

19 The souls of the martyrs under the altar of Christ (6:9–10)

20 The souls being arrayed in white robes by angels (6:11)

21 Opening the sixth seal: 'The great day of his wrath'; the ruin created by earthquakes, the sun with a black sackcloth of hair, and the moon turned to blood (6:12–17)

22 Angels holding back the wind from the land and the ships of the sea (7:1)**

23 The multitude before the throne of God, in white robes carrying palms (7:9–12)**

24 The lamb before the throne, between the four sacred living creatures (7:9–12)

25 St John and an Elder (7:13)

26 Opening the seventh seal (8:1)

27 The seven angels before God being given seven trumpets (8:2)

28 An angel giving incense to the altar (symbolizing the prayers of the saints) (8:3)

29 The prayers of the saints reaching God (8:4)

30 An angel taking the altar fire and casting it upon the earth (8:5)

31 The sounding of the first trumpet. Hail and fire descend (8:6–7)

32 The second trumpet; a burning mountain descends into the sea (8:8–9)

33 The third trumpet; the star Wormwood failing on to the waters (8:10–11)

34 The fourth trumpet – sun, moon and stars darkening, and the eagle as the angel crying Woe, Woe, written beneath it (8:12–13)

35 The fifth trumpet; the star fails from heaven, the key to the bottomless pit, and a huge locust (9:1–6)

36 Locusts as horses prepared for battle, with heads like men, hair like women and tails like scorpions (9:7–10)

37 Abaddon or Apollyon, the angel of the bottomless pit (9:11)

38 The sixth trumpet (9:13) **39** The four angels of the Euphrates unbound (9:14)

40 Some of the two hundred thousand thousand (i.e. two hundred million) warriors destroying a third part of humanity (9:16–19)

41 An angel (on a rainbow) giving St. John an open book (10:1,8)

42 The heads of the seven thunders (in a blue cloud) and St John being forbidden to write (10: 3–5)

43 St John measuring the Temple of God with a reed (11:1)

44 The two witnesses are put to death with a turbaned figure looking on (11:3–11)

45 The resurrection of the witnesses and their ascension (into the blue clouds) whilst the lookers-on are amazed (11:11–13)

46 The seventh trumpet; the Elders prostrate themselves before the throne (11:15)

47 The woman clothed as the sun, the moon under her feet and twelve stars in her nimbus (12:1)

48 The dragon with seven heads and ten horns and a 'third part of the stars' (12:3–4)

49 'War in heaven'; St Michael conquers the dragon (12:7–8)

50 The dragon persecutes the mother of the man-child; but she has wings with which to fly into the wilderness (12:13–14)

51 The beast with seven heads comes out of the sea (13:1)

52 The dragon gives power and authority to the beast (13:2–3)

53 Adoration of the dragon (13:4)

54 The beast makes war against the saints (13:7)

55 Adoration of the beast (13:8)

56 Another beast with ram-like horns calls down the fire from heaven (13:11–14)

57 The lamb on Mount Sion with the 144,000, redeemed (14:1–5).*

58 The angel announces the hour of judgment (14:6–7)

59 Two angels, one announcing Babylon is fallen, the other carrying the wine of the wrath of God (14:8–11).*

60 The time of harvest. The son of man with a sickle on a white cloud (note the Venetian glass in the red and white spirals of the pillar on the right) (14:14–16)

61 The gathering of the grapes with the sickle (14:17–18).*

62 The elect singing the song of Moses (15: 2–4).*

63 One of the four beasts gives the seven angels the vials of the wrath of God (15: 5–7).*

64 The first vial is poured upon the earth (16: 2).*

65 The second vial is poured upon the sea – which turns to blood (16:3)

66 The third vial is poured upon the rivers and streams 16:4–6).**

67 The fourth vial is poured upon the sun, scorching men (16:8).**

68 The fifth vial is poured upon the seat of the beast – a *fauteuil Dagobert* his subjects gnawing their tongues for pain (16:10)

69 The sixth angel pours his vial upon the Euphrates (16:12).*

70 Unclean spirits like frogs, coming out of the mouth of the dragon, subsequently go to the great battlefield of Armageddon (16:13).*

71 The seventh vial is emptied, as a yellow liquid, into the air (16:17)

72 The great earthquake and hailstones as heavy as coins 16:18–21)

73 The seven-headed beast carries the whore of Babylon with a golden cup in her hand (17:3–5).**

74 A mighty angel casting a great millstone into the sea (18:21)

75 'Faithful and true', the king of kings on a white horse, with two other warriors behind (19:11–16)

76 The kings of the earth making war against the beast (19:19–20)

77 The seven-headed beast and the two-horned beast being cast into the lake of fire burning with brimstone (19:20)

78 The angel with the key of the bottomless pit binding the dragon Satan for a thousand years (20:1)

79 The New Jerusalem, coloured 'finegold', an angel at each door, with all manner of stones in the walls and the lamb on the throne in its midst (21:10–24) God in Majesty is in the right-hand trefoil outside the rose, and opposite is the beast with seven heads. Unfortunately both these panels are extensively restored. The rest of the window contains the royal arms (**80, 81, 83**) and the initials of Charles VIII (**82, 84, 85**).

CHAPTER 6
THE GEOMETRY OF LIGHT: DESIGNING AND BUILDING THE ROSE WINDOW

'The whole form of the Gothic cathedral proceeds from the harmonically divided circle,' wrote Titus Burkhardt, adding: 'As if to impress this principle even on the ignorant, there are the large geometrical rose windows that occupy a central position in the walls of the church.'[1] It was Dionysius the Pseudo-Areopagite who wrote that human order on earth should endeavour to reflect the order in heaven.[2] Geometry was seen as the means by which to achieve and express this order. A church or cathedral built according to the basic laws of geometry and number was seen as doing nothing less than imitating Creation itself, organizing its parts according to divine harmonies. This chapter covers the process of commissioning, designing, building and maintaining rose windows, and also gives an insight into the powerful geometry that underlies the structures.

As with so many things in the study of Gothic architecture the roles of geometry and that of the master mason have undergone much reconsideration over recent years. Gone is the view of the architect as a 'numerologist, as a pure pragmatist, as a groping super-mason or as a contract theologian,' operating without plans, proceeding by trial and error. 'The lodges functioned very much like modern offices' concluded François Bucher after studying over two thousand medieval plans and designs, theoretical treatises and working drawings.[3] Of this large number of drawings only a very few relate to the period before 1300, and these too were primarily used in order to communicate ideas to the patron. The famous drawings of the façade of the cathedral in Strasbourg, the earliest dating from around 1255, are almost unique.[4] They show

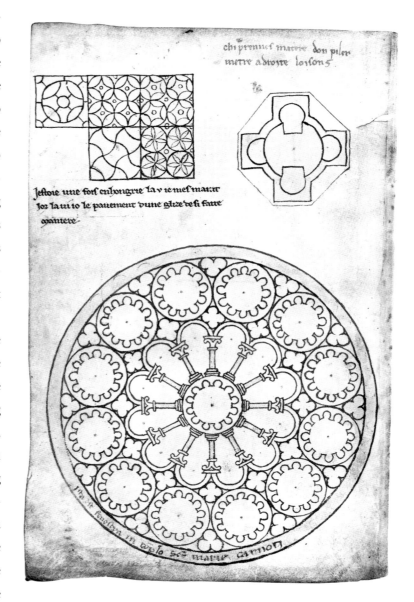

OPPOSITE Viollet-le-Duc's detailed drawing of the rose in the chapel at Saint-Germain-en-Laye shows how the rose window is made up from a series of repeating units

ABOVE RIGHT Villard de Honnecourt's sketch of Chartres west rose window, c. 1235. Either it was drawn from memory, or else he had in mind 'improvements' for another window based on Chartres – in any case, the design deviates significantly from the actual window (see p. 80)

the frequent changes of mind involved. One of these drawings is over four metres (thirteen feet) high and shows a remarkable portrayal of the intended rose window.

The architect did not operate in a vacuum, however. In the Middle Ages architects did not build speculatively, but were commissioned by a patron, almost always the church. The patron would have had general demands and wishes relating to how the building would function, and presumably some aesthetic preferences when it came to such prominent features such as rose windows. The architect and the patrons must have met regularly, the patrons responding to the sort of drawings seen at Strasbourg (and, on occasions, models). Almost certainly the patron would have chosen the theme of the glazing, and in some cases this will have forced the architect's hand. Sometimes the window was paid for by somebody other than the church, a private donor: the most famous examples are the north and south roses at Chartres, which were paid for by Blanche of Castille and the Count of Dreux, respectively. In these cases, the donor's input was probably limited to incidental detail – background pattern, which in the case of the north rose is the fleur-de-lis, symbol both of the French monarchy and of the Annunciation of the Virgin.

When the general approach and programme had been agreed, presumably more detailed drawings would have been made to begin the actual work of fabrication and construction. Sadly no examples of these drawings remain from the early period, but we do find occasional tracings as at Byland Abbey and in the crypt of Bourges (see p. 258). There is also a large drawing of what was probably a clearstorey rosette on the wall on the tribune of the south transept in Soissons, presumably used as a reference during building there, and there used to be a very faint graffito on a wall in Saint-Quentin Cathedral, based on the Chartres west rose, possibly used as a reference in choosing the design of Saint-Quentin's clearstorey rosettes.

That the architects or masons used only compasses, dividers, set-squares, rulers and knotted ropes throughout the Middle Ages is fairly certain. We have already seen God the Creator portrayed with a medieval pair of compasses designing the cosmos in the window at Malvern Priory (see p. 196), and there is no doubt that this was an important tool to the mason. One of the main architects of Reims Cathedral, Bernard of Soissons, was portrayed with compasses on the now-lost plaque at the centre of the labyrinth at Reims, where it was also stated that he built the façade 'up to the "O"'[5] – that is, to the west rose window. And Alexandre de Berneval, who designed at least one of the spectacular roses at St Ouen, Rouen, was depicted on his tombstone drawing a rose.[6] Clearly the architects themselves viewed these creations with pride.

OPPOSITE A drawing of the west rose at Strasbourg Cathedral, made around 1290. The full series of drawings show how the designs changed over a period of years. This indicates the general approach to the rose, but not the specifics of construction.

ABOVE RIGHT A 16th-century model for the Schöne Maria pilgrimage church at Regensburg, made in wood. Such models are believed to have been common in order to demonstrate and discuss designs to the patrons and donors. This design, with a series of huge Flamboyant rose windows at the clearstorey level would have been magnificent, but does not seem to have been realized

ABOVE The south rose at Sens was the gift of Tristan de Salazar, whose arms fill all the outer panels. The rose itself was designed by Martin Chambiges and has glasswork by Hughes Cuvelier, and depicts the Last Judgment (south rose, Sens Cathedral, early 16th century)

OPPOSITE The figures of Pierre Mauclerc and his wife, donors of the rose, appear on their knees before the Virgin Mary at the bottom of the lancets. Beneath the Virgin is a shield depicting their coats of arms (south rose, Chartres Cathedral, glass finished by 1226)

DESIGNING THE ROSE WINDOW

Behind the visible framework of every rose window is a precise hidden geometry. In the greatest roses it defines the exact position of many of the major features, relating the radial elements to the concentric divisions, and all to the centre. The eye probably unconsciously picks up these relationships just as it does with the inner geometry of a Renaissance painting, and the sketchbook of Villard de Honnecourt shows many geometric forms drawn within people, animals and buildings alike. The two simplest and most basic governing principles in geometry at the time of the High Gothic were those of *ad quadratum* (layout based on adjoining squares), and 'right measure', or 'two to one', the proportions produced by drawing one square inside another (see p. 248). This latter technique, which originated with Plato, was transmitted to the Middle Ages via the Classical writer Vitruvius and perpetuated through the Liberal Arts. Apart from the obvious ratios derived from *ad quadratum*, such as the ratio of the side of a square to its diagonal (1:1.4142), designers used the Golden Section proportion of 1:1.618. Such irrational numbers were probably unknown to most masons since such theoretical knowledge was unnecessary: the ratios arose from simple geometrical operations.

Euclid's *Elements*, originally written in the 3rd century BC, was translated from Arabic into Latin in the 11th century (the original, of course, was written in Greek). Euclid's approach enabled essential geometric figures to be drawn without calculation, using only a ruler and a compass. In rose window design, up to the Flamboyant era at least, these traditional tools would seem to have been sufficient, since using them alone it is possible to divide the circle into all numbers from two to twelve with the exception of seven, nine and eleven, as the accompanying illustrations show. (With a protractor it is possible to create any number of divisions but this item of equipment does not seem to have featured in the mason's toolset before the end of the Middle Ages.)

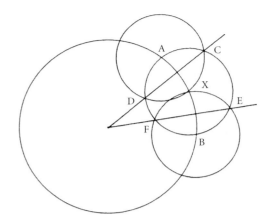

1 TO FIND THE CENTRE OF A CIRCLE
a) Draw any smaller circle on the circumference with centre X: A and B are where it cuts the main circle
b) With the same radius draw two circles using A and B as centres; C, D and E, F are where it cuts the circle with centre X
c) Extend the lines CD and EF and where they meet is the centre

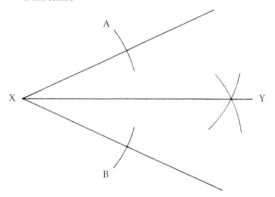

2 TO BISECT AN ANGLE
a) Given any two lines intersecting at X put the compass at X and with any reasonably large radius draw a part of an arc that cuts the two lines at A and B
b) Repeat the operation from points A and B except that the part arcs should be made to intersect at Y
c) Join X and Y: this line bisects the angle

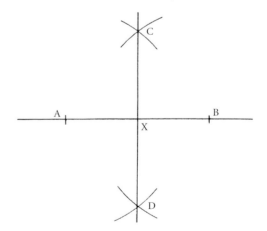

3 TO BISECT A LINE INTO TWO EQUAL PARTS
a) Draw the line AB. With the compass at A and a radius AB draw a part of a curve above and below the line; repeat from B so that the part curves form a cross with those just made.
b) Where the part curves cross at C and D draw a line; this bisects AB at X)

Once the centre of a circle is known the fundamental geometry for rose windows based on 2, 3, 4, 5 or 6 petals (and their multiples 8, 10, 12, etc.) can be created as follows:

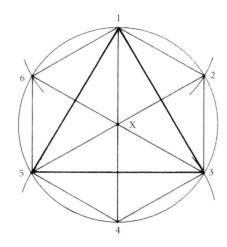

4 DIVIDING A CIRCLE INTO THREE OR SIX

a) Set the compass to the radius of the circle
b) With the same radius mark out six points on the
   circumference starting at 1
c) Three or six radials can be drawn by simply joining
   the lines 1, 3, 5, or all, to the centre X.
d) A triangle or hexagon can be created by joining 1, 3, 5
   (triangle) or 1, 2, 3, 4, 5, 6 (hexagon)

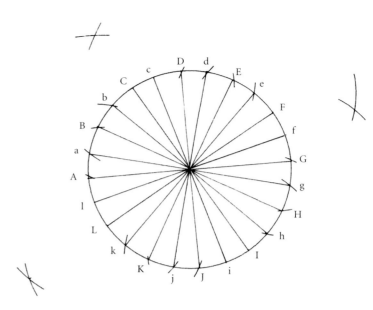

5 DIVIDING A CIRCLE INTO TWELVE AND TWENTY-FOUR

a) Perform 3a and 3b above to give the four points A, D, G, J
b) From A perform 4 above to give six points C, E, (G), I, K
c) Do the same from D to give six further points F, H, (J), L, B.
   This gives TWELVE points.
d) Bisect the angle AXB to give point a
e) Repeat for BXC to give point b and likewise for the remaining angles
   to give points a to l
f) Draw in the twenty-four radials

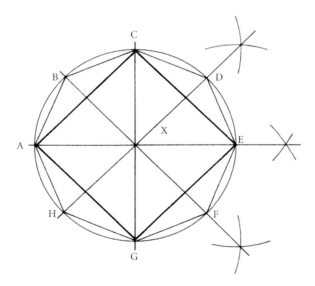

6 DIVIDING A CIRCLE INTO TWO, FOUR, EIGHT, SIXTEEN OR THIRTY-TWO

a) Draw the diameter of the circle AE with centre X. This divides
   the circle into TWO.
b) Perform stages 3a and 3b above, to give the points C and G
c) XA, XC, XE, XG divides the circle into FOUR. Join AC, CE, EG and
   GA to create a square.
d) Bisect the right-angle AXC to give B and repeat for the three
   other sections CXE, EXG and GXA to give the points D, F and H
e) Join all the points to the centre to give a circle divided into eight,
   or successively to their neighbours to give an octagon.
f) To create sixteen and thirty-two subdivisions each of the
   angles containing the sides of the octagon are bisected in
   the normal way for sixteen, and then yet again for thirty-two.

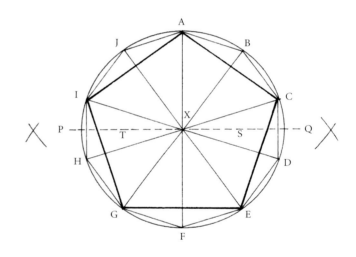

7 DIVIDING A CIRCLE INTO FIVE OR TEN

a) Perform stages 3a and 3b starting with diameter AF to give P and Q
b) Bisect the radius XQ to give point S
c) Set the point of the compass at S and with a radius equal to SA draw
   an arc to cut the diameter at T
d) Set the point of the compass at A and with a radius equal
   to AT draw an arc to cut the circle at I
e) Set the point of the compass at A and with a radius equal to IA draw
   an arc to cut the circle again at C; continue this with the point at C
   to define E, and with the point at E to define G.
f) Join A, C, E, G and I to give a pentagon, and the same points to
   X to divide the circle into five parts
g) With the compass point at F set the radius to FE. Putting the
   point at E an arc defines the point D; putting it at A defines the
   points B and J; putting it at G defines H. This second pentagon F, H,
   J, B, D interlinks with the original pentagon to give the ten points
   A, B, C, D, E, F, G, H, I and J that divide the circle into ten

This overdrawing on the west rose at Notre-Dame
shows the principle of 'right measure' – drawing
a series of squares inside each other to define the
proportions of the different zones within the window.
It is a device illustrated by Villard de Honnecourt who
shows how the method can be applied to define the
tapering units that comprise a spire

The north rose at Chartres has always presented a puzzle
to viewers: the distinctive squares that form the central
layer of openings seem at first sight to have been thrown
in almost randomly. However, nothing was ever left to
chance in these windows, and in fact the small squares
mark the corners of three large rotating squares

THE GEOMETRY OF THE LAUSANNE ROSE

This window is examined in some detail since it well illustrates both a range of design techniques and also the problems that arise in trying to 'decipher' the design. It also gives a useful insight into how the architect, masons and glaziers would have had to accommodate one another. Like the contemporary Dean's Eye rose at Lincoln, it is clearly based on the number four – a scheme that extends into the subjects of the glass, as we saw in Chapter 5. As the sequence of drawings on pp. 252–3 shows, the starting point is a square within a circle: all other elements take their cue from the relationship between these two fundamental elements. So, for example, the smaller circles take as their radius the distance between the square and the edge of the circle. A very distinctive element of the design – the square sitting on top of the central four circles – is derived from the technique of 'right measure' or

diminishing squares, which also informs the design of the contemporary west window of Notre-Dame (see p. 248).

Past attempts at explaining the geometry of this rose are either incomplete or else have failed to realize that the design, as built, takes into account the proposed thickness of the tracery. Simply put, in examining any window there is the problem of where the lines are to be drawn, and without the actual measurements of the window and its components, checking such schemes against photographs has its limitations. However, even from a photograph it can be seen that there are three different sizes for the circular openings that contain the glass: Size 1 for the central panel with God, the four seasons, the four rivers of Paradise and the four elements, all roughly the same size; Size 2 for the groups of three and four circles that surround Size 1; Size 3 for triplets of each of the winds. The part-circles containing the exotic creatures attending the rivers of Paradise are Size 4. Even within the groups there might be variations in dimensions: two of the rivers of Paradise are 66 cm, the seasons are 64 cm (one 63.7 cm), Earth, Fire, Air and Water are all 61 cm, the months and signs of the zodiac together with the sun and moon originally around God are mostly 58 cm (two 57.5 and one 57.7 cm). Most of the half-circles are around 54 by 30 cm, but one is 51.5 by 30 cm. These variations show that even in the most tightly worked rose there are minor inaccuracies – or perhaps, rather, they show that the inaccuracies were tiny considering the complexity and scale of the project.

The success of reconstructing the design of this rose, then, depends upon getting the thickness of the profiled circles and squares right, and choosing a correct average size for Size 2 circles. In other words we need to take account of the fact that medieval masons were not above altering the geometry slightly to fit – there were aesthetic considerations, and the occasional inaccuracy might creep in (see pp. 260–61). Nevertheless, the design of the rose at Lausanne remains a *tour de force* of the art of geometry.

The large rose window at Lausanne Cathedral – some 9.43 metres (31 feet) across – uses simple geometry to create a complex effect, which is compounded by its distinctive layered tracery and profiles. The whole window was taken down in 1907–8 and the stonework replaced and some of the panels moved. The glass was again cleaned in the 1990s (rose, Lausanne Cathedral, after c. 1205)

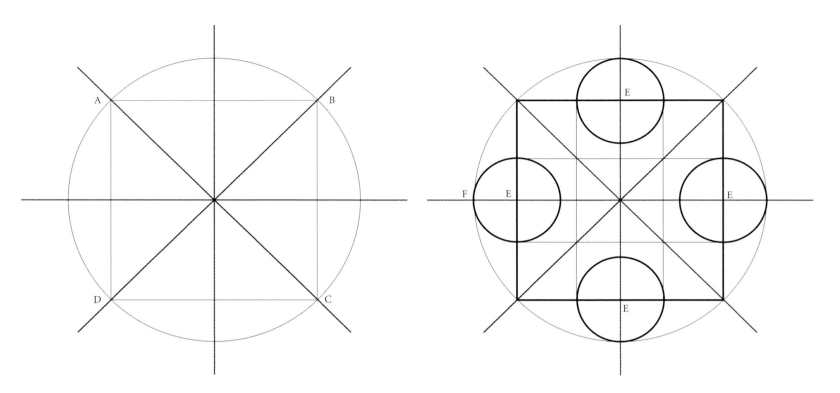

1 Draw the main circle: this is drawn not to the inner edge of the window's circular profiled rim but around the external surface of the visible 'constructional square'. Draw the two 90 degree axes and bisect these to give the diagonals AC and BD

2 Draw the four outer circles: their centres at E are the points of intersection of this square with the axes, the radius, EF, being the distance to the outer circle. Since these circles also have a thick profiled rim, it is important to note that it is the beginning of the central 'hump' of the profile that marks where these circles actually go

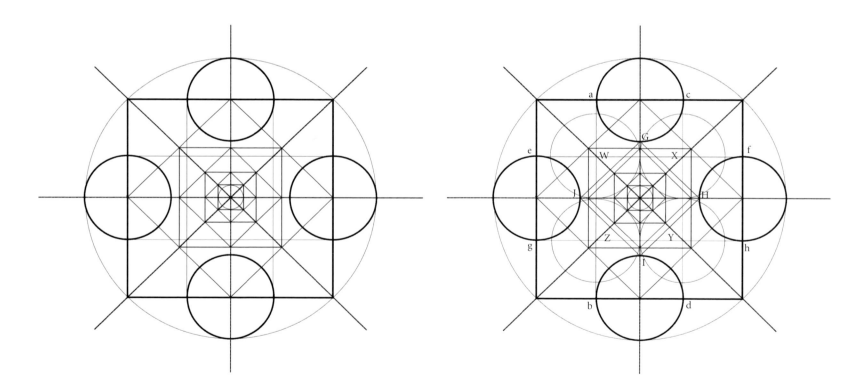

3 Draw a series of squares inside the main square in the traditional manner of 'right measure' until the central circle containing God is created – this is, appropriately, within the seventh square. The fourth of these squares also marks the position of the inner edge of the profiled central square

4 Returning to the outer circles, draw a square from the points where the inner side of each of the circles touches the axes, i.e. at G, H, I, J. This square marks the outer edge of the profiled central square (the inner edge is the fourth square just drawn). The near half-circles that abut the sides of this square are drawn by first drawing the tangents to the outer circles – the lines ab then cd then ef then gh. Where these intersect are the centres of these near half-circles, W, X, Y, Z. Their radii are the same as the outer circles with centres E. As with the outer circles this circle marks the central 'hump' of the profile

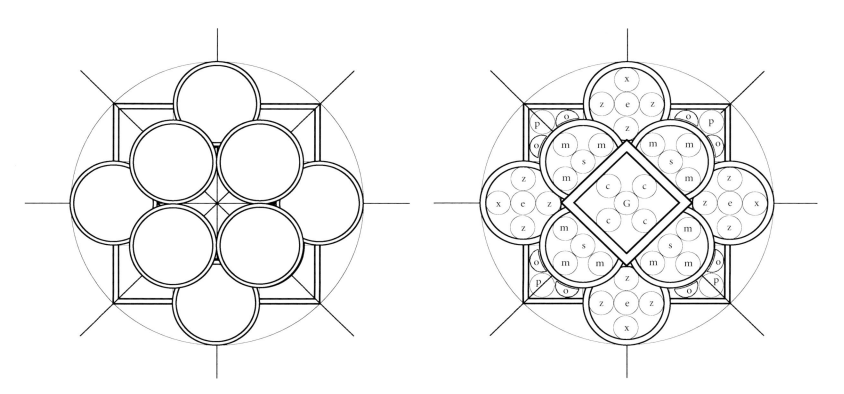

5 Draw the inner edges of the four outer and four inner circles

6 Draw in the central square and erase the parts of the inner circles that lie within it. Sketch in the circles that will contain the glass: in this diagram *e* represents the elements, *s* the seasons, *m* the months, *p* the rivers of Paradise, *o* the creatures at the corners of the world, *z* the signs of the zodiac, *x* the sun, moon and prophecy, *c* the creation, *G* God at the centre

7 The circles that contain the glass can now be drawn in, bearing in mind the small differences in sizes mentioned earlier (these differences are not shown here). The centres of the *x* and *e* circles and some of the *z* circles, lie on the intersection of axes: the centres of *c*, *s* and *p* circles, and and some of *m* circles lie on the diagonals; the other *m* lie on lines parallel to the central square. The groups of three small circles that contain the eight winds (actually one wind and two decorative in each group) are contained within circles that fit into the space between the outer square, outer circles and the outer perimeter: these are now drawn in

8 Within each of these last circles are drawn the groups of three small circles. Each group is arranged so that one of the three points towards the centre of the rose

THE GEOMETRY OF FLAMBOYANT ROSE WINDOWS

At first sight Flamboyant roses – particularly the later ones – seem almost impossibly complex. One is tempted to believe, even, that the designers have dispensed entirely with compasses and elected to draw the flowing curves and exotic shapes freehand. However, as we shall see here, nothing was left to chance, and even such complicated roses as that at the Sainte-Chapelle can be explained geometrically (see pp. 256–7).

The vocabulary of the Flamboyant is extraordinarily rich. The fundamental form is the double curve, which is created by the intersection of two circles (the shape of the curve can be varied by altering the sizes of the circles). The other two key shapes are the mouchette and the soufflet, the first asymmetrical, the second symmetrical. Again, while both appear irrational, they are both constructed using parts of circles. When these shapes are used in conjunction with one another, they generate further shapes in the in-between spaces, which are given such exotic names as 'fish bladders' and 'daggers'. One of the key differences between the Rayonnant rose and the Flamboyant is this use of the void. In deciphering how these roses were designed, meanwhile, the key obstacle is locating the centres of the curves, which are not necessarily part of the visible geometry.

The earliest surviving Flamboyant rose window, on the main façade of Lyon Cathedral from 1393, establishes the approach that was used through to the mid-16th century, though with increasing embellishment. Briefly, the rose is made up of six circles, each one touching its neighbour, all touching the main containing circle. The central hub is created by 'right measure', as at Lausanne – here it is the circle within the fifth square. Six spokes join the six circles to the hub, a Rayonnant throwback, breaking the circles to create the double curve that marks the window out as Flamboyant. Each of the six main circles, meanwhile, contains three smaller circles, which again have their boundaries broken to form two mouchettes

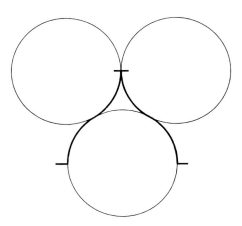

THE DOUBLE CURVE
The double curve is formed when two circles touch tangentially. Here the circles are of identical size, although different-sized touching circles are also used. The ogee arch is formed from three such circles touching

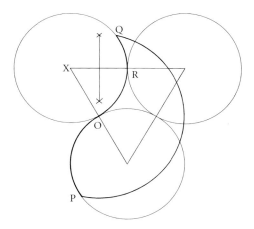

DESIGNING A MOUCHETTE
Combining a double curve with another curve forms a mouchette. Here the double curve PORQ is combined with the segment of a circle PQ. The radius of this latter circle is 1.5 times the radius XQ. A circle is then drawn from Q to P, centred on O

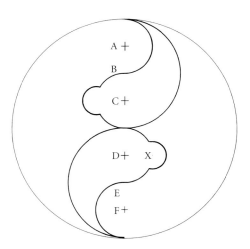

A PAIR OF MOUCHETTES
The diameter is divided into eight parts in order to find the centres A, B, C and D, E, F. Small half circles are then drawn from A, C, D and F while larger ones are drawn from B and E, the radius in each case being the distance from the point to the containing circle. The cusps at the 'heads' of the mouchettes are again formed from part-circles with diameters equal to DE and with centres at X and Y that are in turn on the circles centred on C and D, and at right angles to AC and DF

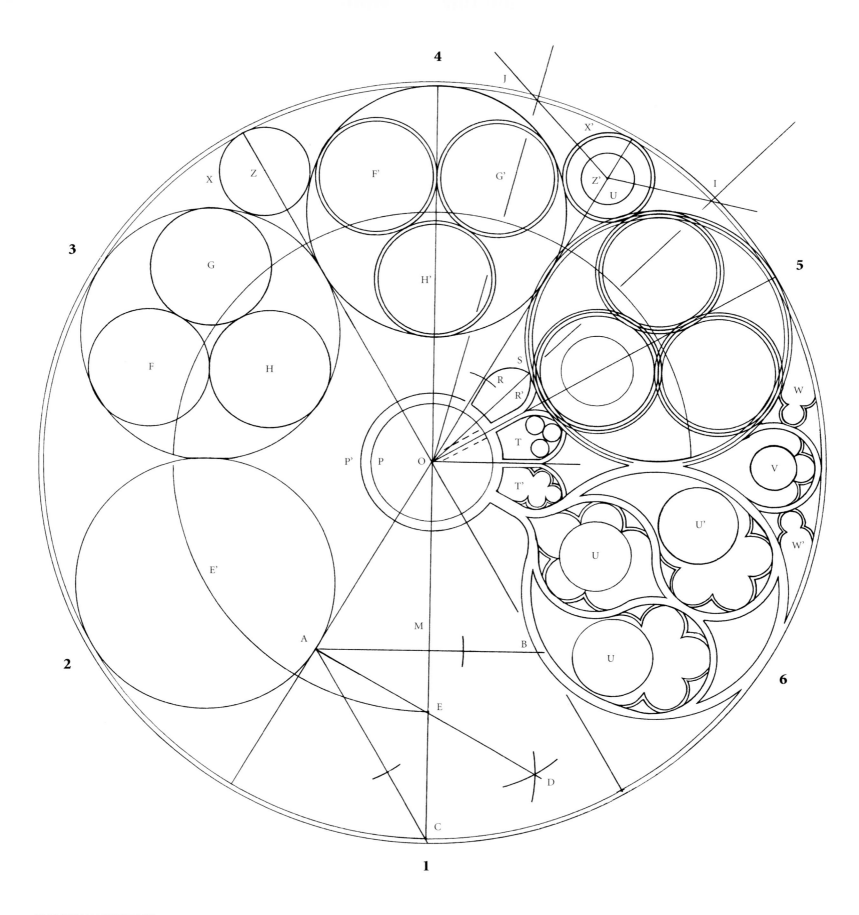

THE LYON WEST ROSE

1   Divide the main circle of the window opening with twelve radials; bisect the radial OC at M and extend the bisecting point to A and B on the neighbouring radials; bisect the angle BAC and where the line crosses the radial OC is the point E, the centre of the circle that will form one of the six main petals; draw a circle radius OE to locate the centres of the other five circles that lie on key radials

2   Draw five diminishing squares within the main circle (see diagram 3 for Lausanne). Within the fifth is the inner surface of the central circular opening, radius OP. (These squares are omitted from this drawing to avoid a confusion of lines); draw the six circles of the main petals on centres E'. Note that they touch their neighbours on a radial and touch the main (structural) circle of the window opening. The thickness of the tracery of these

circles overlaps with its neighbour, so the circles we have just drawn are the centre lines of the tracery

3   Draw three circles, F, G & H within each of the six circles such that they touch each other and the circumference of the main circle; draw the thickness of the central hub PP' and a circle OR to mark where the spokes begin to change into arches

4   Draw in the small circle ZX between each of the six main circles and the outer circle; draw in the thickness of the tracery of the three circles within each circle

5   'Expand' and 'contract' each of the six main circles to create the thickness of the tracery; 'expand' each of the three circles H, G, F so the thickness marries with the containing circle; 'Contract' the ZX circles to ZX' to allow for thickness. Add the circle ZU. Draw the lines ZI

and ZJ, where I and J are the points where the 15 degree radials cut the main circle. Where they intersect the circles ZX is the point of contact for the mouchettes; the cusped mouchettes are then drawn in. Draw the twelve central lancets with their arches: the arches RS and R'S in this drawing are only approximately drawn as precise measurements are needed for this. Likewise the three circles at T that define the curves of the cusps within these lancets are drawn

6   The three circles F, G, H are now metamorphosed into two mouchettes and a soufflet, and the cusps drawn in. The circles U, U' and U" that will contain the scenes within the glass within these openings are drawn

and one soufflet. In between the six main circles, smaller circles are drawn with little mouchettes filling in the last remaining spaces. The ring around the hub is divided with tracery giving twelve small central petals and six small fillets above. The principal innovation of this window, then, is not the underlaying geometry, but the joining, merging, of the shapes to create new forms.

A far greater challenge is posed by the window at the Sainte-Chapelle. Here we would do well to rely on Viollet-le-Duc's description, together with his diagram, opposite:

ab defines the central 'eye', the remainder of the radial bc being divided into three equal parts. The line ae is the diameter of a hexagon on the sides of which have been placed the centres f of parts of the circle bg. On the side ff' of the hexagon has been placed the centre of the part of the circle gi; from the point h a line has been drawn parallel to the main radial aB. A third of the way along the circumference cB is the point j. From this point j a tangent is drawn to the curve gi which gives the axis on which the secondary curves of the main lobes meet. On the line AC, parallel to the main radial aB is the centre K of the arc of the circle lj, the line lK, being parallel to the side of the hexagon. From the point K a perpendicular is drawn to the axis jD; on this line is located n the centre of the arc of the circle il. On this same line Em at an equal distance from the axis Dj, at o, has been placed the centre of the arc mj; on this same line at p has been found the centre of the arc mq; on the extension of this line at r has been found the centre of the arc mB. Thus the main curves of the compartment have been drawn. An equilateral triangle divided by the axis Dj has given the centres of the secondary lobes as other equilateral triangles of this part. The sides of these equilateral triangles have given the positions of the points of the cusps destined to consolidate the system. This diagram gives sufficient information as to the siting of these centres on the sides of the equilateral triangles. The profile G gives the section of the principal members, and H of the secondary members

Every Flamboyant rose window is an individual creation – in many instances the architect's deliberate attempt to break the mould – but all use the language of geometry.

ABOVE LEFT The west rose at Lyon Cathedral, 1393

OPPOSITE Viollet-le-Duc's diagram of the Sainte-Chapelle window, to illustrate the description given above, from his *Dictionnaire raisonné*

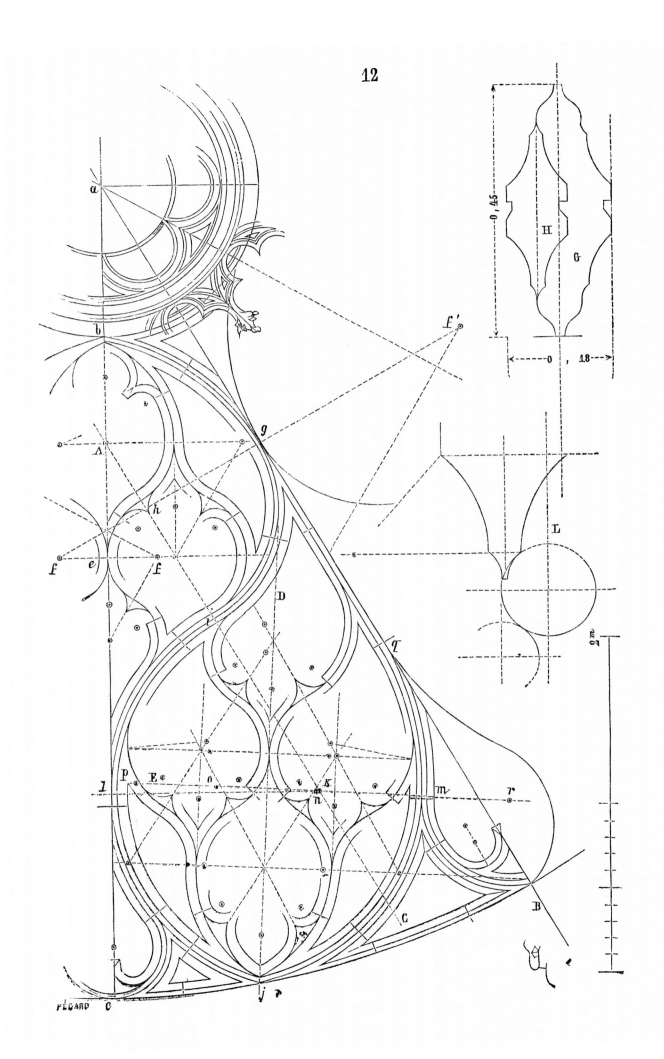

12

BUILDING THE ROSE

So far we have largely considered the architect's role in the design of the rose window and the idealized geometry that governed the scheme. However, it was the job of a team of stone masons to actually carve the components and make the design a reality.

The self-supporting 'O' would have been built first. This had to be accurate, since any departure from a pure circle would cause problems with the tracery (which would also have been cut with great accuracy). Presumably a wooden frame was used to achieve this, as we know was used to construct roof vaults. Meanwhile, the masons would create a section template for the tracery at full-size, which would be used to cut the stone ('full size' would depend on the agreed unit of measurement – Notre-Dame and St Denis, for example, were built using the Parisian foot of 324.84 mm; at Strasbourg it was 285 mm). Presumably this template would have been one sixth or one eighth of the rose, depending on the number of divisions. Examples of templates relating to roses have survived at Bourges and Byland Abbey, carved into the wall or floor of the church; at Girona Cathedral there are some well-preserved wooden tracing boards for lancet windows, and it is possible that a similar technique was used for some smaller roses.

Every rose window is comprised of many pieces of stone and how these pieces lock together is of great structural importance. The actual shapes of the pieces would have been decided using a template, the basic rule being to use as few pieces as possible. Most roses are modular – a detailed analysis of the late 15th-century rose at Lieu-Restauré, for example, shows that only eleven different-shaped pieces were used (the entire rose is made up of sixty-six pieces). Furthermore, it was important to cut the stone in such a way as to preserve its natural strength. In this the mason would draw on experience and intuition. Where the units of the tracery abutted their neighbours, iron dowels set in lead were inserted into rectangular holes; after laying out the components,

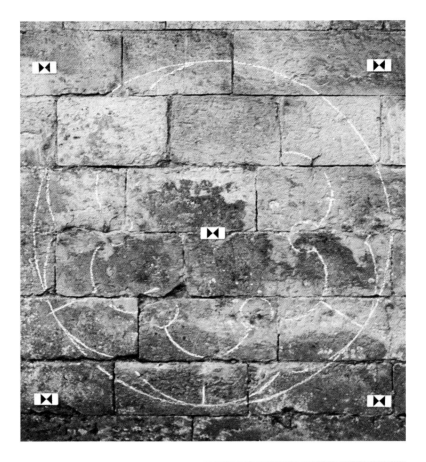

TOP RIGHT This template of the central boss of the rose window at Byland Abbey was buried under rubble for many years, accounting for its survival. It has a diameter of 152 cm (5 feet) and would probably have been used to finish the six components that make up the boss (tracing, west façade, Byland Abbey, early 13th century)

BELOW RIGHT The stone floor of the crypt at Bourges Cathedral has the complete incised design of the blind rose over the gable above the central west portal; this would have been used as the pattern to finish the various pieces of the rose which is about 2.5 metres (8 feet) in diameter. This is a rare surviving example of what was probably a widely used technique for obtaining the final shapes of any decorative item in a church

they were fitted into the circle, building up from the bottom. Sometimes the inner surfaces were painted. Even a sound scheme allows for what François Bucher described as 'deviations from the norm during construction'. He added: 'There is reason to believe that these irregularities were consciously condoned by architects who realized the limitations inherent in too rigid a scheme.'[7] Certainly most roses contain readjustments and corrections that do not follow the architect's pure geometrical scheme. However, they needed to be robust: a one hundred kilometre per hour wind blowing onto the surface of a large rose window of about thirteen metres (forty-three feet) exerts a force of around twelve tons![8]

Finances permitting, at the time of making the template, work would also begin on the glazing; often, however, we find that the glass dates from a few years after the tracery (in the meantime the window would be boarded up or else filled with canvas). In the early period particularly, stained glass was very expensive and time consuming to produce. The designer of the window, working to the agreed programme, would first draw up cartoons, which would then be used to select, cut and paint the glass. The pieces of glass were then joined into panels using lead strips, called cames, and the panels would be slotted into grooves in the stonework, sometimes making last-minute adjustments for a better fit. External ironwork was used to secure large panels of glazing.

The above techniques give the basic radial layout of the geometry for all medieval rose windows in the north of Europe. The Italian wheels with their sometimes strange numbers of spokes often seem to rely on an even more modular system of distinct columns, arcades and wheels. Thus, at S. Rufino in Assisi (see p. 120) the wheel has twelve spokes in the innermost layer, then twenty, and finally thirty-three in the outermost layer – such inconsistencies would have been inconceivable in France, and unless some esoteric significance can be ascribed to the numbers, one must assume that these roses were only quite loosely planned.

In the same town the rose at S. Francesco upper church has twelve, fourteen, then forty-six spokes (see p. 120), while the lower church has fourteen spokes. At S. Chiara (see pp. 119, 120), meanwhile, the numbers are more consistent: fifteen in the centre and then thirty in the outer layer, and the whole composition with its interweaving petals seems to have been very precisely constructed. Spain, too, seems to have shared some of this modular approach: an excellent example is the rose at Armenteira (see p. 121), which uses a brick-like construction, with shapes punched through the blocks, a throwback to the plate tracery seen in France in the late 12th century, though very distinctive – a similar approach is seen at Palermo, Sicily (see p. 156).

A detailed modern drawing by Jean-Luc François of the rose window at Lieu-Restauré, France, made from accurate measurements. The jointing pattern of the sixty-six pieces that comprise the rose can be seen from this section that reveals the eleven basic patterns that are reproduced six times over. A great variety of mouchettes and soufflets are employed

ODDITIES AND FAILURES

Considering their great complexity and delicacy, it is not surprising that from time to time rose windows have come out not entirely as planned. Many were replaced soon after completion, perhaps due to structural failure – for example, Amiens north and south, Laon south, the original Bishop's Eye at Lincoln (the predecessor of the current window), and the giant rose at Palma; at Troyes and Tours insecure or collapsed roses were rebuilt with central props to prevent further accidents. Sometimes this failure was due to subsidence, which can lead to the rose rotating and the spokes snapping (both the west rose at Laon and the south rose at Notre-Dame have suffered from this problem in their histories); sometimes it is due simply to poor or over-optimistic design.

Others were badly designed or built but have not collapsed, and these give us an insight into the difficulties faced by architects and masons. A spectacular example can be found in the south transept of Laon. The designer, clearly trying to create a seven-fold rose (which, being impossible to achieve using Euclidian geometry, he has done using symmetry), would seem to have miscalculated the space between spokes and has had to insert a triangular fillet at the top to compensate. In addition, some of the lancets are shorter than others, with trefoils used to fill gaps, but with no obvious pattern. At Villiers-le-Bel it seems that the circle was not perfectly round to begin with, and as a result the tracery does not fit properly, leading to distortion. As with Laon, it is difficult to comprehend how this rose was allowed to be put up! At Bitonto something else seems to have gone wrong, leading to half of the spokes twisting. It may be an attempt to create a spiral effect; or it may be that half of the spokes are longer than the others.

The vast majority of rose windows are twelve- or six-fold, with many others being eight- or sixteen-fold.[9] This is not surprising, since the number twelve has great symbolic value, and a circle can easily be divided into six and eight. Seven-, nine-, eleven- and thirteen-fold rose windows are not widely found from medieval times simply because such structures cannot properly be designed using only a compass and straightedge. Nevertheless, examples of each exist. Most intriguing are the thirteen-fold roses at St Jacques in Dieppe and on the north façade of Cremona. The number thirteen almost always refers to the Last Supper, at which Judas was present, making the number generally taboo in Christian art. Yet the Dieppe rose is clearly not a mistake on the architect's part, but a deliberate, if rather opaque, statement. Eleven-petalled roses survive at Précy-sur-Oise (see p. 73) and Troia in Apulia, while a seven-fold design can be found at Caussade and Beaulieu Abbey, Ginals (one almost certainly a copy of the other). However, perhaps we should not consider these to be mistakes, but brave attempts to challenge orthodox geometry and create something genuinely new.

ABOVE This unusual seven-pointed rose at Caussade was influenced by a 14th-century rose at Beaulieu Abbey, Ginals. It is impossible to divide a circle into seven using only Euclidian techniques, meaning that either a protractor was used (making the design much later) or else it was designed by trial and error

OPPOSITE Not surprisingly, considering their complexity, rose windows did go wrong sometimes. Clockwise, from top left: south rose, St Jacques, Dieppe, c. 1300, rebuilt 16th century; south rose, Laon Cathedral, c. 1350; west rose, Bitonto Cathedral, mid-13th century; St Didier, Villiers-le-Bel, late 13th century

RESTORING ROSE WINDOWS

While attempts at historically informed conservation began in the 19th century, roses had, as part of the fabric of a functioning church, been repaired for centuries. However, such restoration work, despite the good intentions of the restorers and incumbents alike, has not always been of the highest order, mainly due to ignorance of medieval techniques in the intervening years. The most recent restoration of an important rose has been that of the Dean's Eye at Lincoln Cathedral.[10] By the 1980s it was clear that the window was in a sorry state, and a decision was made to clean and restore the glass – it was taken down and removed to a workshop, leaving a bare stone skeleton. However, it soon became apparent that the stonework itself was fast deteriorating, as numerous fractures, past makeshift repairs and a gradual thinning of the tracery due to environmental erosion, conspired to undermine the structural integrity. Above all, the huge weight of the sagging gable wall above threatened total collapse, and a decision was quickly made to replace the whole of the stonework.

Once the masonry arch above the rose had been propped up, the old stonework was carefully removed and used to create completely new tracery identical to the original. Here there was a question of authenticity, since the only remaining source of the same type of stone was directly underneath the cathedral. Excavating was not an option, so a similar oolitic limestone was imported from France. While it may at the moment appear rather stark, over time the colour will mellow to match the rest of the cathedral. The original design, while distinctive, contained certain weaknesses, so when constructing the new rose it was decided to incorporate a number of invisible modern engineering improvements. The weakest point was the unusual central quatrefoil arrangement with only four 'spokes' to handle the various forces concentrating towards the centre; this has now been countered with the introduction of a stainless-steel hoop around the central four large openings. The

new design is planned to last at least five hundred years and allows even for the increase in extreme weather expected as a result of global warming.

The glasswork, meanwhile, was cleaned and repaired, and when put back into the rose will be protected from the elements by isothermal glazing – a form of secondary glazing often used with stained glass. Over the centuries a number of panels from other parts of the cathedral have found their way into the composition, some soon after the window was completed, and the conservation has given scholars an opportunity to reconsider the original plan. Such interpolation raises a dilemma common to all conservators, including those at Lausanne recently: whether to leave the eroded, damaged or misplaced originals where they are, or to clean them, return them to where they 'should be', or to replace them with facsimiles and put the originals in a museum. While one might feel that without the original stonework the rose loses something, it is wonderful to see the glass recapture its original luminescence.

OPPOSITE ABOVE The old tracery laid out on the floor of the north transept. Note the pieces of the new tracery around the edges

OPPOSITE BELOW Two of the restored panels. The glass at Lincoln is rather jumbled, making the conservationist's job even more difficult. The left-hand panel shows Adam and Eve, delving and spinning being instructed by an angel; the right-hand shows Christ teaching in the Temple. See p. 32 for this window before it was cleaned

ABOVE The newly cut replacement stone, ready to be put into position

GAZETTEER AND MAP

NOTES

BIBLIOGRAPHY

ACKNOWLEDGMENTS FOR ILLUSTRATIONS

INDEX

GAZETTEER

A list of the most important or interesting rose windows, by country. The numbers to the left of entries refer to the map on pp. 270–71.

ABBREVIATIONS

N   *north*
S   *south*
E   *east*
W   *west*
tr   *tracery or stonework*
gl   *glasswork*
bl   *blind rose or rosette in stone*
R   *substantially rebuilt*
r   *ruined or filled (f) in rose window*
C14   *14th century, etc.*
Mod   *modern (i.e. C19 and later)*
Cont   *contemporary (i.e. 1970 and later)*
Oc   *oculus*

ARMENIA
ANI, CATHEDRAL: tr C11 Oc

BELGIUM
AUDENARDE, NOTRE-DAME DE PAMELE: N tr C13
BRUSSELS, NOTRE-DAME DU SABLON: S & W tr C16 & C19
GAND, BILOQUE ABBEY: Refectory pignon tr C14 bl
1   TOURNAI, CATHEDRAL: W tr C13/19
TOURNAI, ST NICOLAS: W tr C13 Oc
2   VILLERS-LA-VILLE, ABBEY: N & S tr C13

CROATIA
3   SIBENEK, CATHEDRAL: W tr C15/16
4   ZADAR, CATHEDRAL: W tr C13

CYPRUS
FAMAGUSTA, CATHEDRAL (MOSQUE): W tr C14

CZECH REPUBLIC
5   PRAGUE, CATHEDRAL: W C20
VYSSIBROD: tr C14

FRANCE
Abbreviations: Alsace (ALSC); Aquitaine (AQUI); Auvergne (AUVN); Bretagne (BRET); Burgundy (BURG); Centre (CENT); Champagne-Ardennes (CHAM); Franche-Comté (FRAN); Ile-de-France (ILE FR); Languedoc-Roussillon (LAN); Limousin (LIM); Lorraine (LOR); Midi-Pyrénées (PYR); Nord-Pas-de-Calais (NORD); Normandy, Basse (NOR B); Normandy, Haute (NORH); Pays de la Loire (LOIR); Picardie (PIC); Poitou-Charente (POIT); Provence-Alpes-Côte d'Azur (PROV); Rhône-Alpes (RHON)

6   ABBEVILLE, ST WULFRAN (PIC): W C16 R; E Cont
AIX, ST JEAN DE MALTE (PROV): tr C14
7   AMIENS, CATHEDRAL (PIC): N 1300, S & W 1500.
ANDELYS (LES), NOTRE-DAME (NOR B): S & N tr C16; W C19
8   ANGERS, CATHEDRAL (LOIR) N & S tr C13, gl C15
ANGERS, LA GALERIE DAVID (FORMERLY TOUSSAINT ABBEY) (LOIR): E tr C18
ANNEVILLE-SUR-SEINE, NOTRE-DAME DE L'ASSOMPTION (NOR H): tr C16
ARCUEIL, ST DENIS & ST JEAN (ILE FR): C13/19 Oc
ARDENNES, ABBEY (NOR B): W tr C15
ARTHONNAY, EGL. (BURG): W tr C14
AUCH, CATHEDRAL (PYR): N, S & W, all C15

AUFFAY, NOTRE-DAME (NOR H): tr C16/20 R
AULNAY, ST PIERRE DE LA TOUR (POIT): S tr C19
9   AUXERRE, CATHEDRAL (BURG): N,S & W all C16
AUXERRE, ST GERMAIN (BURG): N tr C13
AVIGNON, STE CATHERINE (PROV): W tr C14
10   AVIOTH, BASILICA (LOR): W & S tr C14
BAR-LE-DUC, ST ETIENNE (LOR): W C16
BAR-SUR-SEINE, ST ETIENNE (CHAM): W C16
BAYEUX, CATHEDRAL (NOR B): NW tr C13
11   BAZAS, CATHEDRAL (AQUI): W tr C16/17
12   BEAUVAIS, CATHEDRAL (PIC): N tr C16, gl C20; S C16; Choir C13
BEAUVAIS, ST ETIENNE (PIC): N tr C12, E C16
BENISSON-DIEU (LA), ABBEY (RHON): W tr C13
BERSON, ABBEY (AQUI): W C14 Oc
BERTEAUCOURT-LES-DAMES, ST NICOLAS (PIC): W rf C13
BEZIERS, ST NAZAIRE (LAN): W & N tr C14
13   BLENOD-LES-TOUL, ST MEDARD (LOR): W tr C15
BLOIS, ST LOUIS DES JESUITES (CENT): C17
BLOIS, ST NICOLAS (CENT): W tr C13/C17
BONNEVAL, NOTRE-DAME (CENT): W tr C13, gl C20
14   BORDEAUX, CATHEDRAL (AQUI): N C16, S C14
BORDEAUX, ST MICHEL (AQUI): N C15
15   BOURGES, CATHEDRAL (CENT): W C14 (& C15)
16   BRAINE, ST YVED & NOTRE-DAME (PIC): N & S tr C12, gl C20
17   BRIE-COMTE-ROBERT, ST ETIENNE (ILE FR): E C13
BURY, COLLEGIALE ST LUCIEN (PIC): E & S tr C13
BUSSIERE-BADIL, ABBEY (AQUI): W tr C14
18   CAEN, ST PIERRE (NOR B): W tr C14, gl C20
CAHORS, CATHEDRAL (PYR): N, S & W tr C14 and C15
19   CARCASSONNE, CATHEDRAL (LAN): N & S C14
CAROMB, EGL. (PROV): W tr C14
CASSENEUIL, EGL. (AQUI): W tr C15
CASTELNAUDARY, ST MICHEL (LAN): N tr ?C15
20   CAUDEBEC, NOTRE-DAME (NOR H): W C16 & C16
CAUSSADE, NOTRE-DAME DE L'ASSOMPTION (PYR): W C19
CHAALIS, ABBEY (PIC): W tr C13
21   CHALONS-SUR-MARNE, CATHEDRAL (CHAM): N C13; S C20
CHALONS-SUR-MARNE, NOTRE-DAME-EN-VAUX (CHAM): S tr C12 gl C13 & C19; W C13 +19
CHAMBLY, NOTRE-DAME (PIC): N, S & W tr all C13
CHAMPAGNE-SUR-OISE, L'ASSOMPTION (ILE FR): W tr C13; E C19; nave Oc
22   CHAMPEAUX, COLLEGIALE ST MARTIN (ILE FR): nave Oc rf
CHAOURCE, ST JEAN-BAPTISTE (CHAM): N C16/17
CHARS, ST SULPICE (ILE FR): S tr C12
23   CHARTRES, CATHEDRAL (CENT): N, S & W all C13
CHAUMONT-EN-VEXIN, ST JEAN-BAPTISTE (PIC): N tr C15
CINQUEUX, EGL. (PIC): W tr C13/19
24   CLERMONT-FERRAND, CATHEDRAL

(AUVN): N & S tr C14
CLERMONT-FERRAND, CHAPELLE VISITATION (AUVN): E tr C13
CLERMONT-L'HERAULT, COLLEGIALE ST PAUL (LAN): W tr C14
COGNAC, ST LEGER (POIT): W tr C15
COHAN, ST JEAN-BAPTISTE (PIC): W tr C13 (R)
COMPIEGNE, ST ANTOINE (PIC): W C16
CORBIE, ABBATIALE ST PIERRE (PIC): W tr C16-18
CORDES, ST MICHEL (PYR): W tr C14/15
COUCY-LE-CHATEAU, EGL. (PIC): W Oc tr C12
COURMELLES, ST GEORGES (PIC): W C13 Oc
CRECY, EGL. (PIC): W tr C15
25   CREPY-EN-VALOIS, ANC. COLLEGIALE (PIC): W C13 rf
CRUAS, ABBEY CHURCH (RHON): W tr C15
DAMMARD, ST MEDARD (PIC): W tr C12
26   DIEPPE, ST JACQUES (NOR H): W tr C14, N tr C17, S tr C14/17
DIEPPE, ST REMY (NOR H): W tr C16
DIGNE, NOTRE-DAME DU BOURG (PROV): W tr C14
DIJON, ST JEAN (BURG): W tr C15
DIVES-SUR-MER, NOTRE-DAME (NOR B): W tr C14
DOL, CATHEDRAL (BRET): E C13
DONCHERY, EGL. (CHAM): SW tr C13 (R)
27   DOMREMY-LA-PUCELLE, BASILIQUE DU BOIS-CHENU: S C19
28   DONNEMARIE-DONTILLY, NOTRE-DAME (ILE FR): E C13 & C19
EPIAIS-RHUS, EGL. DE L'ASSOMPTION (ILE FR): N & S tr C16
EPINAY-SUR-SEINE, EGL. (ILE FR): C20
EPINE (L'), NOTRE-DAME (CHAM): W tr C15
ETAMPES, COLLEGIALE NOTRE-DAME (ILE FR): S tr C12
EU, COLLEGIALE ST LAURENT (NOR H): S C13/15 r
29   EVREUX, CATHEDRAL (NOR H): N & S C15
FECAMP, ST ETIENNE (NOR H): S C16, N tr C16
FERRIERES-EN-BRIE, ST REMY (ILE FR): W tr C13/19
FIGEAC, NOTRE-DAME (PYR): W tr C13/14
30   FLARAN, ABBEY (PYR): W & S tr C12
FLEURIEL, NOTRE-DAME (AUVN): W Oc C12
31   FOLGOËT (LE), NOTRE-DAME (BRET): S tr C15/19
FONTMORIGNY, ABBEY (CENT): E tr C13 Oc
FOUGERES, ST LEONARD (BRET): W tr C16
32   GASSICOURT, STE ANNE (ILE FR): W C12 Oc
33   GISORS, ST GERVAIS & ST PROTAIS (NOR H): N tr C15, E C20 Cont
GORZE, ST ETIENNE (LORR): N, S, W tr C15
GOUZON, ST MARTIN (LIM): W C13 Oc
GRIGNAN, ST JEAN (RHON): W tr C15
34   GUIGNICOURT, ST PIERRE (PIC): N tr C12
35   HARBONNIERES, ST MARTIN (PIC): W tr C15
36   IVRY-LA-BATAILLE, ST MARTIN (NOR H): N & S tr C16
JOIGNY, ST THIBAULT (BURG): C16
KERNASCLEDEN, CHAP. NOTRE-DAME (BRET): S tr C15
LACHALADE, ABBEY (LOR): S tr C15
37   LAON, CATHEDRAL (PIC): N tr C12, gl C13; E & W C13/C19; S tr C14
LAVAUR, CATHEDRAL (PYR): W tr C16
LESGES, NOTRE-DAME (PIC): W tr C13 (R)
38   LIEU-RESTAURE, ABBEY (PIC): W tr C15 r
LILLE, NOTRE-DAME DE LA TREILLE

(NORD): W C20
LILLERS, ST OMER (NORD): N, S & W tr C12
LIMOGES, CATHEDRAL (POIT): S C14; N C15/16
39   LONGPONT, ABBEY (PIC): W C13 r
LOUVECIENNES, ST MARTIN (ILE FR): E tr C13 gl Mod
40   LYON, CATHEDRAL (RHON): N & S C13; W C14
LYON, STE BONAVENTURE (RHON): W tr C16 gl Mod
LYON, ST PAUL (RHON): N C12 Oc: W tr C16
41   MAILLERAYE-SUR-SEINE (LA), ST MATHURIN (NOR H): W tr C16 gl Mod
42   MANS (LE), CATHEDRAL (LOIR): N C15/16
43   MANTES, CATHEDRAL (ILE FR): W C13
MAREIL MARLY, ST ETIENNE (ILE FR): W tr C13 R
MARMANDE, NOTRE-DAME (AQUI): tr C14/19
MARVILLE, ST NICHOLAS & ST HILAIRE (LOR): W tr C14/19
MEAUX, CATHEDRAL (ILE FR): W tr C16 gl Mod
44   MELLO, COLLEGIALE NOTRE-DAME (PIC): S & W tr C14 gl Mod
MENDE, CATHEDRAL (LAN): W C17
45   METZ, CATHEDRAL (LOR): W C14
MEZY-MOULINS, NOTRE-DAME (PIC): W tr C13
MOLOMPIZE, NOTRE-DAME DE VAUCLAIRE (AUV): W C13 Oc
46   MONS-EN-LAONNOIS, ST PIERRE & ST PAUL (PIC): S tr C13
MONTFERRAND, NOTRE-DAME DE LA PROSPERITE (AUVN): W tr C15 gl Mod
MONTPEZAT-DE-QUERCY, COLLEGIALE ST MARTIN (PYR): W tr C14
47   MONTREAL, EGL. (BURG): N,S,E,W tr C12/13/19
MONTREUIL-BELLAY, COLLEGIALE (LOIR): W tr C14
MONT-ST-MARTIN, EGL. (LOR): W tr C13
48   MORLAIX, ST MELAINE (BRET): W tr C15
MOSLES, EGL. (NOR B): W tr C13/19
MOUZON, ABBEY (CHAM): N,S (Oc) & W tr C13
NANTEUIL, NOTRE-DAME (PIC): EC12 Oc
NESLES-LA-VALLEE, ST SYMPHORIEN (ILE FR): W tr C12/19
NEUBOURG (LE), SS PIERRE & PAUL (NOR H): W tr C16/17 gl Mod
49   NIEDERHASLACH, ST FLORENT (ALSC): W tr C14 gl C14+19
50   NOGENT-LE-ROI, ST SULPICE (CENT): S C16
NORVILLE, ST MARTIN (NOR H): W tr C16
NOTRE-DAME D'AULPS (RHON): E C12 r
51   NOYON, CATHEDRAL (PIC): Chapterhouse E tr C12
OGER, ST LAURENT (CHAM): E tr C13 gl C19
52   ORLEANS, CATHEDRAL (CENT): gl C17
ORTHEZ, ST PIERRE (AQUI): S tr C13 R
53   OTHIS, NATIVITE-DE-LA-SAINTE-VIERGE (ILE FR): W tr C16
54   OUTINES, ST NICHOLAS (CHAM): W C20 Mod
PARIS, CATHEDRAL (NOTRE-DAME) (ILE FR): W, N & S C13
PARIS, SAINTE-CHAPELLE (ILE FR): W C15
PARIS, ST DENIS (ILE FR): W C12; N & S tr C13 gl Mod
PARIS, ST EUSTACHE (ILE FR): N & S C17
PARIS, ST GERMAIN L'AUXERROIS (ILE FR): S & W C16

PARIS, ST MERRI (ILE FR): N & S tr C16
PARIS, VINCENNES, CHAPELLE DU
   CHATEAU (ILE FR): W tr C16
55 PETIT NIORT, ST MARTIN (POIT): N C11
56 PITHIVIERS, ST SALOMON-
   ST GREGOIRE (CENT): W tr C17
PLOUNEVEZ-DU-FAOU, ST HERBOT
   (BRET): tr C14 gl Mod
PLOUNEVEZ-MOËDEC, ST PIERRE (BRET):
   N tr C15
PLOVAN, CHAPELLE DE LANGUIDOU
   (BRET): C15 r
POITIERS, CATHEDRAL (POIT): W tr C13
57 POITIERS, STE RADEGONDE (POIT):
   N nave C13
PONT-À-MOUSSON, ABBEY (LOR):
   W tr C15
58 PONT-CROIX, NOTRE-DAME DE
   ROSCUDON (BRET): bl C15
PONT-L'ABBE, EGL. DES CARMES (BRET):
   E + W tr C15 gl Mod
59 PONTIGNY, ABBEY (BURG): S + N Oc C12
60 PONTOISE, ST MACLOU (ILE FR): Wtr C15
61 PRECY-SUR-OISE, EGL. (PIC):
   E tr C13 gl Mod
62 REIMS, CATHEDRAL (CHAM): N C13;
   S tr C13 R gl Mod; W C13 + W C20
REIMS, ST REMI (CHAM): W tr C13 gl Mod
63 RENWEZ, NOTRE-DAME LA TRES SAINTE
   VIERGE (CHAM): S tr C14/15
64 RETHEL, ST NICOLAS (CHAM): S tr C14
RIOUX, NOTRE-DAME (POIT): W C12 Oc
ROCHEFOUCAULD (LA), ST CYBARD
   (POIT): W tr C16 gl Mod
65 RODEZ, CATHEDRAL (PYR): W & S tr C16
   gl Mod
66 ROMAINVILLE, ST LUC (ILE FR): C20
67 ROUEN, CATHEDRAL (NOR H): N & S tr
   C13; W tr C16 gl all Mod
ROUEN, ST MACLOU (NOR H): N, S & W tr
   C15 gl all Mod
ROUEN, ST OUEN (NOR H): N & S C15;
   W tr C16 gl C19
ROUFFACH, ST ARBOGAST (ALSC):
   W tr C13/14
68 ROYAT, ST LEGER (AUVN): N & S C13 Oc
ROYAUCOURT, ST JULIEN (PIC): W tr C16
ROYE, ST LEGER (PIC): W tr C12 R
ROYE-SUR-MATZ, ST MARTIN (PIC):
   W tr C12 R
SAINT-AMAND-SUR-FION (CHAM):
   N & S C16
SAINT-BRIEUC, CHAPELLE DU
   SEMINAIRE (BRET): W tr C15
69 SAINT-FARGEAU, ST FERREOL (BURG):
   W tr C13/14
SAINT-FORT-SUR-GIRONDE, EGL. (POIT):
   W tr C13
70 SAINT-GABRIEL (NR. TARASCON) (PROV):
   W C12 Oc
71 SAINT-GENEROUX (POIT): E C10/11 Oc
72 SAINT-GERMAIN-EN-LAYE, CHAPELLE
   DU CHATEAU (ILE FR): W tr C13
73 SAINT-GERMAIN-LES-CORBEIL,
   ST VINCENT (ILE FR): E C13
74 SAINT-GERMER-DE-FLY, ABBEY (PIC):
   W tr C13
75 SAINT-HILAIRE-ST-FLORENT, OLD ABBEY
   (LOIR): tr C16
SAINT-JEAN-AUX-BOIS, ABBEY (PIC):
   W tr C13
76 SAINT-LEU-D'ESSERENT, ABBEY (PIC):
   W tr C15 gl Cont
SAINT-MACAIRE, ST SAUVEUR (AQUI):
   W tr C15
77 SAINT-MALO, CATHEDRAL (BRET):
   W C20 Cont
78 SAINT-MICHEL-EN-THIERACHE, EGL.

(PIC): N tr C12
SAINT-NICOLAS-DE-PORT, BASILICA
   (LOR): N & S tr C16
SAINT-PERE-SOUS-VEZELAY, NOTRE-
   DAME (BURG): W tr C14
SAINT-POL-DE-LEON, CHAPELLE NOTRE-
   DAME DU KREISKER (BRET): tr C14
79 SAINT-QUENTIN, CATHEDRAL (PIC):
   N C13; S tr C15
SAINT-SEINE-L'ABBAYE (BURG): E tr C13/14
SANTEUIL, SS PIERRE & PAUL (ILE FR):
   W tr C13
80 SEES, CATHEDRAL (NOR B): N C13; S tr
   C13, gl C19
81 SELESTAT, ST GEORGES (ALSC):
   S aisle C14
82 SENLIS, CATHEDRAL (PIC): W tr C12;
   N & S tr C16 gl Mod
83 SENS, CATHEDRAL (BURG): W tr C12;
   N C16, S C15
SERVON, STE COLOMBE (ILE FR): E tr C13
SEURRE, ST MARTIN (BURG): W tr C14
SEYNE, NOTRE-DAME-DE-NAZARETH
   (PROV): W C13/C18
84 SILVACANE, CISTERCIAN ABBEY (PROV):
   E C12
85 SOISSONS, CATHEDRAL (PIC): N C13;
   W tr C13 (R) gl C20
SOISSONS, ST-JEAN-DES-VIGNES (PIC): W
   C13 r
86 STRASBOURG, CATHEDRAL (ALSC):
   S C13; W tr C14 gl C14/19
STRASBOURG, MUSEE DE L'OEUVRE
   (ALSC): Wheel & designs
STRASBOURG, ST BARTHOLOMEE (ALSC):
   E C14
STRASBOURG, ST THOMAS (ALSC): W C13
SYLVANES, ABBEY (PYR): E C13 Oc
THANN, ST THIEBAUT (ALSC): W tr C14
THÔNES, ST MAURICE (RHON): W ?C17
THOUARS, ST MEDARD (POIT): W tr ?C15
TOUL, CATHEDRAL (LOR): W tr C13
87 TOULOUSE, CATHEDRAL (PYR): W C13
TOULOUSE, NOTRE-DAME DE LA
   DALBADE (PYR): W tr C16 gl Mod
88 TOURS, CATHEDRAL (FRAN):
   N & S C13/14; W C16
89 TROYES, CATHEDRAL (CHAM):
   N C13/C15; S C19; W C16
TROYES, ST NICOLAS (CHAM): W tr C16
VAILLY-SUR-AISNE, NOTRE-DAME (PIC):
   W tr C15
VALMAGNE, ABBEY (LAN): C13 rf
90 VAUX-DE-CERNAY (LES), ABBEY (ILE FR):
   W C12 r
91 VAUX-SOUS-LAON, ST JEAN-BAPTISTE
   (PIC): tr E C13
VERNON, NOTRE-DAME (NOR H):
   W tr C15 gl Cont
VIAS, ST JEAN-BAPTISTE (LAN): W tr C15
VIGNORY, ST ETIENNE (CHAM): E tr C12
93 VILLENEUVE-SUR-YONNE, NOTRE-DAME
   (BURG): W tr C17
94 VILLIERS-LE-BEL, ST DIDIER (ILE FR):
   S tr C13
VORGES, ST JEAN-BAPTISTE (PIC):
   W tr C13 gl C13/19
95 WISSEMBOURG, SS PIERRE & PAUL (ALSC):
   N C12/13; S C13

Rose windows, interesting oculi (oc) or ruins
(r) can also be seen at the following places
(although the list is by no means exhaustive!):
Agen, Cathedral (AQUI); Ambierle (RHON);
Anet (CENT); Arcy-Ste-Restitue, St Martin
(PIC); Auxi-le-Château (NOR H); Avrechy (PIC);
Azelot (oc) (LOR); Bayonne, Cathedral (AQUI);

Beaulieu-en-Rouergue (nr. Ginals) (PYR);
Beaumont (AQUI); Beaune (BURG); Belley
(RHON); Belleville-sur-Saône (RHON); Bergues
(NOR H); Blainville-Crevon (NOR H); Bordeaux,
St Sernin (AQUI); Bourg Dun (NOR H); Breuillet
(oc) (POIT); Brigueil, St Martial (oc) (POIT);
Broualan (BRET); Caen, St Jean (NOR B); Caix,
St Croix (PIC); Chaillevois (PIC); Champigny-
sur-Veude (CENT); Chartres, St Aignan (CENT);
Châteaudun, Notre-Dame du Champdé (r)
(CENT); Chissey-sur-Loue (FRAN); Cirey-les-
Bellevaux (oc) (FRAN); Condom (PYR); Congis-
sur-Thérouanne, St Rémi (ILE FR); Couronne
(La) (r) (POIT); Couvrelles (PIC); Croissy (oc)
(ILE FR); Croix Hékélan, Chapelle St Mande
(BRET); Dieppe, St Rémy (NOR H); Dole, Notre-
Dame (FRAN); Domrémy-la-Pucelle (LOR);
Dreux, Cathedral (CENT); Drosnay (NOR H);
Eauze (PYR); Ennery, St Aubin (ILE FR);
Épernay (CHAM); Ermenonville (POIT);
Eymoutiers (POIT); Ferté-Bernard (La) (LOIR);
Ferté-Milon (La) (PIC); Fontfroid, Abbey (oc)
(LAN); Ganagobie (oc) (PROV); Genouillé (oc)
(POIT); Giroussens (PYR); Gorze, St Etienne
(LOR); Gourdon, St Pierre (PYR); Grâces (BRET);
Guingamp, Notre-Dame des Grâces (BRET);
Havre (L'), Notre-Dame (NOR H); Hermonville
(CHAM); Houdan (ILE FR); Journet (oc) (POIT);
Labbeville (ILE FR); Laon, St Martin (oc) (PIC);
Lapalisse (AUVN); Lavans-les-Dole (FRAN); Le
Faouët (Brit); Leoncel (oc) (RHON); Les Hauts-
de-Clée (LOR); Lévignac (PYR); Lévis-St-Nom
(ILE FR); Ligescourt (PIC); Lille, Chapelle du
Palais Rihour (NOR H); L'Isle-Adam (ILE FR);
Loches, St-Ours (CENT); Lodève (LAN); Loges
(Les) (NOR H); Longpont-sur-Orge (ILE FR);
Longuyon, Ste Agathe (oc) (LOR); Lons-le-
Saunier (FRAN); Luzarches (ILE FR); Magné
(POIT); Magny-en-Vexin, Notre-Dame (ILE FR);
Mailly-Maillet (PIC); Malestroit (BRET);
Mamers (oc) (LOIR); Mareuil-en-Dole (PIC);
Mareuil (AQUI); Marmoutier (ALSC);
Megemont (AUVN); Melun, Notre-Dame (ILE
FR); Melun, St Aspais (ILE FR); Mériel, Abbe du
Val (r) (ILE FR); Miradoux (PYR); Monpazier
(AQUI); Montolieu, St André (LAN); Montreuil-
aux-Lions (PIC); Montreuil-sur-Mer (NOR H);
Mortemer (oc) (NOR H); Mothe-St-Héray (La)
(POIT); Moutier (LIM); Mouy (PIC); Neuwiller,
SS Pierre & Paul (ALSC); Neuwiller, St Adelph
(ALSC); Noyon (PIC); Orchamps (FRAN); Orgeval
(ILE FR); Pagny-le-Château (BURG); Paris,
St Merri (ILE FR); Pencran (BRET); Pierrefonds,
St Sulpice (PIC); Plume (La) (PYR); Pluneret,
Ste Anne (BRET); Poissy-la-Fôret (ILE FR);
Pontant (AQUI); Puiseaux (CENT); Quimper,
Cathedral (BRET); Rabastens (PYR); Réole (La),
St Pierre Priorale (AQUI); Rieux (oc) (PIC);
Romieu, La (AQUI); Ronquerolles (ILE FR); Rots
(NOR B); Rue (PIC); Saint-Brieuc, Cathedral
(BRET); Saint-Contest (NOR B); Saint-Jean-de-
Sorde (LAN); Saint-Jean-le-Blanc (NOR B);
Saint-Macaire (AQUI); Saint-Manvieu-Norrey-
en-Bessin (NOR B); Saint-Nolff, Chapelle Ste
Anne (BRET); Saint-Omer, Cathedral (NOR H);
Saint-Paul-de-Maxence (PIC); Saint-Rémi-
Blanzy (PIC); Saint-Sever, Couvent des
Jacobins (POIT); Saint-Suliac (BRET); Sainteney
(NOR B); Santeuil, St Pierre (ILE FR); Sauviat, St
Michel (oc) (AUVN); Savigny (FRAN); Sénanque
(oc) (PROV); Silvacane (oc) (PROV); Simorre
(PYR); Songy (CHAM); Taverny, Notre-Dame (ILE
FR); Terrasson (AQUI); Thiéville (NOR B); Toulon
(PROV); Toulouse, Musee des Augustins (PYR);
Toulouse, Les Jacobins (PYR); Tréguier (BRET);
Trie-Château (PIC); Uzeste (AQUI); Varangéville
(LOR); Vémars (ILE FR); Ver-sur-Launette (oc)
(PIC); Verneuil-sur-Avre (NOR H); Vienne, St
Maurice (RHON); Vieux (PYR); Viroflay (ILE FR);
Vivier-en-Brie (Le) (r) (ILE FR).

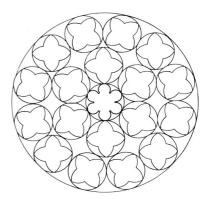
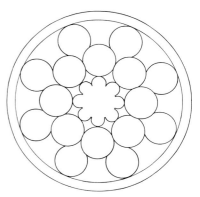

FROM TOP TO BOTTOM Arthonnay; Chars; Cognac;
Saint-Pol-de-Leon; Strasbourg Cathedral

FROM TOP TO BOTTOM Ebrach, Germany; Milan Cathedral, Italy; Trapani, Italy; Santes Creus, Spain; Exeter Cathedral, United Kingdom

GERMANY

Abbreviations: Brandenburg (BRAND), Bayern (BAY), Baden-Würtemberg (B-W), Hessen (HESS), Niedersachsen (NIE), Nordrhein-Westfalen (N-W), Rheinland-Pfalz (R-P), Schleswig-Holstein (S-H), Sachsen (SACH), Sachsen-Anhalt (SACH AN), Thüringen (THÜR)

AACHEN, KORNELIMÜNSTER (N-W): C20
AACHEN, SUERMONDT-LUDWIG-
  MUSEUM (N-W): C20
AUGSBURG, ST ANNA (BAY): C18/19
96 BRANDENBURG,
  FRONLEICHNAMSKAPELLE (BRAND):
  C14/15 (blind)
97 CHORIN, ABBEY (BRAND): C14 (blind)
98 EBRACH, ABBEY (BAY): N,S,E,W tr all
  C13/14 R
ERFURT, ST SEVERUS (THÜR):
  S/W tr C13/14
FREIBURG-IM-BREISGAU, CATHEDRAL
  (B-W): N C13; SW tr C14
GELNHAUSEN, ST MARY (HESS): S tr C13
99 LIMBURG, CATHEDRAL (HESS):
  W tr C13 gl Mod
MEISSEN, CATHEDRAL (SACH): E tr C16
100 MINDEN, CATHEDRAL (N-W):
  N tr C13/19, N + S nave tr C13/14
101 NUREMBERG, ST LORENZ (BAY): W tr
  C13/14
102 OPPENHEIM, ST KATHERINE (R-P):
  S nave tr C14 gl C14 + C19
103 OTTERBERG, ABBEY CHURCH (R-P):
  W tr C13
PADERBORN, CATHEDRAL (N-W):
  SW tr C12 Occ & C13
104 PRENZLAU, MARIENKIRCHE (BRAND):
  C14 bl
RATZEBURG, CATHEDRAL (S-H): C20
REGENSBURG, ST ULRICH: S tr C13, W
  Oc C14
REMSCHEID, ST JOSEPH (N-W): C20
SALEM, ABBEY: N tr C13
SANKT THOMAS AN DER KYLL (R-P):
  N & W nave tr C13/14
SCHWÄBISCH-GMÜND, HEILIG-KREUZ-
  MÜNSTER: W tr C14
SINZIG (R-P): N nave tr C13/14?
SPEYER, CATHEDRAL (R-P): W C19
105 TANGERMÜNDE, TOWN HALL (SACH AN):
  C15 blind
TRIER, CATHEDRAL (R-P): tr C13 rosettes
106 WORMS, CATHEDRAL (R-P): W tr C13

HUNGARY

BELAPATFALVA: tr ?C14
BUDAPEST, ST MATTHIAS: W tr C13
LEBENY, ABBEY: tr C13 Oc
ZSAMBEK, PRAEMONSTRATENSIAN:
  W tr ?C12 Oc

ITALY

Abbreviations: Abruzzo & Molise (ABRUZ); Apulia (APUL); Calabria & Basilicata (CALAB); Campania (CAMP); Emilia-Romagna (EMIL); Friuli-Venezia Giulia (FRIU); Liguria (LIG); Lombardy and the Lakes (LOMB); Marche (MARC); Piemonte & Valle d'Aosta (PIEM); Rome & Lazio (ROME); Sardinia (SARD); Sicily (SIC); Trentino-Alto Adige (TRENT); Tuscany (TUSC); Umbria (UMB); Venice & the Veneto (VEN)

n.b. All windows are on the west façade and are tracery only unless stated otherwise.

107 ACQUAVIVA, CATHEDRAL (APUL): C16
ALATRI, S. MARIA MAGGIORE (ROME): ?C13
108 ALTAMURA, CATHEDRAL (APUL): C14
ANCONA, CATHEDRAL (MARC): C12/13 Oc
ARDAULI, NOSTRA SIGNORA DI
  BUONCAMMINO (SARD): ?C15
109 ASSISI, S. RUFINO (UMB): tr C13
ASSISI, S. CHIARA (UMB): tr C13, gl C20
ASSISI, S. FRANCESCO (UMB): tr C13, gl
  C20
ASSISI, S. PIETRO (UMB): tr C13
ATRI, CATHEDRAL (ABRUZ): ?C14
BARI, CATHEDRAL (APUL): S ?C16
110 BITETTO, CATHEDRAL (APUL): C14
111 BITONTO, CATHEDRAL (APUL): C13
BOLOGNA, S. MARIA DEI SERVI (EMIL): C13
112 BOVARA, ABBEY OF S. PIETRO (UMB):
  C12/13
CAMPI, S. SALVATORI (UMB): C14/5
113 CARRARA, CATHEDRAL (TUSC): C14
CASTEL RITALDI, CAMPANILE (UMB):
  C12 Oc
CASTELSARDO, S. MARIA IN TERGU
  (SARD): C13 Oc
CEFALU, CATHEDRAL (SIC): C12 Oc
114 CERRETO DI SPOLETO, S. MARIA DI
  PONTE (UMB): C12/13
CHIARAVALLE DEL CHIENTI, ABBEY
  (MARC): C12/13
CHIARAVALLE DELLA COLOMBA, ABBEY
  (EMIL): C12/13
CHIARAVALLE MILANESE, ABBEY (LOMB):
  C12 Oc
COMO, CATHEDRAL (LOMB): W C14/15
CORIGLIANO, S. NICCOLO (APUL): C16
115 CREMA, CATHEDRAL (LOMB): C13/14
116 CREMONA, CATHEDRAL (LOMB):
  N, S & W C13
CREMONA, S. MICHELE (LOMB): C12/13
117 FERMO, CATHEDRAL (MARC): C14
118 FLORENCE, CATHEDRAL (TUSC):
  Dome (x 7) C15 Oc + gl
FLORENCE, S. CROCE (TUSC): C15 Oc
FLORENCE, S. MARIA NOVELLA (TUSC):
  C14 Oc
FOLIGNO, CATHEDRAL (UMB): S C13 +
  C19
119 FOSSANOVA, ABBEY (ROME): W C13,
  E C12 Oc
GENOA, CATHEDRAL (LIG): C13
GIOVIANAZZO, CATHEDRAL (APUL): C13
GRAVINA, CATHEDRAL (APUL): C17
120 GRAVINA, MADONNA DELLE GRAZIE
  (APUL): C17
GROSSETO, CATHEDRAL (TUSC):
  C13/16/C19
GUALDO TADINO, S. BENEDETTO (UMB):
  C13/19
LANCIANO, S. MARIA MAGGIORE (ABRUZ):
  S/W tr C13
L'AQUILA, S. MARIA DI COLLEMAGGIO
  (ABRUZ) (3); C13
LAVAGNA, S. SALVATORE (LIG): C13
LECCE, S. CROCE (APUL): C16 Oc
LUCCA, S. LEONARDO E TREPONZIO
  (TUSC): (one-piece tympanum rose) C12
LUGNANO IN TEVERINA, S. MARIA
  ASSUNTA (UMB): C13/14
MARTIS, S. PANTALEONE (SARD): C14
121 MATERA, CATHEDRAL (CALAB): C13
MATERA, S. MARIA DELLA PALOMBA
  (CALAB): C13/17?
122 MILAN, CATHEDRAL (LOMB): E apse tr C15,
  gl Mod, W C16
MILAN, S. MARCO (LOMB): C14/19
MILAN, S. EUFEMIA (LOMB): C19
123 MODENA, CATHEDRAL (EMIL): C12/13
MONTALCINO, S. AGOSTINO (TUSC): C14
124 MONTELEONE SABINO, S. VITTORIA
  (ROME): C12
MONZA, CATHEDRAL (LOMB):
  tr C14, gl C19
125 MONZA, S. MARIA IN STRADA (LOMB): C14
NICOSIA, S. BENEDETTO (SIC): ?C14
NUGHEDU, S. VITTORIA (SARD): ?C14
126 ORVIETO, CATHEDRAL (UMB):
  tr C14, gl Mod
127 OSTUNI, CATHEDRAL (APUL): C15
128 OTRANTO, CATHEDRAL (APUL): C14
PADUA, S. ANTONIO (VEN): N C13/14;
  W C13
129 PALERMO, CONVENT OF S. AGOSTINO
  (SIC): C14
130 PAVIA, S. MARIA DEL CARMINE (LOMB):
  C14/15
PERUGIA, ABBEY OF S. MARIA DI
  VALDEPONTE (UMB): C13/14
PERUGIA, S. COSTANZO (UMB): C12/19
PIACENZA, PALAZZO DEL COMMUNE
  (EMIL): C13/14
PIACENZA, CATHEDRAL (EMIL): C13/14
PIEDIVALLE, ABBEY OF S. EUTIZIO (UMB):
  C13
131 POMPOSA, ABBEY (EMIL): C11
ROBBIO, S. MICHELE (LOMB): W Oc C15
132 RUVO, CATHEDRAL (APUL): C13
SAN GALGANO, ABBEY (TUSC): C13 r
SAN GIMIGNANO, S. IACOPO (TUSC):
  C12/13
SAN GIOVANNI IN MONTE (VEN):
  gl C16 Oc
SANTA MARIA DEL PATIR (CALAB): C13 Oc
133 SIENA, CATHEDRAL (TUSC): E gl C13;
  W gl C16 Oc
SORGONO, S. MAURO (SARD): C16
SPELLO, S. CLAUDIO (UMB): C12/13
134 SPOLETO, CATHEDRAL (UMB): C13
SPOLETO, S. PIETRO (UMB): C13
SPOLETO, S. FELICE DI NARCO (UMB):
  C13
SPOLETO, VALLO DI NERA, S. MARIA
  (UMB): C13
135 SYRACUSE, S. GIOVANNI (SIC): C16 (r)
TARQUINIA, ANNUNZIATA (ROME): C13
TARQUINIA, S. FRANCESCO (ROME):
  C13/14
TARQUINIA, S. GIOVANNI (ROME): C13
TARQUINIA, S. MARIA DI CASTELLO
  (ROME): S C13
TERMOLI, CATHEDRAL (ABRUZ): C12 Oc
136 TODI, CATHEDRAL (UMB): tr C14, gl C20
137 TRANI, CATHEDRAL (APUL): S C13, W C19
138 TRAPANI, ANNUNZIATA (SIC): C14
TRAPANI, S. AGOSTINO (SIC): C13/14
139 TRENTO, CATHEDRAL (TRENT):
  N & W C13
140 TRIESTE, CATHEDRAL (VEN): C13
141 TROIA, CATHEDRAL (APUL): C12/13
142 TUSCANIA, S. PIETRO (ROME): C13
TUSCANIA, S. MARIA MAGGIORE (ROME):
  C13
UZZANO, SS IACOPO E MARTINO (TUSC):
  C12 Oc
VALVISCIOLO, ABBEY (ROME): C13
143 VERCELLI, S. ANDREA (PIEM): E, S W C13
144 VERONA, S. ZENO MAGGIORE (VEN): C13
VOLTERRA, CATHEDRAL (TUSC): C13 Oc
ZURI, S. PIETRO (SARD): E (2) C14

Rose windows, wheels or oculi can also be seen at: Anagni; Ardola; Arezzo, Oratorio dei SS Laurentino e Pergentino; Arezzo, Pieve; Assisi, S. Maria Maggiore; Bazzano, S. Giusto; Bellano, SS Nazaro & Celso, Bominaco, S. Pellegrino; Borutta; Bulzi; Brescia, S. Francesco, S. Agostino; Caravaggio, Cathedral; Casamari, Castiglione Olone, Coll.; Abbey, Cecima; Civita Castellana; Codrongianus, SS Trinita di Saccargia; Erice, Matrice dell'Assunta; Escalaplano; Falleri; Galatina, S. Caterina;

Gubbio, Cathedral; Gubbio, S. Francesco; Lodi, S. Francesco, Cathedral; Lodi (Vecc), S. Bassiano; Lucca, S. Michele; Lucca, S. Maria del Giudice, Pieve Nuova; Mantua, S. Francesco; Massa Marittima; Matera, Palazzo del Licco; Matera, S. Giovanni; Matera, S. Giovanni Battista; Milan, S. Colso; Milan, S. Cristoforo; Milan, S. Maria del Grazia; Minervino, Cathedral; Morimondo, Abbey; Mortara, S. Lorenzo; Nicosia, Cathedral; Norcia, Cathedral; S. Benetto; Norcia, S. Francesco; Orvieto, Palazzo del Capitano del Popolo; Orvinio (Sabino), S. Maria del Piano; Pontecurone, S. Maria Assunta; Pozzuoli Martesana, S. Francesco; Sannazzaro Sesia; Vigevano, S. Francesco

LUXEMBOURG

ECHTERNACH, ST WILLIBRORD: W tr ?C14

NORWAY

[145] TRONDHEIM, CATHEDRAL: W tr C14

POLAND

KOLBACZ: W pignon tr C13/14 bl
SULÉJOW: W tr ?C13; S C13/20
KOPRZYWNICA: W tr C13 r
WACHOCK: tr S & E tr C14

PORTUGAL

ALCOBAÇA, ABBEY: W ?C17/18
ALCOCHETE, IG. MATRIZ: W ?C16
[146] ALGOSINHO, IG. MATRIZ: ?C13
[147] BATALHA, S. MARIA MONASTRY
BELEM, JERONIMO MONASTERY: W C16
CEDOFEITA: E Oc C13
EVORA, CATHEDRAL: S ?C15
FONTE ARCADA, IG. MATRIZ: S ?C13
GUIMARAES, S. DOMINGOS: W C18
LECA DO BAILO, MONASTERY: W ?C16
LISBON, CATHEDRAL: W
LOURINHA, MATRIZ ANTIGA: W
MATOSINHOS, BOM JESUS: W C16/20
[148] PACO DE SOUSA, MONASTERY OF S. SALVADOR
PALMELA, CONVENT: W Oc C12/13
POMBEIRO DE RIBAVIZELA, IG DO MOST. BENEDITO: W ?C13
PONTE DE LIMA, IG. MATRIZ: W ?C16
PORTO, S. FRANCISCO: W? C18
PORTO, CATHEDRAL: W ?C18
[149] SANTAREM, IG. DA GRACA: C15/16
TAROUCA, S. JOÃO: ?C14
[150] TOMAR, NR. SR. DO CLIVAL: W ?C13/14
VIANA DE CASTELO, CATHEDRAL:W?C18

Rose windows can also be seen at: Barcelas; Bravaes; Caminha; Cete; Fizurara; Montemor-o-Velho; Outeiro; Paderne; Pitoes; Reriz; Rates; São Salvador de Anciaces; São Sebastiao, Terceira, Azores; São João de Tarouca, Convent; Vila do Conde, Mosterio de Santa Clara; Vilas de Frades, Mosterio dos Loios

SPAIN

Abbreviations: Andalucia (AND); Aragon (ARA); Asturias (AST); Balearic Islands (BAL); Castille (CAST); Catalonia (CAT); Extremadura (EXTR); Galicia (GAL); Navarra (NAV); Valencia (VAL)

[151] ARMENTEIRA, MONASTERY (GAL): W tr ?C13/14 gl C20
[152] BARCELONA, SAGRADA FAMILIA (CAT): C20, gl Cont
BARCELONA, SANTA MARIA DEL MAR (CAT): W C15

BARCELONA, SANTA MARIA DE PEDRALBES (CAT): C14
BARCELONA, SANTA MARIA DEL PI (CAT): W C14
[153] BETANZOS, SAN FRANCISCO (GAL): S & E tr C14/15
BETANZOS, SANTA MARIA DEL AZOGUE (GAL): W tr C14
BREAMO (GAL): E & W tr C12
BURGOS, MONASTERIO DE LAS HUELGAS (CAST): N/W tr
[154] BURGOS, CATHEDRAL (CAST): S C13; W C19
BURGOS, SAN ESTEBAN (CAST): W C13/14
CAMBRE, SANTA MARIA (GAL): W tr C12/13
CIUDAD RODRIGO, CATHEDRAL (CAST): W tr C14
CIUTADELLA, CATHEDRAL (BAL): W tr C14/15
[155] CORDOBA, SAN MIGUEL (AND): W tr C13/14
CORDOBA, SAN PABLO EL REAL (AND): W tr C14/15
CORDOBA, SAN FRANCISCO (AND): W tr C13
CORUÑA (A), SANTA MARIA (GAL): E tr C13
COVET, SANTA MARIA (CAT): W tr C12/13
EL PLA DE SANTA MARIA, SANT RAMON (CAT): N tr C13
[156] GIRONA , CATHEDRAL (CAT): W gl C16 and C17
GIRONA, SANT DOMENECH (CAT): W tr C14
GIRONA, SANT PERE DE GALLIGANTS (CAT):
GIRONA, SANT FELIU (CAT):
GUADALUPE, MONASTERY (EXT): W C17/18
HUERTA, STA MARIA (CAST): S & W tr C13
[157] HUESCA, SAN PEDRO DE SIRESA (ARA): N, S, E, W in choir
JEREZ DE LA FRONTERA, LA CARTUJA (AND): W C15/6
JUNQUERA DE AMBIA (GAL): E tr ?C12/13
[158] LEON, CATHEDRAL (CAST): W C13; N C13/15; S C13/19
LEON, MONASTERIO DE SAN MARCOS (CAST): W C12 Occ; tr C18
LLEIDA, OLD CATHEDRAL (CAT): W tr C13; (N & S C19/20 R)
[159] MEIRA, SANTA MARIA (GAL): W tr C13
MEZONZO, SANTA MARIA (GAL): E tr C12/13
MONDONEDO, CATHEDRAL (GAL): W tr C13/14 gl C19
MORELLA, SANTA MARIA (VAL): tr ?C14
[160] NOIA, SAN MARTIN (GAL): W tr C14
OLITE, SAN PEDRO (NAV): W/N tr C14
OLIVA (LA), SANTA MARIA (AST): W tr ?C12/13
OVIEDO, CATHEDRAL (AST): W, N & S tr C16
[161] OVIEDO, SAN MIGUEL DE LILLO (AST): tr C9
[162] PALMA DE MALLORCA, CATHEDRAL (BAL): E tr all C14; W C16/17; gl all C20
PALMA DE MALLORCA, SANT FRANCESC (BAL): W tr C17/18
PAMPLONA, CATHEDRAL (NAV): S tr C15
PORTOMARIN, SAN NICOLAS (GAL): W tr C13
[163] PRIESCA, SAN SALVADOR (AST): tr C10
PUIG, SANTA MARIA (VAL): C13
[164] SAN ESTEBAN DE RIBAS DE MINO (GAL): W tr C13
SAN PEDRO DE LA MEZQUITA (GAL): W ?C12/13

[165] SANT CUGAT DEL VALLES, SANT CUGAT (CAT): W tr C14 gl Mod
SANTA MARINA DE AGUAS SANTAS (GAL): E tr C13/19
[166] SANTES CREUS, MONASTERY (CAT): E tr C13
[167] SEVILLE, CATHEDRAL (AND): N, S & W tr and gl C16
SIGÜENZA, CATHEDRAL (CAST): W C15/16
SORIA, SANTO DOMINGO (CAST): W tr C12/13
[168] TARRAGONA, CATHEDRAL (CAT): W C14
[169] TOLEDO, CATHEDRAL (CAST): N C14, W C15, S C16
TORO, SANTA MARIA LA MAYOR (CAST): E & S tr C13
TRUJILLO, SANTA MARIA (EXTR): tr C13
[170] VALENCIA, CATHEDRAL (VAL): W C14/19 gl Mod
VALL DE ROURES (CAT): tr C14/15
[171] VALLADOLID, SAN PABLO (CAST): W tr C15
VILLAFRANCA DE LOS BARROS, SANTA MARIA (EXTR): W tr ?C13/17

Rose windows can also be seen at: Agramunt, Santa Maria (CAT); Barbastro, (); Barcelona, Sant Pau del Camp (CAT) (oc); Cuenca, Cathedral (CAST); Huesca, Cathedral (ARA); Murcia, Cathedral (MUR); Piedra, Nuestra Señora (ARA) (r); Poblet, Monasterio (CAT) (oc); San Miguel de la Escalada (CAST) (oc); San Pedro de Dozón (GAL); Santa Maria del Huerta (VAL); Seu d'Urgell, Cathedral (CAT) (oc); Valbuena (CAST) (oc); Valdedios, Santa Maria (AST) (oc); Veruela, Monastery (CAST); Vic, Cathedral (CAT)

SWEDEN

NYDALA, CATHEDRAL: tr C13
[172] UPPSALA, CATHEDRAL: N,S & W tr C14

SWITZERLAND

[173] BASLE, CATHEDRAL: S tr C12/19
BERNE, ST VINCENT: W porch tympanum tr C15 bl
FRIBOURG, CATHEDRAL: W tr C15
[174] LAUSANNE, CATHEDRAL: S C13
NEUCHATEL, COLLEGIALE: W tr C13
POSIEUX, HAUTERIVE ABBEY: W tr C13
VALANGIN, COLLEGIALE: W tr C16
SION, ST THEODULE: tr C15

UNITED KINGDOM

Abbreviations: Angus (ANG); Avon (AVON); Borders (BORD); Cambridge (CAM); Cheshire (CHES); Corwall (CORN); Denbighshire (DENB); Devon (DEV); Dorset (DST); Dumfrieshire (DUMFS); Durham (DURH); Essex (ESSEX); Gloucestershire (GLOS); Hertfordshire (HERTS); Kent (KENT); Lincolnshire (LINCS); Lothians, E, N (LOTH); Moray (MRY); Northhamptonshire (NHNT); Norfolk (NORF); Orkney (ORK); Oxfordshire (OXON); Suffolk (SFK); Staffordshire (STAFFS); Yorkshire (YORKS); Warwickshire (WARW); Wiltshire (WILTS)

[175] BARFRESTON, ST NICHOLAS (KENT): W tr C12
[176] BEVERLEY, MINSTER (YORKS): N & S tr C14
[177] BOYTON, SS COSMAS & DAMIEN (WILTS): tr C14 gl C19
[178] BRISTOL, ST JAMES (AVON): W C12
[179] BYLAND, ABBEY (YORKS): C13 (r)
[180] CANTERBURY, CATHEDRAL (KENT): N C12; S C19
[181] CHELTENHAM, ST MARY (GLOS): E/N tr C14, gl C19

[182] CHESTER, CATHEDRAL (CHES): C21
[183] DURHAM, CATHEDRAL (DURH): E tr C13/C16, gl C19
[184] ELGIN, ABBEY (MRY): C13 (r)
[185] EXETER, CATHEDRAL (DEV): W tr C15, gl C19
[186] FOUNTAINS, ABBEY (YORKS): C12 r
IFFLEY, ST MARY (OXON): W C19 (Oc)
KINGSTON, ST JAMES (DST): W C19
LEAMINGTON SPA, ST PETER (WARW): N & S C19
[187] LINCOLN, CATHEDRAL (LINCS): N C13, S C14
[188] LONDON, WINCHESTER PALACE: C15 r
LONDON, ST KATHERINE CREE: E C17
LONDON, ST LUKE CAVERSHAM RD: C19
LONDON, WESTMINSTER ABBEY: N C18; S tr C13/19 gl C19
MELROSE, ABBEY (BORD): C13 (r)
[189] MINCHINHAMPTON, HOLY TRINITY (GLOS): tr C14 gl C19
PATRIXBOURNE, ST MARY (KENT): tr C13
[190] PETERBOROUGH CATHEDRAL (NHNT): C13
ROSSLYN CHAPEL (LOTH): E tr C15
[191] SELSLEY, ALL SAINTS (GLOS): C19
[192] ST ALBANS, CATHEDRAL (HERTS): tr C19, gl C20
SWEETHEART, ABBEY (DUMF): C13 (r)
TRURO, CATHEDRAL (CORN): N & S C19
[193] WALTHAM, ABBEY (ESSEX): C19
WILTON, ST MARY (WILTS): tr C19, gl C17
[194] YORK, MINSTER (YORKS): S tr C13, gl C15/16

Rose windows can also be seen at : Arbroath Abbey (ANG); Bury St Edmunds Cathedral; Cley-next-the-Sea (NHNT); Coningsby (LINCS); Dryburgh Abbey (BORD); Hunstanton (CAM); Leek (STAFFS); London, Southwark, St George; London, St Pancras Old Church; Oxford, Christchurch Cathedral (OXON); Oxford, Merton College Chapel (OXON); Temple Balsall (WARW); Terrington, St John (YORKS); St Magnus Cathedral (ORK); Valle Crucis (DENB)

UNITED STATES

BOSTON, ISABELLA STEWART GARDNER MUSEUM: ?C15
MALDEN (MASS), FIRST BAPTIST CHURCH: C20
NEW YORK, CENTRAL SYNAGOGUE: C20
NEW YORK, CHURCH OF THE BLESSED SACRAMENT: C20
NEW YORK, ST JOHN THE DIVINE: C20
NEW YORK, ST PATRICK: C20
NEW YORK, ST THOMAS: C20
NORTH ADAMS, ST JOHN'S EPISCOPAL CHURCH: C20
PETERBOROUGH (NEW HAMPSHIRE), ALL SAINTS: C20
POCANTICO HILLS, UNION CHURCH: C20 (by Henri Matisse)
SAN FRANCISCO, GRACE CATHEDRAL: C20
SEATTLE, ST JOSEPH: C20
WASHINGTON, D.C., CATHEDRAL: N, W, S C20

KEY ROSE WINDOWS IN EUROPE

145

172

184

183

186
179
194 176

182

187
190

181
189
178 191
177
192 193
188
185
180
175

104
97

105
96

100

99
102
103 106

1 2
6 78
26 7 63

18
20 12
10
45

. Paris
95

80
13 49
27 86
81
23

42
8
9
75 see box opposite 47

71
57 15

98

5

101

24 40
68

174

14

11

139
125
143 122 115 144
130 116

140

131

123

30

3

87 65 70 84
113
4
19 118
47
133
136 109
157 112 117
134 114

156
165 142 126
168 166 152 124

119

141
137
132 111
120 107 110
108 127
121 128

153
160
151 164 159 163
161
158

148 146 171

147
150
149

169

170
162

138 129

167 155

135

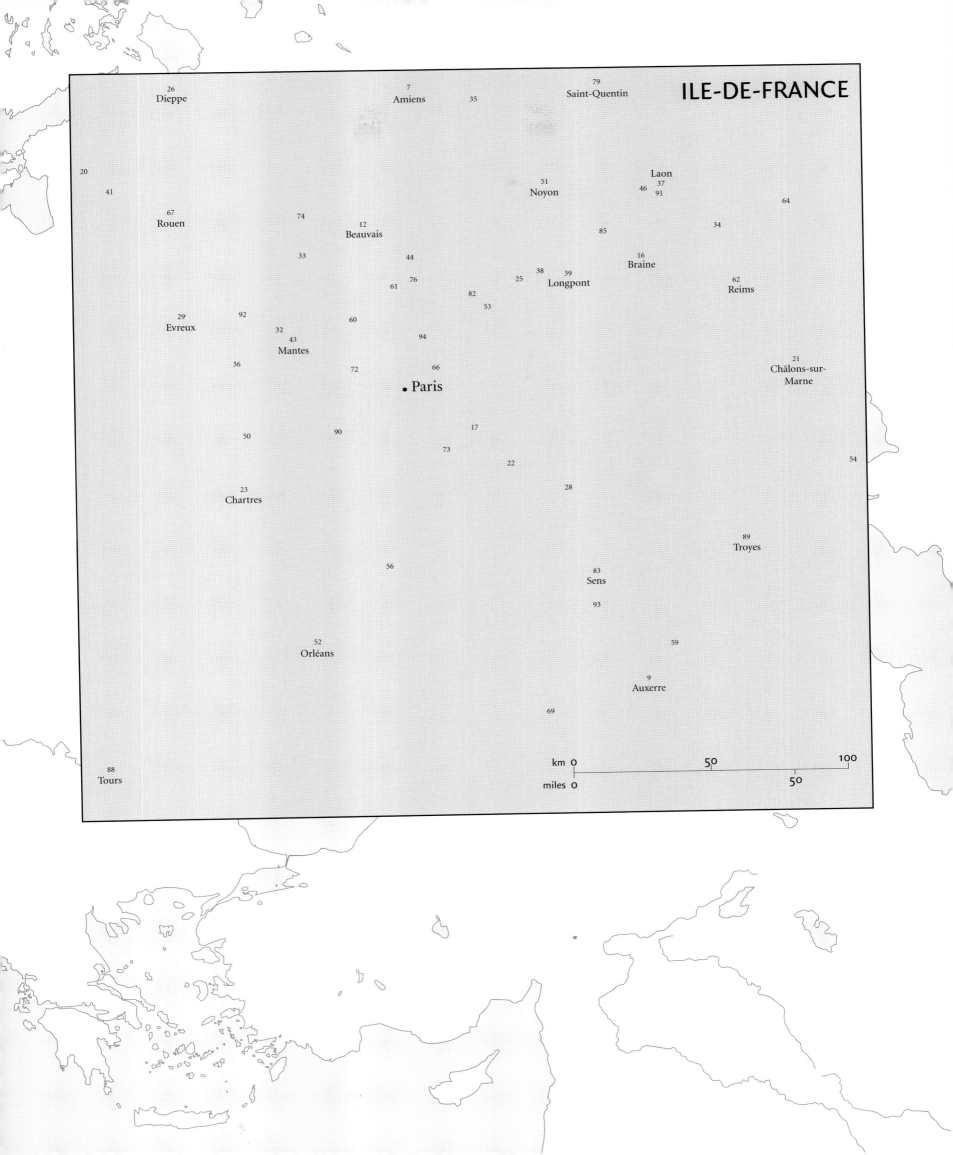

ILE-DE-FRANCE

26 Dieppe

7 Amiens

35

79 Saint-Quentin

20

41

67 Rouen

74

51 Noyon

Laon
46 37 91

64

12 Beauvais

85

34

33

44

16 Braine

76

25 38 39 Longpont

62 Reims

61

82

53

29 Evreux

92

60

32 43 Mantes

94

36

72

66

21 Châlons-sur-Marne

• Paris

17

50

90

73

22

54

23 Chartres

28

89 Troyes

56

83 Sens

93

52 Orléans

59

9 Auxerre

69

88 Tours

km 0   50   100

miles 0   50

NOTES

See Bibliography opposite for full bibliographic references.

INTRODUCTION pp. 13–39

1 Aubert et al., 1959, p. 18
2 O. Latry, sleeve notes to *The Organ Music of Olivier Messiaen*, CD, 2001
3 Blomme, 1994, p. 52, quotes the 19th-century architect Mérindol who refers to the architect François le Duc who in 1687 referred to a fire-damaged window as 'la rose'
4 Dow, 1958, cites C. Enlart, *Manuel d'Archéologie Française depuis les temps mérovingiens jusqu'à la Renaissance*, Paris, 1902, p. 310
5 Jean de Landun, *Traité de Louanges de Paris*. See Aubert et al., 1959, p. 18
6 From Hugh of St Victor's *Didascalicon*. Quoted in Rudolph, 1990
7 'Two of his modes are external and corporeal, two are internal and spiritual,' says Madeleine Caviness (Caviness, 1983). The first is the opening the eyes to the exterior and visible world, so that we can see 'the figures and colours of visible things'. The second is the 'mystical significance' of the outward appearance or physical action, for example, the allegorical level of scripture. The third mode is a higher one, belonging to the internalized spiritual level. It consists in 'the eyes of the heart' discovering the 'truth of hidden things', but this is still to be achieved 'by means of forms and figures and the similitude of things'. The fourth is entirely spiritual or visionary involving the 'ascent of the spirit to celestial contemplation without the intermediary of visible forms.' Dante also said that his Divine Comedy could be understood at four levels of appreciation: the literal, allegorical, moral and anagogical (mystical).
8 The Metrical Life of St Hugh, Bishop of Lincoln, was written between 1220 and 1235 by either another Bishop Hugh (of Wells) or Master John of Leicester.
9 Quoted in U. Eco, *Art and Beauty in the Middle Ages*, New Haven, 1986
10 Quoted by Panofsky, 1970, p. 162
11 Shrine of Wisdom, 1923
12 See also Van de Meulen, 1966
13 Quoted in Von Simson, 1962, p. 51
14 The four elements were Earth, Fire, Air and Water, and the four humours were Sanguine, Phlegmatic, Cholic, Melancholy; see Caviness, 1983, p. 107
15 Other tombs with pignon roses can be seen at Châlons-sur-Marne Cathedral.
16 See Gaborit-Chopin (ed.), et al., 1996, for a definitive account of this treasure.
17 Emile Mâle's books are still, despite (or perhaps because of) their age, the most empathetic readings of medieval iconography.

CHAPTER 1: FROM DARKNESS TO LIGHT
pp. 41–87

1 Henwood-Reverdot, 1982
2 Bony, 1983, pp. 234–5, and Panofsky, 1951, p. 70

3 As can be seen from the photograph published in Butler's *Early Churches in Syria*, 1929, p. 150
4 Dow, 1958, pp. 249–50
5 Conant, 1974, p. 43ff.
6 As, for example, at Lecce in Apulia, Italy, and Mailly Maillet, Piccadie, France.
7 However, the fact that both of the figures are ascending, and the presence of two crouching people below (reminiscent of the Atlantes beneath some Italian roses), suggests it may be something other than a straightforward Wheel of Fortune
8 A rose on the south side of Orvietto Cathedral, for example, is filled with attractive patterned sheets of alabaster.
9 There are a number of other examples in the National Museum in Damascus. See Franz, 1956, pp. 7–9
10 Franz, 1956–7, p. 266
11 Fine Chi-Rho symbols can be seen in the tympanums of churches in the French and Spanish Pyrenees, notably at San Pedro el Viejo, Huesca, the cathedral in Jaca, at Santa Cruz de la Seros, Huesca, and the church of St Engrace, Plaisance.
12 For example, St Mark's, Venice; Palatine Chapel, Palermo; Kariye church (now a museum), Istanbul
13 There is usually a space between the roof and the vaults.
14 There are also two fine wheel/rose windows at Beverley, and remains at Kirkham Abbey and Arbroath Abbey, while at Ripon Minster there is evidence that there was a round window very early on, probably in the 1150s. Ripon was 'the first non-Cistercian building in the region to reflect the new mode (of architecture),' according to Hearn. It was influenced by Kirkstall, possibly via Roche Abbey (see Hearn, 1983).
15 Others can be seen in the Raymond Pitcairn Collection, Bryn Athyn, Pennsylvania. See Hayward and Cahn, 1982, pp. 125–29
16 See Caviness, 1990
17 See Lillich, 2001
18 Laon, with its cathedral and the church of St Vincent, influenced much ecclesiastical design in north France thereafter. See Héliot, 1972
19 See Cowen, 1979, pp. 122–3, and James, 1973
20 The Evangelists on the shoulders of the Prophets echoes the words of John of Salisbury quoting Bernard of Chartres, a Chancellor of the School of Chartres early in the 12th century: 'We are as dwarfs mounted on the shoulders of giants, so that we can see more and further than they; yet not by virtue of the keenness of our eyesight, nor through the tallness of our stature, but because we are raised and borne aloft upon that giant mass.' See R. L. Poole, *Illustrations of Medieval Thought and Learning*, New York, 1962, p. 102
21 The scenes in the lancets below the large figures contain Old Testament incidents that relate by contrasting virtues with vices: thus Melchisedek (twice anointed as priest and king) represents Faith, while Nebuchadnezzar, below, represents idolatory. King David is Hope, while

King Saul, below, is Despair; Solomon is Wisdom while Jereboam worshipping golden calves is Folly. The High Priest Aaron represents Humility above Pride, portrayed as the Pharaoh.

CHAPTER 2: THE AGE OF THE ROSE
pp. 89–121

1 See Branner, 1965
2 Some of the twelve apostles and the Virgin and Child in the centre are in modern glass, one with a 16th-century head.
3 There are nine 12th-century panels relating to the legend of St Matthew, as well as the Annunciation, the Flight into Egypt, a Healing scene, the Judgment of Solomon and a number of saints, all 13th century and introduced by Gerente under Viollet-le-Duc's guidance in *c.* 1861. The original scheme probably comprised Christ in majesty with twelve apostles, then martyrs and confessors and angels. Twelve out of eighty-five are probably original, but only nine are modern, the rest being medieval substitutions. See Aubert et al., 1959, pp. 52–67, for a complete analysis of this window.
4 At Troyes, the central prop was inserted in the 1460s, some fifty years after the window was finally completed. For the full story of building the north rose at Troyes, see Murray, 1987.
5 An attempt to establish what the north rose at Westminster Abbey originally looked like can be found in Wilson et al., 1986
6 For an illustration of this see Sherlock, 1978, p. 98. See line 132 of 'The Miller's Tale', in *The Canterbury Tales*
7 The rose as it appears in De Son's engraving is almost certainly the replacement rose, installed in *c.* 1550, after the original was destroyed in a storm. Viollet-le-Duc's drawing, however, seems to be an attempt to reconcile this later Flamboyant rose with his idea of what the original Rayonnant rose might have looked like.
8 See Lillich, 2001, p. 161ff. for an account of this evolution and influence of the design of the Reims transept roses.
9 It was restored again in the 19th century, but there is some original glass in the panels. See Lillich, 2003, for an account of this window.
10 12th- and 13th-century wheels with the four Evangelists can also be seen at Castel Ritaldi, Cerreto di Spoleto, Lignano in Teverina, Norcia Cathedral, S. Costanzo, Perugia, Piedivalle, Spoleto Cathedral, and S. Felice di Narco.
11 The transept roses at León hint at Chartres, although the west rose is more reminiscent of the Châlons-sur-Marne north rose.

CHAPTER 3: EXPERIMENTS IN FORM
pp. 123–61

1 Other smaller examples can be seen in England at Winchester Cathedral (north transept pignon) and in France at Réthel, Vailly sur Aisne, and in the

transept windows at Meaux Cathedral.
2 In this north window at Amiens the 'paired lancets' alternate with paired segments that are almost identical to the Rayonnant windows of Notre-Dame – probably a hangover from the design of its predecessor.
3 The double-curve arises from the intersection of two circles (see p. 254), and the ogee arch first appears in England in the late 13th century (the Eleanor Crosses, from *c.* 1291–94), but a few decades earlier in Venice where it probably arrived from the East. The Strasbourg south rose windows show the feature and date from 1230–40.
4 The tracery of the windows in the two La Grange chapels at the western end of the north side of the nave of Amiens Cathedral show an early example of the Flamboyant in France, *c.* 1373.
5 The CVMA volume only deciphers three of the St Stephen panels: the Stoning (below), Disputing with the Jews (right), and being ordained Deacon (above to left). The scenes of John the Baptist are more legible and the cycle begins lower left with the Annunciation to Zachariah, then the birth of St John, the Visitation with Mary, two unidentifiable scenes, Salomé bringing the saint's head to Herod, SS. Elisabeth and Joachim, the Glorification of St John, the dispute with Herod, the Baptism of Christ, John the Baptist, the crowd at the River Jordan, John preaching in the desert. Heads of children and satirical figures can be seen in the smaller windows.
6 The roses at St Antoine, Compiègne, and St Etienne, Fécamp, have a similar design although the tracery thicknesses are different.
7 There is a small spiral rose window at the centre of the west façade of Milan Cathedral (see p. 268), although this may date from the 16th century.
8 The tracery is of a distinctly non-Flamboyant design, reminiscent of the 14th-century experiments seen at Mello or Niederhaslach.
9 The three windows at Toledo Cathedral date from different centuries: the north with plate tracery vaguely reminiscent of Laon north is from the 14th century, the south with radiating petals from the 15th, and the west from the 16th.

CHAPTER 4: DECLINE AND REVIVAL
pp. 163–93

1 Following in the footsteps of Prosper Merimée and Victor Hugo.
2 The window features the Death, Assumption and Coronation of the Virgin Mary, by Duccio (and possibly Cimabue?), 1287–8. This is one of the earliest representations of the Assumption of the Virgin Mary. The other figures are the Four Evangelists and the four patrons of Siena. It was taken down when the choir was extended in 1365 and fitted into the new opening.
3 There is another spectacular late 16th-century rose window in the church of St Nicolas, Troyes.

4 There are some interesting medieval lookalikes dating from the 19th century: for example at Kingston in Dorset there is a simplified structural version of the Lausanne rose window, while at Leamington Spa in Warwickshire the south window is highly reminiscent of the south rose at St Ouen, Rouen, and the north window of the north rose at Sées.

CHAPTER 5: CYCLES OF MEANING
pp. 195–239

1 See *The Metrical Life of St Hugh of Lincoln*, Garton, 1986
2 Mâle, 1958, p. 14
3 See Van de Meulen, 1966, p. 90
4 Krautheimer, 1942, p. 9
5 The quotation '… the nature of God is a sphere …..' is generally ascribed to St Augustine. The *Oxford Book of Quotations* says it comes from Empedocles.
6 See Panofsky, 1955, p. 157ff.
7 Thomas Aquinas quotation from Duby, 1966–7, vol. II, p. 129
8 Cited by Wilkins, 1969, p. 86
9 The ecclesiastical directions of north, south, east and west are all based on the assumption that the altar is placed in the east. In most cases this is true, but considerable deviations are sometimes to be found around this orientation – such as the 47° north of east orientation of Chartres Cathedral which results in the sun appearing in the 'north' rose window on late summer afternoons when it sets near the north-west.
10 Dow, 1958, p. 275
11 A smaller version can be seen on the façade at S. Caterina, Pisa
12 Dow, 1958, p. 275
13 Mâle, 1958, n. 19, p. 96
14 Dow cites Strabo from M. L. W. Laistner, *Thought and Letters in Western Europe, A.D. 500 to 900*, New York, 1931, p. 330
15 Leyerle, 1976, p. 283
16 W. L. Tronzo, 'Moral Hieroglyphics: Chess and Dice in San Savino in Piacenza', *Gesta*, 16/2, 1977, p. 15
17 See Caviness, 1990, for a discussion on this building and its glass.
18 The Evangelist symbols as the tetramorph or 'Sacred Beasts' do not seem to appear in church architecture in France after *c.* 1200, St Gabriel, Tarascon, being the prime example. In Italy, however, there are many examples from the 13th century, though few thereafter.
19 The authoritative works on this window are the two publications by Ellen Beer, 1952 and 1970, and Amsler, 1999.
20 See Wilkins, 1969, for a good discussion on this imagery. Also the rose features in wondrous mystical terms in Dante's *Paradiso*.
21 Lillich, 2001, p. 121, citing Y. Christe, 'The Apocalypse in the monumental art of the Eleventh through Thirteenth centuries' in R. Emmerson and B. McGinn (eds), *The Apocalypse in the Middle Ages*, Ithaca, 1992
22 Lillich, 2001, pp. 117–42

CHAPTER 6: THE GEOMETRY OF LIGHT
pp. 241–63

1 Burkhardt, 1995
2 See Von Simson, 1962, 'Measure and Light' chapter
3 F. Bucher, 'Design in Gothic Architecture: A Preliminary Assessment,' in *The Journal of the Society of Architectural Historians*, 27, 1968, pp. 49–71
4 These drawings can be seen in the Musée de l'Oeuvre de Notre-Dame at Strasbourg.
5 The Reims Labyrinth was removed in 1778. The plaque at the centre was copied a number of times, but the copies contain irregularities. The plaque commemorates Jean d'Orbais, Jean Loup, Bernard de Soissons and Gauchier de Reims. Bernard was said to have 'Ouvra a l'O' and it was one of the copyists, Cocquault, who supposedly saw a figure with compasses, but 'le personnage du centre dont la silhouette est imprecise'. See A. L. Paris, *Le Jubé et le Labyrinth dans la cathédrale de Reims*, 1885, pp. 26–31 for a drawing made before removal.
6 See Colombien, 1973, p. 65, for an illustration of this.
7 Bucher, 1968, p. 53
8 The calculation is mentioned by Stephen Murray in his 1996 publication.
9 A rough survey that I have made of the basic geometry/numerology in 522 in medieval rose windows indicates:

No. of spokes	No. of windows	%
2	2	0.4
3	13	2.5
4	43	8.2
5	11	2.1
6	87	16.6
7	1	0.2
8	110	21.0
9	2	0.4
10	22	4.2
11	3	0.6
12	142	27.1
13	2	0.4
14	5	1.0
15	4	0.8
16	49	9.4
18	6	1.1
19	1	0.2
20	5	1.0
22	2	0.4
24	9	1.7
26	3	0.6
30	1	0.2
33	1	0.2
	522	100.0

10 The 'Dean's Eye' at Lincoln was started in 1220 and completed by 1235. In 1770 there were minor repairs to the tracery and some rearrangement of the medieval glass. In 1855 major masonry and glazing repairs with some new stonework: Ward and Hughes worked on the glass. Recent restoration started in 1990 and will be completed in 2006. The rose is the subject of a forthcoming publication.

BIBLIOGRAPHY

Note: The key sources for information on stained glass windows are the various volumes published by the Corpus Vitrearum Medii Aevi (CVMA), an international stained glass research project. Broken down into regions or monuments, these currently cover France, Germany, Italy, Spain, Great Britain, Portugal, among other places.

Amsler, C., *La rose de la cathédrale de Lausanne: histoire et conservation récente*, Lausanne, 1999
Aubert, M., *Notre-Dame de Paris*, 1929
——, *Les Eglises de France*, 5 vols, 1932
——, *L'Architecture Cistercienne en France*, 2 vols, Paris, 1943
——, et al., *Les Vitraux de Notre-Dame et de la Sainte-Chapelle de Paris* [CVMA volume], Paris, 1959
——, and S. Coubet, *Cathédrales et Abbatiales Romanes de France*, Paris, 1970
Barral i Altet, X., *Vidrieras Medievales de Cataluña*, Barcelona, 2001
Baltrusaitis, J., 'Roses des vents et roses de personnages a l'époque Roman', *Gazette des Beaux Arts*, 1938, pp. 265–76
Barbieri, F., [*Vincenzo Scamozzi*] *Taccuino di Viaggio da Parigi a Venezia, 14 Marzo–11 maggio 1600*, Florence, 1959
Baudot, A. de, *Archives de la Commission des Monuments Historiques*, 5 vols, Paris, 1900
Bayer, V., 'Rosaces et roues de fortune a la fin de l'art roman et au debut de l'art gothique', *Zeitschrift für Schweizerische Archaeologie und Kunstgeschichte*, 22, 1962, pp. 34–43
Beer, E. J., 'Die Rose der Kathedrale von Lausanne', *Berner Schriften zur Kunst*, 6, Berne, 1952
——, 'Nouvelles reflexions sur l'image du monde dans la cathédrale de Lausanne', *Revue de l'Art*, 1970 p 57-62
Bénard, P., 'Récherches sur la patrie et les travaux de Villard de Honnecourt', in *Transactions de la Société Académique des Sciences, Arts etc de St Quentin*, 3rd ser., vol. 6, pp. 66, 260–80
Binding, G., *Le Gothique rayonnant: le temps des cathédrales*, Paris, 1999
Blomme, Y., 'La Construction de la cathédrale de Poitiers', *Bulletin Monumentale*, 152, 1994, pp. 50–6
Bony, J., *The English Decorated Style. Gothic Architecture Transformed 1250–1350*, Oxford, 1979
——, *French Gothic Architecture of the 12th and 13th centuries*, Berkeley, 1983
Branner, R., 'Paris and the Origins of Rayonnant Gothic Architecture down to 1240', *Art Bulletin*, 44, 1962, pp. 39–51
——, 'St Louis and the Court Style in Gothic Architecture', *Art Bulletin*, 47, 1965
Bucher, F., 'Medieval Architectural Design Methods, 800–1560', *Gesta*, 11, 1972, pp. 37–51
——, *Architector, The Lodgebooks and Sketchbooks of Medieval Architects*, New York, 1979
Bulteau, Abbé M. T., *Monographie de la cathédrale de Chartres*, Chartres, 1887
Butler, H. C., *Early Churches in Syria*, Princeton, 1929
Cahier, Ch., and A. Martin, *Mélanges d'Archeologie*, 4 vols, Paris, 1847–56
——, *Nouveaux Mélanges d'Archeologie*, 4 vols, Paris, 1874–7

Cali, F., *L'Ordre Flamboyant et son temps*, Paris, 1967
Caviness, M. H., 'Images of Divine Order and the Third Mode of Seeing', *Gesta*, 22/2, 1983
——, *Sumptuous Arts at the Royal Abbeys in Reims and Braine*, Princeton, 1990
Cirici, A., *Arquitectura Gotica Catalana*, Barcelona, 1968
Colombien, P. du, *Les Chantiers des Cathédrales*, Paris, 1973
Conant, K. C., *Carolignan and Romanesque Architecture 800–1200*, London, 1974
Connick, C. J., *Adventures in Light and Colour*, New York, 1937
Cowen, P. D., *Rose Windows*, London, 1979
——, *Stained Glass in Britain*, London, 1984
Crosby, S. M., *The Royal Abbey of St Denis. From its Beginnings to the Death of Suger* (ed. P. Blum), New Haven and London, 1987 (orig. pub. as *L'Abbey Royal de Saint Denis*, 1953)
Crossley, P., 'Medieval Architecture and Meaning. The Limits of Iconography', *Burlington Magazine*, 130, 1988, 116–21
De Vogüé, M., *Syrie Centrale*, Paris, 1867–77
Dehio, G., and G. Bezol, *Die Kirchliche Baukunst des Abenlandes*, Stuttgart, 1884–1901
Dictionnaire des Eglises de France, 5 vols, Paris, 1967
Dow, H., 'Rose Windows', *Warburg Institute Journal*, XXI, 1958
Dubourg-Noves, P., 'La Roue et la rose dans le symbolism medieval', *Archaeologia*, 23, 1968
Duby, G., *History of Medieval Art* (3 vols), 1966–7
Duzas, P.-M., 'Viollet-le-Duc et la restauration de Notre-Dame de Paris', *Acts du Coloque Int. Viollet-le-Duc, 1980*, Paris, 1982
Fergusson, P., *Architecture of Solitude. Cistercian Abbeys in Twelfth Century England*, 1984
Florival, A., and Midoux, *Les Vitraux de Laon*, Paris, 1882–91
François, J.-L., 'La Rose de Lieu-Restaurée', *Bulletin de la Société Historique de Compiègne*, vol. 29, 1985
Frankl, P., *Gothic Architecture* (rev. P. Crossley), New Haven and London, 2000
Franz, H., 'Gerhard Die Fensterrose und Ihre Vorgeschichte in der Islamischen Baukunst', *Zeitschrift fur Kunstwissenschaft*, vol. 10, 1956, pp. 1–22
——, 'Les Fenêtres circulaires de la cathédrale de Cefalù', *Cahiers Archeologiques*, 8/9, 1956–7, pp. 253–70
Gaborit-Chopin, D. (ed.), et al., *Un Trésor Gothique. La Chasse de Nivelles*, exh. cat., Réunion des Musées Nationaux, Paris, 1996
Garton, C., *The Metrical Life of St Hugh of Lincoln*, Lincoln, 1986
Gilmore-House, G., 'The Transept windows of Angers Cathedral', from *Selected papers from the 11th Congress* [CVMA], 1982
Grodecki, L., *Gothic Architecture*, London, 1978
——, and C. Brisac, *Le vitrail gothique au XIIIè siècle*, Freibourg, 1984
Hahnloser, H. R., *Villard de Honnecourt*, 1935
Hamann-MacLean, R., and I. Schüssler, *Die Kathedrale von Reims*, Stuttgart, 1997, 8 vols

Hardy, C., 'Les Roses dans L'élévation de Notre-Dame de Paris', *Bulletin Monumental*, 149, 1991, pp. 153–99

Harrison, S., 'Kirkstall Abbey. The 12th Century Tracery and Rose Window', *British Architectural Association Conference Transactions*, 1995

——, and P. Barker, 'Byland Abbey, North Yorkshire; The West Front and Rose Window Reconstructed', *Journal of the British Architectural Association*, CXL, 1987, pp. 134–51

Hayward, J., and W. Cahn, *Radiance and Reflection*, New York, 1982

Hearn, M. F., 'Ripon Minster: The Beginning of the Gothic Style in North England', *American Philosophical Society Transactions*, vol. 73, pt 1, 1983

Héliot, P., 'Le Chevet de la cathédrale de Laon, ses antecedents français et ses suites', *Gazette des Beaux Arts*, 1972, pp. 193–214

Henwood-Reverdot, A., *L'Eglise St Etienne de Beauvais. Histoire et architecture*, Beauvais, 1982

James, J., 'Medieval Geometry: The Western Rose of Chartres' in *Architectural Association Quarterly*, vol. 5, no. 2, 1973, pp. 4–10

Katzenellenbogen, A., *Allegories of Virtues and Vices in Medieval Arts*, London, 1939

Kidson, P., 'Panofsky, Suger and St Denis', *Journal of the Warburg and Courtauld Institutes*, L, 1987, pp. 1–17

Kimple, D., and R. Suckale, *L'Architecture Gothique en France (1130–1270)*, Paris, 1990

King, G. G., *Pre-Romanesque Churches of Spain*, New York, 1924

Kobler, F., 'Fensterrose' in *Reallexikon zur Deutsche Kunstgeschichte*, vol. viii, Munich, 1982, pp. 65–203

Krautheimer, R., *Studies in Early Christian, Medieval and Renaissance Art*, London, 1971

——, 'An Introduction to an Iconography of Medieval Architecture', *Warburg Institute Journal*, V, 1942, pp. 1–33

Lassus, J. B. A., and P. Durand, *Monographie de la cathédrale de Chartres*, 1842–81

Lasteyrie, R. de, *L'Architecture religieuse en France a l'epoque romane*, 1929

Leyerle, J., 'The Rose Wheel design and Dante's Paradiso', *University of Toronto Quarterly*, 1976, vol. XLVI, no. 3, 1977, pp. 260–308

Lillich, M. P., *The Armour of Light*, Berkeley, 1994

——, 'La Rose Verte de la Cathédrale de Châlons', *Cahiers Archaeologique*, 49, 2001, pp. 117–42

——, 'Observations on the Gothic Rose Window with Centripetal Tracery', in *Studies in Medieval Stained Glass and Monasticism*, London, 2001

——, 'The Genesis Rose Window of Reims Cathedral', *Arte Medievale*, 17, Rome, 2003/2, pp. 41–65

Mâle, E., *The Gothic Image* (trans. D. Nussey) New York, 1958

Mersmann, W., *Rosenfenster und Himmelskreise*, Mittenwald, 1982

Murray, S., *Building Troyes Cathedral. The Late Gothic Campaigns*, Indiana, 1987

——, *Notre Dame de Amiens. The Power of Change in Gothic*, Cambridge, 1996

Nieto Alcaide, V., *La Vidriera Española*, Madrid, 1998

Nodier C., et al., *Voyages pittoresques et romantiques dans l'ancienne France*, various vols, Paris, 1824–46

Nussbaum, N., *Deutsche Kirchenbaukunst der Gotik*, Darmsdadt, 1994 (trans. as *German Gothic Church Architecture*, New Haven and London, 2000)

Palol, Pedro de, *Arte Hispánico de la Epoca Visigoda*, Barcelona, 1968

Panofsky, E., *Gothic Architecture and Scholasticism*, Latrobe, 1951

Prache, A., *Chartres. Image of Heavenly Jerusalem*, Chartres, 1993

Reuterward, P., 'The Forgotten Symbols of God, and Windows of Divine Light', *Stockholm Studies in History of Art*, 25, 1982 and 1985

Rudolph, C., *Artistic Change at St-Denis: Abbot Suger's program and the early 12th century controversy over art*, Princeton, 1990

Sandron, D., *La Cathedrale de Soissons. Architecture de pouvoir*, Paris, 1968

Sanfacon, R., *L'Architecture flamboyant en France*, Quebec, 1971

Shelby, L. R., *Gothic Design Techniques. The C15 Design booklets of Mathes Roriczer & Hanns Schmuttermayer*, Carbondale, 1977

Sherlock, D., 'The Drawing of old St Pauls in Ashwell Church', in *Hertfordshire Archaeology*, VI, 1978

Shrine of Wisdom (The), *Mystical Theology and the Celestial Hierarchies*, 1923

Suckale, R., 'Thesen zum Bedeutungswandel der Gotischen Fensterrose' in K. Clausberg et al. (eds), *Bauwerk und Bildwerk im Hochmittelalter. Anschauliche Beitrage zur Kulture und Sozialgeschichte* (Kunstwissenschaftliche Untersuchungen des Ulmer Vereins für Kunst und Kulturewissenschaft 11), Geissen, 1981, pp. 259–94

Van de Meulen, J., 'A Logos Creator at Chartres & Its Copy', *Journal of the Warburg and Courtauld Institutes*, XXIX, 1966, pp. 82–100

Viollet-le-Duc, E., *Dictionnaire raisonné de l'architecture française du XI au XVe siècle*, Paris, 1858–68

Von Simson, O., *The Gothic Cathedral*, New York, 1962

White, J., *Art and Architecture in Italy 1250–1400*, London, 1966

Wilkins, E., *The Rose Garden Game*, London, 1969

Wilson, C., *The Gothic Cathedral. The Architecture of The Great Church 1130–1530*, London, 1990

Wilson, C., et al., *Westminster Abbey*, 1986

Woillez, E., *Description de la cathédrale de Beauvais*, Beauvais, 1838

ACKNOWLEDGMENTS FOR ILLUSTRATIONS

All photographs and drawings by the author except the following:

p. 13 From B. Winkles, *French Cathedrals*, London, 1836. Drawn by H. Brown from a sketch by R. Garland. Engraved by B. Winkles.

p. 19, top Collection Biblilothèque Nationale, Paris

p. 21 Sonia Halliday Photographs

p. 22, bottom from Dehio, *Kirchliche Baukunst*

p. 22, top From Dehio, *Kirchliche Baukunst*

p. 23, top, left From Dehio, *Kirchliche Baukunst*

p. 23, top, right From J. H. Parker, *An Introduction to Gothic Architecture*, London, 1888

p. 23, bottom, left From Dehio, *Kirchliche Baukunst*

p. 23, bottom, right from Dehio, *Kirchliche Baukunst*

p. 24 Collection Ste Marie Madeleine, Aix-en-Provence. Lauros/Giraudon/Bridgeman Art Library

p. 30, top, left Copy made in 1818 by Christian Moritz Engelhardt of the original 12th-century *Hortus Deliciarum*, which was kept in the municipal library of Strasbourg but which was destroyed by fire in 1870.

p. 30, top, right Copyright Dean and Chapter of Westminster

p. 30, bottom, right Nivelles reliquary, now destroyed. Unknown photographer

p. 31 Fol. 83r of *La Vraye Histoire du Bon Roy Alixandre* (British Library MS Royal 20 B XX). Courtesy British Library

p. 41 From Butler, *Early Churches in Syria*

p. 46 Photo by Painton Cowen for Sonia Halliday Photographs

p. 48 From Dehio, *Kirchliche Baukunst*

p. 49, top, left and right From De Vogüé, *Syrie Centrale*

p. 49 Collection Museo de Córdoba. Hirmer Fotoarchiv

p. 52 Tapis de la Creació, Cathedral Treasury, Girona

p. 53 Photo Nicolo Orsi Battaglini

p. 54, right 19th-century photograph of San Miguel de Lillo. Conway Library, Courtauld Institute of Art

p. 54, bottom Visigothic screen, Oviedo

p. 61 All drawn by Stuart Harrison

p. 68 From Dehio, *Kirchliche Baukunst*

p. 76 From Dehio, *Kirchliche Baukunst*

pp. 78–9 Chartres during (or shortly after) Second World War. Bildarchiv Photo Marburg

p. 84 Sonia Halliday Photographs

p. 85 Sonia Halliday Photographs

p. 89 Hirmer Fotoarchiv

p. 90, bottom From Dehio, *Kirchliche Baukunst*

p. 100 From B. Winkles, *French Cathedrals*, London, 1836. Drawn by H. Brown from a sketch by R. Garland. Engraved by B. Winkles

p. 101 From Viollet-le-Duc, *Dictionnaire raisonné*

p. 107 From a copy in Westminster Abbey Library

p. 110 left Collection Biblilothèque Nationale, Paris

p. 110, right From Viollet-le-Duc, *Dictionnaire raisonné*

p. 125, bottom, left Sonia Halliday Photographs

p. 130 J. Britton and C. Wild, *The History and Antiquities of the Cathedral Church of Lincoln*, London 1819

p. 133 Canterbury Cathedral archives

p. 149 E. Woillez, *Description de la Cathédrale de Beauvais*, Paris, 1838

p. 161 Sonia Halliday Photographs

p. 162 Photos by the author, taken with the permission of the Servizio Musei Comunali

p. 182, top © Copyright The Connick Foundation

p. 182, bottom © Copyright The Connick Foundation

p. 183 Matisse window, Pocantico. Historic Hudson Valley, Tarrytown, New York. © Succession H. Matisse/DACS 2005

pp. 184–5 Photo from the Cathedral Church of St Peter and St Paul, Washington

p. 187 Photo by Joan Vila-Grau

p. 190, top, right Photo Ramon Roca i Junyent. Arxiu de l'Institut d'Estudis Catalans, Barcelona

p. 200 St John's College, Oxford. MS 17 f 7v. Courtesy of The president and Scholars of St John the Baptist College in the University of Oxford

p. 205, top, right Corpus Christi. MS 66 p. 66. Copyright Corpus Christi College, Cambridge University

p. 205, bottom, left Collection Biblilothèque Nationale, Paris

p. 208 MS. Hist. fol. 415, folio 17v. Württembergische Landesbibliothek, Stuttgart

Lausanne diagram/key drawn by the author and Tad Mann

p. 227 From Cahier & Martin

p. 236 Collection Biblilothèque Nationale, Paris

p. 240 From Viollet-le-Duc, *Dictionnaire raisonné*

p. 241 Collection Biblilothèque Nationale, Paris

p. 242 Collection Musée de l'Oeuvre de Notre-Dame, Strasbourg

p. 243 Collection Museum der Stadt Regensburg

pp. 246–7 Geometry drawings by the author and Tad Mann

p. 248 Photo CNRS Editions (lines added by current author).

pp. 252–3 Diagrams drawn by the author and Tad Mann

p. 257 From Viollet-le-Duc, *Dictionnaire raisonné*

p. 258, top Photo by Stuart Harrison

p. 259 Drawing by Jean-Luc François

p. 262, top Lincoln, 'Dean's Eye' old tracery. © Copyright Dean and Chapter of Lincoln

p. 262, below, left and right Photos by Aukett Brockliss Guy Limited

p. 263 © Copyright Dean and Chapter of Lincoln

INDEX